American Indian Cowboys in Southern California, 1493–1941

American Indian Cowboys in Southern California, 1493–1941

Survival, Sovereignty, and Identity

David G. Shanta

LEXINGTON BOOKS
Lanham • Boulder • New York • London

Published by Lexington Books
An imprint of The Rowman & Littlefield Publishing Group, Inc.
4501 Forbes Boulevard, Suite 200, Lanham, Maryland 20706
www.rowman.com

86-90 Paul Street, London EC2A 4NE

Copyright © 2024 by The Rowman & Littlefield Publishing Group, Inc.

All rights reserved. No part of this book may be reproduced in any form or by any electronic or mechanical means, including information storage and retrieval systems, without written permission from the publisher, except by a reviewer who may quote passages in a review.

British Library Cataloguing in Publication Information Available

Library of Congress Cataloging-in-Publication Data Available

ISBN 978-1-66695-704-4 (cloth)
ISBN 978-1-66695-705-1 (ebook)

I dedicate this modest work to all the peoples in the world, whose homelands having been invaded, their resources taken, and their very lives put at risk, fight to survive, assert their God-given human rights, and incorporate stories of their ultimate triumphs into their family histories, their cultures, and their identities.

Contents

List of Illustrations ix

Acknowledgments xi

Introduction 1

1 Spanish Origins of California Mission Cattle 9

2 Marches to New California, 1769–1781 31

3 California Mission Cattle and Native American *Vaqueros* 1769–1833 49

4 Hides and Tallow: Native American Labor and the Rise of Californio Society, 1833–1848 65

5 The Early American Period, 1848–1890 83

6 "Subjects But Not Citizens," 1891–1920 109

7 A New Economy Based on Cattle, 1921–1941 131

Conclusion 149

Bibliography 155

Index 171

About the Author 179

List of Illustrations

FIGURES

Figure 0.1	Morongo Indian Cowboy Charles Largo	xiv
Figure 4.1	Californio *Ranchero* with Roped Steer	68
Figure 7.1	Roundup on the Morongo Reservation, Banning, CA	132
Figure 7.2	Roundup on the Morongo Reservation, Banning, CA	144
Figure 8.1	Cahuilla Indian Cowboys, Cahuilla Reservation	152

TABLES

Table 6.1	Combined Total Incomes in Dollars, of Malki and Soboba Superintendencies, 1911–1920	123
Table 6.2	Rapid Expansion of Reservation Farm and Ranch Productivity during the Great War	126

Acknowledgments

This book culminates my years of study, research, and writing at the University of California Riverside and at California State University San Bernardino. I am indebted to the faculty members of the History Department at the University of California Riverside for their sustained support of my candidacy in the Doctoral program. The department members backed my acceptance with the prestigious Chancellor's Fellowship that funded my early academic career at the university. The department also assisted my research through direct grants for travel to the National Archives in Washington, DC, and to the Huntington Library in San Marino, California. They indirectly supported me through Graduate Assistance in Areas of National Need, funded by the U.S. Department of Education. I must also acknowledge the Madrigal Research Initiative of the Rupert Costo Endowment for additional support in uncovering primary source material related to Indian Cowboys and Cattlemen.

I am deeply grateful to Distinguished Professor Clifford E. Trafzer, who chaired my dissertation committee, inspired and challenged me to tell an important story, and guided my path through all aspects of the Doctoral program. Committee member Professor Rebecca Kugel generously shared her vast knowledge of Native American histories in research seminar classrooms and in my meetings with her. I always came away enlightened and inspired to try and live up to her example. Professor Robert Perez enthusiastically agreed to join my committee. His enthusiasm and his own work influenced and supported my efforts to make a contribution to truth and justice in the history of the American West.

Many other faculty members shared the generosity of spirit that comes from the love of history. These include Denver Graninger, who allowed me to connect Post-Hellenic Greece to the American West; Catherine Gudis and Molly McGarry, who opened my eyes and mind to the history close at hand; and I thank Kiril Tomoff for a new, transnational perspective. Professor Steven Hackel's studies on the colonial history of this region informed and supported my own work. I also thank Graduate Student Affairs Officers Alesha Jaenette and Iselda Salgado for their counsel, guidance, and friendship at UCR. I must also pay tribute to my mentors at California State University San Bernardino—Timothy Pytell, Cherstin Lyon, Joyce Hanson, Richard Samuelson, and Michal Kohout.

Conceiving, developing, and finishing work in this field does not happen without the help and encouragement of Native people. I sincerely thank the many members of the Southern California Indian community for their patience and generosity in sharing and helping me to better understand their histories and cultures. An incomplete list includes former Morongo chairman Robert Martin, Morongo elders Mrs. Doris Sanchez, Roderick Tyron Linton, and Ernest Siva; Kim Marcus, Raymond Huaute, Aaron Saubel, Gerald Clarke, Bill Madrigal Sr., Luke Madrigal, William Madrigal, Joshua Little, Amanda Wixon, and Sean Milanovich. I hope that my work is worthy of their trust.

Finally, I wish to thank family and friends who encouraged me in my work and who also impatiently asked "When are you going to finish already?" A few are brother James, sister Bonnie, Brativ Dann and Josh E., and old friends Tim, Jon, Bob, Cheryl, Cindy, Andy, and Lafaye. I posthumously thank my old friend Major Bill Helwig, U.S.A. Retired, my mother Madeline Petro Shanta and my father George Shanta, a son of immigrants who defended our country in World War II and passed on to me his love of American history.

Figure 0.1 Morongo Indian Cowboy Charles Largo. *Source*: photCL 39 (146), William H. Weinland Collection. The Huntington Library, San Marino, CA.

Introduction

The Indigenous peoples of Alta California had no knowledge of the massive historical forces that played out on the Iberian Peninsula in the medieval period 1100–1300 CE. The outcome of that struggle set a chain of events in motion that drastically altered the Indigenous world of the Americas. Christian Spaniards and Portuguese launched the *Reconquista*, a war of reconquest, determined to remove Muslims from that land in the name of the Christian God. All aspects of Iberian life adapted to wartime expediencies, especially food production. In the borderlands between the combatants, where one side might harvest or burn crops planted by the other, cattle herding offered food mobility and security. The war that eventually ended Islamic rule in Spain and Portugal in January 1492, opened up multiple horizons for the triumphant royal partners, Queen Isabel and King Fernando.

These Christian heroes had an opportunity to return multiple Mediterranean locations to Christian rule by force, including the Holy Land. Instead, they turned westward. Isabel and Fernando were determined to compete with their erstwhile allies, the Portuguese, for coveted trade goods like black pepper and silk from India and China, respectively. Isabel agreed to fund Christopher Columbus's proposed expedition to reach India and China by heading westward across the Atlantic Ocean. The horse and cattle culture that had evolved during the Iberian *Reconquista* supported the twin imperatives of conquering the newly discovered lands of the Americas for God and king and of returning great wealth to *Los Reyes*, the Royals. Columbus' second voyage disembarked in 1493 after loading horses from Andalucía in Spain and bull and heifer calves, and other livestock from the Canary Islands. Columbus and the men of the expedition landed on the island of Hispaniola, one of the four large Caribbean islands known as the Greater Antilles, including Cuba, Jamaica, and Puerto Rico.

Spanish military leadership intended to plant crops and enable their various livestock animals to reproduce rapidly in order to quickly make the new colony self-sufficient. Missionaries sought to feed the Indigenous people whom they called *Indios*, in order to make them more amenable to religious conversion to the Catholic faith, and hopefully, to recruit them to work on the farms and ranches. Accordingly, they taught the Natives to plant, tend, and harvest crops, and to tend, slaughter, and butcher the new domesticated animals. In a process that repeated itself wherever the Spanish founded missions, horses and cattle thrived on the natural vegetation and reproduced beyond the ability of the *padres* and the few soldiers to control. Mission priests and *presidio* soldiers selected trusted converts or neophytes and taught them to ride horses and herd the cattle. The first Indigenous American who mounted up to control the herds became the first American cowboy.

Many historians have chronicled the building of the Spanish empire in the Western Hemisphere, in all its myriad aspects, locations, and Spanish heroes, including the devastating impacts on the Indigenous civilizations, whose lives they had fractured. Studies of the massive demographic collapses due to infectious European diseases alone can easily fill many bookshelves. Historians have paid much less attention to the nearly anonymous American Indians who herded and branded Spanish Longhorn cattle and then worked the *matanzas* or slaughtering of the animals, to feed with the meat, and to clothe, build, and protect with the hides and the tallow. They labored on the mission ranches and built up herds of horses and cattle that they then pushed forward to found the next mission. First, the Spanish transported livestock by ship to the other Antilles of Puerto Rico, Jamaica, and Cuba and then to the mainland of New Spain. After defeating the Aztecs, the Spanish implanted missions outward from Mexico (City) and northward to what became the American Southwest in Sonora, Arizona, New Mexico, and the California's. Native Indian herdsmen not only brought the cattle for each new mission; they stayed and taught the local Natives about horses and cattle. Those newly taught Natives then became agents of change—the messengers and the teachers for the next move northward.

The few histories that are entirely dedicated to telling of American Indian cowboys, focus on Native cattlemen on the Great Plains, the northwestern Plateau, or Arizona. This book focuses entirely on California Indians as cowboys and cattlemen. The entry of Spanish Longhorns into Alta California in 1770 spelled doom for the ancient way of life of Alta California Indians. In southern California, this fate befell the Kumeyaay, Acâgchemem, Luiseño, Cahuilla, Serrano, and Tongva.

Horses and Spanish Longhorn cattle multiplied rapidly on the California ranges and consumed Indigenous food sources and other plants used for medicines, tools, and weapons. This attrition of the traditional diet forced the first of many Native adaptations to the new and uninvited occupants of their lands—adopting the raising and herding of cattle as a survival strategy. Cattle provided food security in their ability to thrive on dry California grasses but also in their mobility, to move to greener pastures, seasonally or in times of drought. Survival literally gave California Indians the strength to assert sovereignty by resisting the preemptions of their ancestral lands by the missions, by seeking land grants after the secularization of the missions, in their *ranchería(s)* within the Mexican *ranchos*, and finally on lands reserved for them by Executive Order or Act of Congress. Conversely, some Natives living in the missions surreptitiously honored their tribal traditions within an institution dedicated to erasing Indigenous language and culture, by violence when deemed necessary. They had asserted a personal sovereignty to keep their cultures alive. Over generations, cowboying became part of California Indian family traditions, passed down by fathers and mothers to sons and daughters, and in this organic way, these family traditions formed part of tribal identities.

Mission herds proliferated on the multiple *estancias* or ranches attached to each mission from San Diego to Monterrey. As the herds increased, Spanish soldiers or padres trained Native neophytes to be *vaqueros* or cowboys. California Indian cowboys earned their reputations as highly skilled riders and ropers. The best also assumed leadership as *majordomos* or ranch foremen. Missions regularly slaughtered cattle for meat to feed the missionaries, soldiers, and Native workers who planted, tilled, and harvested crops as well as managed the cattle. For the slaughter, they rounded up the cattle, and one by one, threw them to the ground, where other Indian ranch workers killed and skinned the animals. After butchering for the best cuts of beef for consumption, they removed the tallow to make soap and candles. They started the process of preparing the hide for tanning by staking it to the ground and scraping off the meat residue. Other neophytes tanned those hides into leather for boots, shoes, *chaquetas* or jackets, and saddles. Some worked with rawhide to produce bindings and straps used to hang doors and church bells, and all manner of furnishings for the mission churches and living quarters. They also learned to braid thin and very long strips of rawhide into *reatas* or leather ropes. By making a large loop at the end of it, mounted California Indian cowboys threw the *lazo* (lasso) over the animal's head and horns to control it, for branding, doctoring, or *matanza* (slaughter). Eventually, the mission *padres* traded surplus hides to foreign traders, in return for household items, tools, and other luxuries in the remote Spanish province of Alta California.

In the early 1800s, historic events in Spain reverberated throughout New Spain when Spanish patriots rose up to overthrow Napoleon Bonaparte's puppet king of Spain. The patriots incorporated ideals of the Enlightenment into their cause, including denial of the king's divine right to rule, which inspired Spanish people in New Spain to reevaluate their relations and to break with the Crown. Ultimately, Mexico gained her independence in 1821. The now-legalized hide and tallow trade flourished throughout Alta California, bringing British traders from England and Yankee traders from Boston. Demand for hides from the vast herds of California cattle roused the ambitious Californios to campaign for the release of all mission lands to private development. Secularization became law in 1833.

Overnight, land grant *ranchos* covered the map of southern California, where hundreds of thousands of cowhides fueled the international market and conferred the aristocratic title of *Don* to the new ranch owners. Throughout this massive transformation of the landscape, Indigenous American families provided the back-breaking farm and ranch labor that literally built Californio society, brick-by-adobe-brick. Cowboying elevated neophyte laborers from the mission field. Their indispensability to the success of the hide and tallow economy necessitated and justified the system of debt peonage that the *rancheros* imposed on them. Nearly insurmountable financial obligations virtually bound California Indians to the land and to their *Don*.

Except for the very small number of land grants made to Native groups, most southern California Indians continued to work cattle as they had done on the missions, answering to the *Don* instead of the *padre*. They clustered in *ranchería(s)* or small villages within the bounds of the big ranch that also rested on some portion of their own ancient domains. Despite the oppression of peonage, *rancho* life provided stability to Indian groups, in terms of feeding and housing their families—basic elements of survival not guaranteed to them, after ships and soldiers of the United States military invaded California to make it part of yet a third country.

The Treaty of Guadalupe Hidalgo (1848) made California a territory of the United States. The treaty also clearly stated that all Mexican citizens had automatically become citizens of the United States. The Indigenous peoples of Mexico possessed Mexican citizenship. However, Americans did not recognize American Indian citizenship and generally viewed any California Indian-occupied land as public land, open to preemption. Many American settlers encroached or even squatted on Indian land. Their cattle fed on Indian pastures and drank from Indian water sources. Ironically, once gold had been discovered in the north in early 1848 and gold-seekers flooded into California, Indian cowboys took active parts in the difficult and dangerous work of driving herds from southern California to feed hungry immigrant prospectors in mining camps in the north.

In the 1850s, demand for beef made fortunes for ranchers who had only been able to sell a Longhorn's hides and tallow just a few months before. Indian cowboy nerve and skill contributed to those fortunes while immigrants tried to box them and their families out of even modest parcels of land. Cattlemen from the Midwest and Texas seized the opportunity and drove their herds into California to sell for beef, and some of those drives included American Indian cowboys among their ranks.

The demand for cattle in the new state eventually peaked and then hit bottom, taking prices down with it, but the herds continued to grow, straining range capacities to support them until natural forces intervened to restore equilibrium. Flood and drought cut the state's cattle numbers in half by 1865 and put many of the old land grant ranchers out of business. At the same time, the introduction of American breeds continued to improve the quality of California cattle, specifically to produce much more beef per animal than the Spanish Longhorn. Combined with the rising power of agriculture, open-range cattle ranching of Spanish Longhorns ultimately yielded to smaller stock-raising farms. Fences maintained breeding quality, and more intensive care produced significantly more beef per animal.

To survive, California Natives still found wage work on ranches in the 1870s and 1880s, and they maintained small herds of livestock wherever possible with their minimal resources. However they still had no clearly surveyed and patented reservations with enforceable boundaries. Great leaders like Jose Panto and Olegario Calac adapted their tactics in these dark times to seek legal redress of grievances through the American legal system, and when necessary, make a show of force to resist the erasure of their people's legacies on the land. Meanwhile, non-Native advocates like Helen Hunt Jackson raised the consciousness of the American people to the ongoing injustices, while groups like the Indian Rights Association simultaneously pressed the U.S. Congress to act. In January 1891, Congress passed *An Act for the Relief of the Mission Indians in the State of California.*

The Native peoples in southern California had the beginnings of recognized sovereignty for their tribal groups, although assimilationist rhetoric and paternalistic policies persisted for decades. From these small bases of land, though, southern California Indians did run horses and cattle, for food security, to supplement wage income with livestock sales, and to provide a measure of autonomy from outside interference in tribal affairs.

To be sure, trespassing cattle still fed on reservation pastures, and California Indian cattlemen and farmers still lived with the specter of drought. In the time before Euro-American fences went up, the Native peoples of southern California had traditionally accepted what nature provided during times of drought or times of abundant rains, and adjusted consumption to match the available foods. In the fence-bound American system of property distributions, coupled with reliance on a few planted crops, droughts often ruined the people on the land. Poverty and starvation lay close at hand. With restricted access to alternative (traditional) foods, Kumeyaay and Cahuilla, Serrano, and Luiseño had also become dependent on plentiful rains for crops and good market prices for livestock. Yet, they adapted, often with wage work, or non-agricultural businesses like freighting, cutting firewood, and crafts like basket-making. They adapted, they survived, and they stayed on the land into the twentieth century.

A good cowboy can find work, and non-Native cattlemen hired and worked with southern California Indian cowboys, whether up in the San Bernardino Mountains, or on large non-Native-owned ranches in the vicinity of the San Gorgonio Pass, San Jacinto Mountain valleys, or Temecula. Non-Native cowboys tell of Indians who had a special way with unbroken horses, or who could precisely throw a looped reata over the horns of a "bronco" or renegade bull in the brush country. Some of these top hands worked cattle well into their sixties and seventies, and some even into their eighties. These men stand as icons of a bygone era.

Some of the Office of Indian Affairs programs did benefit southern California Indians by helping them to grow and improve their herds. Some of the Indian Service personnel cared about the people they sought to serve, and sometimes outside forces brought prosperity to people who had not seen much of it. During the 1910s, Farming Agents and the Reimbursable program helped to increase reservation cattle herds and crops. Combined with the strong national demand for grain and meat during the Great War of 1914–1918, these factors stimulated a brief period of significant prosperity in terms of overall reservation incomes among the people of the Mission Indian Superintendency.

Southern California Native people sold more beef, more crops, and earned more wages in that decade than they ever had before but it could not and did not last. The post-war decline of demand and prices returned to the norm, as did poverty and suffering but they did not give up. Most of the southern California reservation land is more suited to raising livestock than farming, so in 1925, the reservations contained as many head of cattle on their ranges as the ranges would carry. They worked with what they had and maximized their assets.

The Stock Market Crash of 1929 served as the official start to the greatest economic crisis in American history. Without knowing it, many Americans began to experience the same kind of poverty and struggle that Native Americans had lived with for decades. The rescue plans of the New Deal benefitted some of the Native groups, especially the Civilian Conservation Corps—Indian Division. As the 1930s wore on, forestry experts sought to slow and eventually stop range depletion and Farming Agents encouraged cooperative marketing to sell cattle at the highest prices possible. Both efforts aimed to make cattle a more sustainable product and to increase incomes by working cooperatively. Morongo Reservation Indians saw real benefits in the later 1930s from the cooperative aspect and established a cattlemen's association and a tribal herder to apply the spirit of continuous improvement across all aspects of their cattle business. Some southern California Indian cattle families built their businesses off the reservation or had decided to lead their lives outside the reservation borders. Those families measured success in the pursuit of their dream, as well as by running productive and profitable ranches.

As the decade drew to a close, war erupted once again in Asia and Europe. The U.S. federal government began to rapidly mobilize the national economy and the American people. These measures had a stimulative effect on the economy that began to reach southern California reservations, not only in off-reservation wage work but also in the increased demand for beef. For these Native peoples, survival meant the ability to adapt to a changing world. They adopted ideas and processes that provided real benefits and resulted in progress for them, strengthened their sovereignty, and reaffirmed their identities as Indian cowboys and cattlemen.

NAMES AND NAMING

Names and naming of Indigenous tribal groups carry great potential for harm and insult. I approached this work with respect and consideration for the people of history who cannot speak for themselves. Language matters. In this study, using any given group's tribal name offered the first and best choice—Acâgchemem, Cahuilla, Kumeyaay, Luiseño, Serrano, and Tongva, to name a few.

However, when speaking of the Indigenous peoples of California in aggregate, I faced a dilemma, especially in the use of the term "Indian."

Dr. Michael Yellow Bird's article "What We Want to Be Called" provided guidance. Dr. Yellow Bird is an enrolled member of MHA Nation (Mandan, Hidatsa, Arikara) in North Dakota and has written and taught about Indigenous peoples of North America at universities in the United States and Canada. His first preference is to use specific tribal names whenever possible, and he states that "Native American" or "Indian" pose their own problems: the former in its usage for people of any ethnicity born in the United States; the latter label can be confused with Asian Indians, a growing demographic group in the United States.

The National Congress of American Indians is the oldest Indigenous political organization in the United States and has retained that name by choice. The National Museum of the American Indian offers that Native, Native American, American Indian, and Indigenous American are acceptable descriptors of aggregated Indigenous or Native groups. In southern California, thirteen local Indigenous groups formed the intergovernmental Tribal Alliance of Sovereign Indian Nations nearly thirty years ago. Their mission is to protect sovereign tribal rights and cultural identity, among other goals. The website uses both Native American and Indian as descriptors.

In writing about Native American cowboys and cattlemen and when the use of individual tribal names is insufficient or inaccurate, I used a specific variant of American Indians: California Indians or southern California Indians. I introduce that phrase early in the paragraph and thereafter may use Indian for brevity. The term Native, as in "Native cattlemen," communicates an ethnic and cultural distinction from Euro-American and adds variety. Indigenous also distinguishes Native histories and cultures from those of European and Euro-American immigrants to the territory.

In each and every instance, I intend my writing to convey respect, compassion, and admiration toward the Native peoples of southern California, some of whom are Acâgchemem, Cahuilla, Kumeyaay, Luiseño, Serrano, and Tongva, among others. With gratitude and humility, I present their story of courage, sacrifice, determination, and triumph.

David G. Shanta

Chapter 1

Spanish Origins of California Mission Cattle

The California Indian cattle industry of the nineteenth century originated in the practices and traditions that the Spanish had developed over centuries on the Iberian Peninsula, which they later brought to their colonies in New Spain, including Alta California. Spanish colonial strategies eventually included teaching Native Americans to be *vaqueros* or mounted herders. The Spanish used different methods in dealing with the Indigenous populations of New Spain, including their use of missions as institutions of control and conversion to Catholicism. Once on the missions, Spanish *vaqueros* (including some who were Native Americans from Mexico) taught the local Indigenous people the art of cattle raising. Soldiers and priests impressed Native converts or *neofitos* into hard labor on farms and ranches that gradually destroyed traditional economies and broke down related religious and cultural practices. Each colonial settlement provided people and animals to found the next one, on Caribbean islands and on the mainland of New Spain. Mission by mission, in Mexico and Baja California, the Spanish marched northward, with horses and cattle in the vanguard, providing food security until crop farming took hold. In 1769 and 1770, led by Father Junipero Serra and Governor Gaspar de Portolá, soldiers, missionaries, and Baja California Indians drove Longhorn cattle into Alta California. In a short time, mission cattle and horse herds in California multiplied out of control of the soldiers and padres, who then trained trusted neophytes to work as *vaqueros*, away from mission crops, gardens, and orchards. Alta California Indians learned quickly and mission economies came to rely on Indian *vaqueros* to manage the large cattle herds on mission lands.[1]

In 1493, the Spanish brought the first cattle and horses to the Americas aboard the ships of Columbus's second voyage and landed on the island of Hispaniola, shared by the present-day nations of Haiti and the Dominican

Republic. Spanish cattle and horse culture in the Caribbean, in Mexico, and eventually among California Indians, originated in Spain, most notably on the coastal plains of Andalucía in southern Spain. Spanish *Conquistadores* also brought cattle and horses to the New World from the *Meseta*, the high plains of the Extremadura region to the north of Andalucía.

Between the years 1100 and 1300 CE, Christians on the Iberian Peninsula launched the *Reconquista* to expel Muslims in order to reclaim the land for Christianity. The armies of Christian Spain and Portugal required many horses and fed their armies on beef. The centuries-long struggle impacted land use and shaped the horse and cattle culture that served Christian armies in Spain and empire-building in the Americas. Power on the Iberian Peninsula shifted slowly but inexorably from Muslim to Christian hands. Christian forces raided Muslim territory for cattle and sheep, and vulnerable Muslims withdrew southward. At length, they took refuge in the last Muslim kingdom of Granada.[2] Aside from the men lost in battle, the continual warfare of the *Reconquista* prompted Christian and Muslim migrations that disrupted farm output. In this landscape shaped by war, Spanish herds of cattle emerged as the most economical use of the land, not to mention a highly portable form of food and wealth in times of danger. From these herds, a relatively few *vaqueros* provided meat and milk that fed many people and by running the herd, they denied food to the enemy.[3]

During the long *Reconquista*, Andalusians and Extremadurans had established a significant cattle-ranching industry in large numbers and over an extensive range. Further, the region contained plentiful horses that made large-scale herding possible and democratized horse ownership. Riding became more commonplace and not an exclusive privilege of the aristocracy.[4] The Crown issued land grants during the fourteenth and fifteenth centuries to religious orders, military orders, municipalities, and a few private individuals. Those grant holders controlled sizable cattle herds in the region. Several centuries later, the Spanish Crown used this same instrument of imperial policy to establish the missions, *presidios*, and *pueblos* of Alta California.[5]

Over centuries, Andalusian and Extremaduran *señores de hato* (herders) also developed methods to control their animals, in order to graze them on fresh pastures, to round them up for counting and branding, to rescue them from danger on the landscape, or to take them to slaughter. The bases of these methods and materials later transferred to the Americas, where for the most part, New World *vaqueros* adapted Spanish experiences and techniques to their new surroundings. The braided leather *reata* replaced spun grass rope, and a looped rope, thrown over their horns from horseback, replaced the prodding of cattle from behind. One change often prompts another and that single change required new American saddle designs. On the open ranges, far from corrals, new American saddles made the *vaquero's* horse a mobile platform from which he controlled a calf for branding or a steer for doctoring.[6]

Driven by the forceful leadership of Queen Isabel of Castile and King Fernando of Aragon, Christian forces conquered the last Muslim stronghold on the Iberian Peninsula in the Battle of Granada. Isabel and Fernando took possession of the city in January 1492 and set about converting, expelling, or enslaving the Muslim population. Jews suffered a similar fate. The victors also mandated changes to the landscape in which church bells now called the faithful to prayer from the surrounding countryside.[7]

The prestige of these champions of Christendom soared throughout Europe's capitals, for having countered the loss of Constantinople to the Ottomans just thirty-nine years prior. To Isabel and Fernando, their victory at Granada suggested possibilities of empire in Africa, Asia, the Atlantic, the Mediterranean, and perhaps even the recapture of Jerusalem from the infidels, God willing. With the reconquest behind them, Isabel made the decision to give full financial support to Christopher Columbus. The Genoese navigator proposed a new route to the lucrative Asian trade centers, heading west across the Atlantic. Isabel partly based her decision on a sense of duty to continually uncover the mysteries of God's creation in order to spread the Holy Faith. But supporting Columbus's voyage also legally entitled the Spanish Crown to any resulting wealth in trade and territory, at least by European custom. In addition, her contract with Columbus preempted his acceptance of Portuguese overtures, whose own explorations had recently confirmed the eastward route to India around the coast of Africa.[8]

Columbus's first voyage set sail on August 3, 1492, aboard three small *caravels*—Portuguese-designed and developed sailing ships that looked slow and "tubby" but were known in Columbus's time for their speed and "excellence in windward work."[9] Isabel commandeered two of the vessels from known smugglers, who provided the ships at their own expense to avoid imprisonment. The expedition reached land in October and found seven islands, including Cuba, mistakenly assumed to be continental Asia. Columbus left one of the caravels and crew on the island of Hispaniola and returned to Spain. Isabel and Fernando received him warmly in April 1493, during which reception Columbus presented them with gold, cotton, cinnamon, pepper, and several of the Indigenous Taino people. *Los reyes* congratulated him on his successes to date and urged that he return to the Indies as soon as they could organize and equip a second voyage with a much larger fleet.[10]

Columbus's second voyage embarked from Cadiz on September 25, 1493. The fleet consisted of seventeen ships and some twelve hundred men. Since this venture intended to establish a permanent colonial presence, the men loaded the ships with arms, tools, and provisions intended to support the colony, including cuttings and seeds from a variety of fruits and vegetables.

Isabel also ordered that a mounted, twenty-man security force be added to the expeditionary party. The lancers received twenty-five stallions and mares from the surrounding region of Andalucía, donated by the Holy Brotherhood of Granada.[11] The expedition then put in at Gomera in the Canary Islands, where they loaded yearling bull and heifer calves, as well as goats, sheep, chickens, pigs, and sugarcanes. The cattle had also descended from Andalusian stock, brought to the archipelago following the Castilian occupation in the early 1400s. The horses and cattle represented tried and true military and economic strategies of the *Reconquista*, now applied to external conquest and colonization. Just as Christian cavalry had played a key role in the assaults on Granada, Spanish-mounted soldiers overmatched Indigenous warriors on foot. Just as cattle and sheep had filled the void in food production during the *Reconquista*, the Spaniards wisely came to the Americas prepared to live off meat and milk if and when crops failed or yielded poorly.[12]

The queen viewed the expeditions as acts of empire-building and religious proselytizing but expected returns on her investments. In this regard, Columbus failed in his mission to return great treasure to the Crown in the form of gold. Conscious of this deficiency, Columbus touted the approximately one million Taino Indians as the most plentiful "resource" on Hispaniola. He proposed their value as impressed labor under the system of *encomienda* or in the form of currency if sold into slavery.[13] However, Isabel asserted her royal prerogatives regarding the treatment of the Taino by claiming them as her vassals. Columbus also proved unable to manage the diverse self-interests of the Spanish contingent, from *hidalgos* of lesser nobility who sought their own fortunes, to convicts who signed on to work off their sentences. Many Spanish men sought the company of Indigenous women often by force. Defense of their women set the stage for violence between Taino men and the Spaniards and forced Columbus to have several of the Spanish perpetrators hung.[14] The queen eventually relieved Columbus of his viceregal authority but supported two additional exploratory missions for the Admiral of the Ocean. Despite Columbus's personal limitations, Spanish colonization of the Americas had taken hold. Cattle and the horses that *vaqueros* rode to control them multiplied on the rich forage of the Caribbean islands.[15]

Approximately twenty-four *caballos* or stallions and ten *yeguas* or mares landed on Hispaniola on November 28, 1493, along with cattle, sheep, hogs, sows, mules, and goats.[16] More horses arrived with each succeeding expedition, and in 1503, Governor Nicolás de Ovando had the capacity to lead sixty to seventy mounted men against a Native uprising. On Hispaniola, the Crown centralized livestock breeding and usage on the first *ranchos del rey* or royal ranches, in the Americas. The *ranchos* served as an instrument of royal authority by accepting livestock for payment of taxes in the accelerated natural increase gained from a larger breeding pool, and in the distribution of horses for expeditions to other islands and as compensation to colonial officials. By the early sixteenth century, some 60 breeding mares and 1,650 cattle grazed on the *rancho del rey* at Santo Domingo.[17]

In 1507, Ovando informed King Fernando that the natural increase had risen to a level that satisfied the demand for horses, and that the colony needed no further shipments of mares. Over time, Hispaniola developed into a logistical base that underwrote the military and economic efforts to extend Spanish dominion over Puerto Rico, Jamaica, and Cuba, achieved with horses, cattle, foodstuffs, weapons, and soldiers. Governor Diego Velásquez landed an expedition of conquest on Cuba in 1511 and, among others, granted an *encomienda* to Hernán Cortés, who established the first *estancia* (cattle station) on the island.[18]

Between Columbus's second voyage in 1493 and Cortés's campaign to conquer the Aztec empire in 1519–1521, the Spanish had fully embedded horse and cattle culture on the Greater Antilles. Cattle and horses fed on the lush grasslands that the Taino people called *sabana*.[19] Cattle had increased so rapidly that the Governor of Hispaniola ordered the stockmen to corral their herds, in order to prevent the destruction of local crops. To comply with the order, *rancheros* built enough corrals to accommodate ten thousand head of Spanish cattle. The Hispaniolan *rancheros* absolutely depended upon Indigenous labor and controlled that labor source under their farm labor system of *encomienda*. They trained select Taino men to work as mounted herders or *vaqueros*.[20] Taino *vaqueros* rounded up the large herds for branding, for slaughter, and for shipment to other islands and eventually, to the mainland of New Spain.[21] Taino Indians continued to work as cowboys, even after massive depopulation by disease. Their decline ruled out large-scale crop farming until the Spanish imported replacement workers but survivors did serve as cowboys through the old system and continued on as hired hands even after *encomienda* died out.[22]

Andalusians from southern Spain constituted the majority of the first wave of Iberian immigrants to the Caribbean (1493–1520) and applied their experience and expertise in the newly implanted cattle and horse culture of the Antilles.[23] In 1519, Capitan-General Hernán Cortés loaded horses from Cuba onto his ships and landed them on the North American continent with his expeditionary force at present-day Vera Cruz, Mexico.[24] Cortés sought gold and treasure, and though his landing party constructed small shrines that venerated "Our Lady" along the road to the Valley of Mexico, his company's primary purpose remained fortune hunting. Aztec attempts to derail his approach only hardened his resolve. The Extremaduran *Conquistador* shrewdly allied with the formidable Tlaxcalans and other subject peoples of the Aztecs. His soldiers carried at least ten artillery pieces, muskets, and crossbows, and wore steel armor. A detachment of mounted troops supported the main force. A smallpox epidemic that decimated the Indigenous populations then emboldened Cortés to make his move. His drive on the Aztec capital of Tenochtítlan with his small force catalyzed a general uprising against Emperor Moctezuma, and culminated in the desperate struggle on the steps of the *Templo Mayor.* In the aftermath, Cortés proclaimed victory for God and king.[25]

As governor of New Spain, Cortés implemented the same colonial strategies that had transformed the landscapes of the big Caribbean islands—cattle and other livestock economies for their inherent values in meat, milk, hides, and tallow, and to buffer against underperforming crops. Spanish soldiers, *vaqueros,* and at times, priests trained trusted neophytes among their Tlaxcalan allies to ride horses and herd cattle, strategies that spread northward and northwesterly in New Spain. All *vaqueros,* Native or Spanish, rode the descendants of Cortés's horses and benefited from continuing experiences and adaptations of cattle economies in the New World.[26]

Cortés had come to the New World to conquer and reap great riches. Consistent with his character and ambitions, he was determined to find out if the unnamed island off the west coast of New Spain in any way resembled the land of legend, described by Ordóñez de Montalvo in his novel *Esplandián*: a land ruled by warrior women, carrying weapons made of gold. Cortés led a colony there in the 1530s and named it Santa Cruz. The colony failed but Cortés's ambition did not. In 1539, he sent Francisco de Ulloa at the head of a second expedition. Ulloa actually found that what came to be called California was a peninsula, not an island. Fantasies of great riches there persisted even though Ulloa found none.[27]

For the Spanish immigrants, beef, hides, and tallow provided a reliable food staple, helped to clothe and armor soldiers and civilian colonists, and generated candlelight by which they wrote orders to administer the colony and reported on their needs, successes, and failures to the Crown. Throughout the Spanish American Empire, the livestock ranching economy enabled missions, *presidios,* and *pueblos* to gain a foothold in previously unexploited territory. However, for the Indigenous peoples of northern New Spain, Spanish cattle, horses, and sheep altered their ecosystem, and so became an adaptive economy, that is, a survival strategy. The nascent industry proved to be especially well suited to the semi-arid grasslands of northern and northwestern New Spain, which eventually included the California provinces in the eighteenth century.[28] In addition to employing local Natives as *vaqueros,* the Spanish learned that Christianized Indians acted as examples if not agents of the new colonial way of life.[29]

From the Antilles to central Mexico, the Spanish sought wealth from cash crops like sugar and from the mining of precious metals like silver. These ventures required forced Indigenous labor and the appropriation of their tribal lands, causing the degradation of traditional societies by conversion to Catholicism. These changes also destroyed traditional economies and caused demographic collapses from multiple epidemics. From Cortés's victory over the Aztec empire, the Spanish learned the value of Native allies. In pursuit of wealth and the expansion of military and political control, they pushed northward, establishing missions, *pueblos,* and *estancias,* or cattle stations. In central Mexico, the rainfall supports unirrigated corn crops, but northward of that zone, the land transitions to semi-arid grasslands.[30] Chichimeca Indians had hunted and gathered their traditional foods there long before the Spanish arrived, and they put up a fierce resistance to the encroachments of the silver mines and horses and cattle on the *estancias* that supported them.[31] War ensued during the latter half of the sixteenth century as the Chichimecas killed *rancheros* and plundered the cattle, horses, and material goods like tools and weapons. And then, they burned the *estancias* to the ground.[32] Defensive measures and attempted punitive expeditions by the Spanish produced no decisive or lasting victories, and lack of funding meant undermanned *presidios.* Frontier Captains adapted by enlisting friendly Chichimecas to scout and spy on warring *ranchería(s)*, and some *estancieros* went so far as to arm and pay their own Native security force.[33] Leading colonial families, churchmen, and viceroys worked to end the decades-long violence. Miguel Caldera, born of a Spanish father and a Huachichil mother, played a pivotal diplomatic role in achieving a peaceful solution to the endless wars in 1590. Caldera's words carried great weight with his mother's people. To achieve peace, the Spanish government made annual donations of cattle, clothing, and food to the Chichimecas. To ensure that the peace endured, Chichimecas agreed to allow Christianized Indians to settle among them and teach them pastoral ways. Tlaxcalans, traditional allies of the Spanish since the time of Cortés, lived among the Chichimecas and taught them to herd their own horses and cattle. Chichimecas survived by adapting to new economies without entirely surrendering their sovereignty. More broadly, at a very granular level, "Hispanic stockmen" pushed their herds slowly into Indigenous domains and employed local Natives as *vaqueros.* Perhaps they shared Spanish beef to feed hungry Native families, and, over time, incorporated and acculturated former and potential adversaries.[34]

Spanish leadership took the lessons of their experiences on the Caribbean islands and in north-central Mexico and applied them on the frontier of northwestern New Spain, in Sonora, Arizona, and the California provinces. Even before Jesuit priest Eusebio Kino arrived in the region in 1687, Spanish horse and cattle herds had increased in Sonora to the point that Spanish (and likely Indian) *vaqueros* drove four thousand head of cattle to Mexico City. In March of that year, Kino founded what became his headquarters mission, Nuestra Señora de Los Dolores, a few leagues north of *Cucurpe* and *Tuape* on the San Miguel River. He stocked the Dolores *estancia* with hundreds of cattle from those missions and built his largest herd at Dolores. There he trained Natives of the Pimería Alta to ride, rope, and brand. From Dolores, Kino projected Spanish culture and the Catholic faith among the Piman- and Yuman-speaking tribes in the Pimería Alta. Their domain extended roughly from the San Pedro and San Miguel Rivers on the east to the Sea of Cortés, and from northern Sonora to the Gila River Valley in southern Arizona.[35] In addition to his religious efforts, Kino made scientific contributions as a first-rate geographer and cartographer.

An Italian of humble birth, Kino chose a life of service as a priest in the Society of Jesus, with the intent of serving as a Catholic missionary. As part of his rigorous Jesuit training in Germany, he studied and excelled in mathematics, geography, astronomy, and cartography. An offer of a professorship of mathematics from the Duke of Bavaria attests to Kino's stature as a scholar. He declined such a prestigious position in order to fulfill his vow to serve God, made while deathly ill as a young student. In addition to missionary zeal and his expertise with horses and cattle, Kino traveled the Pimería extensively, with the trained eye of a geographer and astronomer. He navigated by the stars and kept meticulous records that he used to produce one of the most accurate maps ever made in North America. His journey from Germany to the Pimería Alta began at the age of thirty-three in 1678. After many delays and disappointments, he landed on Mexican soil at Vera Cruz in 1681.[36]

In his very first assignment in New Spain, Kino served as a missionary and geographer with the military-Jesuit siting expedition on Baja California in 1683. That survey led to the founding of Mission San Bruno on the Sea of Cortés in the same year.[37] In late 1684, *Almirante* (Admiral) Isidro de Atondo y Antillón and Kino led a trans-Baja exploration from San Bruno that succeeded in reaching the Pacific Ocean. Along that shoreline, Kino found blue abalone shells. The memory of those shells later contributed to Kino's reasoning that Baja is a peninsula and not an island.[38] Nonetheless, lack of water and fertile soil forced the Jesuits to abandon San Bruno in 1685. Divided leadership with contending priorities also contributed to the failure in California. Kino objected to the harsh and at times violent treatment of (Baja) California Indians by the military. In one instance, Admiral Atondo's men fired a cannon at a group of supposedly threatening Indians killing and maiming a dozen. Soldiers and civilian colonists wanted access to neophyte labor, which Jesuits saw as exploitative only. The loss of his first mission stung Kino. He determined to apply the hard administrative lessons learned there toward a second chance at settling in California. First, future mission sites must have better water, pasturage, and cropland. Second, success also required guaranteeing the mission's survival with livestock transfers and other abundant food resources from Sonora. Lastly, leadership must be unified under Jesuit command. His work in the Pimería kept him close.[39]

From 1687 to 1711, Kino introduced and distributed cattle and horses to dozens of Native villages, as well as sheep and goats. Through this introduction of cattle and other livestock economies, Kino gained the trust of the Indigenous peoples he sought to convert to Catholicism. By prioritizing food security for the Natives, the Padre hoped to open their hearts to his spiritual message. Consistent with this desire, Kino invited groups like the O'Odham people of San Xavier del Bac to visit Mission Dolores and see for themselves the abundance of grains and meat on the hoof, enjoyed by neophytes at a Spanish mission.[40] This work along with his explorations and map making stand as his great contribution to the Spanish empire and to the sustenance of peoples who had suffered great losses to multiple European diseases. They suffered the losses both through European-Indigenous contact and possibly through direct Indigenous contact with domesticated animals.[41] He regularly worked alongside his Native assistants and allies as they herded, rounded up, and branded cattle—the hard work that such a vast enterprise required.[42]

Kino's distribution of livestock took hold in those areas where Kino or other Spanish padres formally established a mission with a permanent padre. This presence reinforced and sustained the cattle culture. Without that presence, however, herds declined or even disappeared. Apache raiding also suppressed livestock populations in the region. Kino's altruistic motives notwithstanding, livestock animals damaged Native ecosystems by consuming traditional wild plant foods, cultivated crops, and precious water. They also scared off wild game. Working on mission farms signified a tacit acceptance of Spanish authority and the preeminence of their Catholic religion. It also forced Pimería Alta Indians to neglect their own crops when they were most vulnerable in an arid land. Many Indians objected vociferously. Violent efforts to rid their territories of the Spanish colonizers and their religion invariably included the slaughter of cattle.[43] Despite these sobering realities, Kino forged ahead with his characteristically energetic devotion to duty—to spread Christianity and cattle ranching among the unconverted Natives. Even in the aftermath of a deadly rebellion in 1695, Kino persisted in driving more cattle to missions such as San Xavier del Bac. By 1700, the herd there had swelled to over a thousand head.[44]

Kino's evangelical work and livestock transfers played an essential role in extending the frontier in Sonora and into Baja California. Specifically, the northern Sonoran herds provided the seed cattle for new missions in both provinces. Even knowing how rugged the Baja country was, Kino still dreamt of returning there to establish successful missions. He and his friend Padre Juan Maria de Salvatierra proposed the idea to both Jesuit and imperial authorities and persistently politicked for it. Finally, the venture gained approval but to Kino's deep disappointment, his superior and the governor petitioned the viceroy against releasing him from his duties in the Pimería. In the face of Native unrest, they said Kino's influence exceeded the presence of a *presidio*. Instead, Father Francisco María Piccolo joined Salvatierra, and Kino never set foot on California soil again.[45]

In October 1697, Jesuit Padre Juan Maria de Salvatierra and a small party of nine men, including Christianized Indians from the mainland, landed on the eastern shore of Baja California. That place, the Indigenous people called *Conchó*, was located about thirty miles south of the failed San Bruno site and in proximity to Isla Del Carmen.[46] There, they situated the new mission that Salvatierra christened Nuestra Señora de Loreto Conchó, in honor of the Catholic Blessed Virgin, who manifested to the faithful in the small Italian town of Loreto.[47] The newcomers unloaded sheep, goats, and pigs at that site along with equipment and provisions. Although they did not transport live cattle at that time, they did bring the dried beef of thirty animals. The Baja Natives who met them on the shore included the Cochimí. For Baja California Indians, whose struggle for existence Padre Kino once described as "laborious and unrelieved," the sight of animal flesh and other foods drew them to the budding mission.[48] Most kept their distance until the Spanish began feeding those few who had volunteered to help unload equipment and supplies from the ship. When the large group of Indians pressed close to the food, the Spanish reacted with alarm and tried to build barriers to protect their food, which angered the Natives. Two separate skirmishes followed, in which European guns and steel solidified the control that food gave the Spanish over Baja Natives.[49]

In 1700, Padre Kino's Mission Dolores donated two hundred head of cattle to Mission Loreto. The cattle helped make Loreto the first sustainable mission on the Baja peninsula, generally believed to be an island at that time. At least seven other missions in Sonora donated another three hundred head of cattle, as well as sheep, goats, and horses, to Loreto.[50]

During his twenty-four-year tenure, Kino made fifty arduous journeys in the arid Pimería, some of which he undertook as exploratory probes to the northern and northwestern frontiers of the region. In 1692, Father Salvatierra accompanied Kino northward to the large Indian village of San Xavier del Bac near present-day Tucson. Kino also explored northwesterly, along the Gila River to its mouth at the Colorado River. By 1702, he had followed the Colorado down to the Gulf of California (or Sea of Cortés). He had also seen blue abalone shells in the Pimería on numerous occasions and knew that the Indigenous peoples of New Spain did not possess ocean-going vessels. Hence, standing where the Colorado River emptied into the Gulf, Kino concluded that Native people brought those shells to the Pimería by land. His map of the region, published in 1705, showed California as firmly attached to the mainland. This news, *California no es isla, sino penisla*, once confirmed by witnesses, promised overland movements of horses, cattle, and sheep in support of Baja California missions—but at a later date. Kino's work also inspired kindred spirits like Father Francisco Garces and Captain Juan Bautista de Anza to fulfill the promise of overland support for new settlements, ultimately in what became Alta California.[51]

Kino chose to make these journeys partly to satisfy his scientific curiosity and his wanderlust. However, the promise of safely supplying large numbers of livestock for the needs of the Baja missions superseded personal satisfactions.[52] Prior to his discovery, the Spanish had no choice but to supply the Baja missions entirely by sea, on board ships that crossed the Sea of Cortés or fought northward from the mainland against the Pacific current. Manila *galleons* also rode that same current all the way from the Philippine Islands to Baja and on to Acapulco. Without the knowledge that Kino's discovery provided, the Sonoran missions had no choice but to transport the donated livestock in 1700 across the Sea of Cortés, on board ships in danger of being wrecked in fierce storms or dashed upon uncharted hazards.[53]

The sad tale of the supply ship *Capitana* illustrates the hazards of cross-gulf transport and the need for an overland alternative. In 1683, the survival of the original military-Jesuit mission at San Bruno (led by Admiral Atondo and Padre Kino) hung on the ability of the ship's Captain Guzmán to bring supplies and livestock from the mainland. After four tries to re-cross the gulf failed, the storms had so battered the small ship that, in order to save the crew, Guzmán ordered all 150 head of livestock dumped overboard. The heartbreaking loss included cattle, sheep, and fourteen horses.[54]

Overland re-supply eventually took place but seagoing transport persisted. In 1709, Father Salvatierra wrote to his *Provincial* (regional supervisor) about the delayed transfer of two hundred head of cattle from Puerto Yaqui (present-day Guaymas on the Sonoran coast) to Loreto. The transport vessel that had been shuttling supplies of all kinds to the Baja missions was down for repairs.[55] In this instance, an overland caravan presented a logical alternative at least until the ship received its repairs. But doubts about California's peninsularity persisted; so much so that the Jesuits commissioned yet another expedition to foreclose the debate some forty-six years later.[56] An overland supply route held its own risks but such caravans promised travel and transport, unthreatened by treacherous seas or shipboard space limitations.[57]

Between 1697 and 1767, the Jesuits founded eighteen missions in Baja, nine of which they relocated, one they abandoned, and one they depopulated, primarily on account of poor water resources.[58] The problem did not lie with poor siting; the Jesuits employed rigorous specifications in choosing a site prior to beginning construction but had no way to determine the long-term availability of water at a given site. Large-scale agriculture, essential to supporting a mission community of neophytes, padres, and soldiers, taxed the existing sources. Cattle and other livestock often served as the primary sources of food when droughts threatened the very existence of a mission. In Baja, the Indigenous peoples had survived for thousands of years by staying on the move, following the available seasonal resources. This held especially true for the Cochimí of central Baja, less so for the Yumans in the north and the Monquí (Guaycurá) and Pericú in the south. But water supplies made all life tenuous on the peninsula, for man or beast. Conversely, the stationary Mission Loreto community lived with the hard reality that they either survived on locally available water or they relocated or they abandoned that venture entirely.[59] Steer meat and cow milk mitigated the harsh effects of drought on mission crops, as they had on the Iberian Peninsula and throughout the Spanish colonizing experience. Sometimes, though, they only forestalled the inevitable.

The dangers of crossing the Gulf of California greatly curtailed connections, supplies, and visitors from the mainland and isolated the peninsula population. Outside the rebellion of 1734–1738, the danger of combat with Native Californians had been remote.[60] So by necessity, the Jesuits selected soldiers from the mainland who had mastered at least one trade and preferably more. Soldiers worked with wood, stone, metals, and leather to build, maintain, repair, and replace all structures, tools, and pieces of equipment. Only officers wore standard uniforms appropriate to their rank. Soldiers' wives, tailors, or seamstresses created non-standard attire for the enlisted men intended to denote their military status with one exception. The *chaqueta de cuera* or leather jacket, made of seven layers of soft deerskin, distinguished the soldiers from all others in California, hence their legendary name, *soldados de cuera*.[61]

In the eighteenth century, soldiers of the king carried a variety of weapons, including the lance and shield that had been used against organized Moorish armies on the battlefields of Iberia. Up against Baja Natives like the Uchití on their own rugged and barren ground, California *soldados* adapted to what worked and likely dispensed with the excess weight.[62]

Most of these unconventional soldiers who arrived in the early years of colonization had emigrated from Sinaloa and Sonora and came from cattle-ranching families. They brought those experiences and skills with them, along with ambitions to pursue ranching on the peninsula. In a theme that recurred on many frontiers of Spanish America, immigrants, whether padre or soldier-rancher, had to rapidly adapt to the landscapes, climates, and Indigenous inhabitants they encountered if they hoped to survive. And as frontiersmen, what they did mattered more than how they looked doing it.

During rare instances when fighting was necessary, great distances had to be traversed in intense heat, and an elusive enemy sought out in vast areas of broken, nearly waterless land. Soldiering under these conditions favored men who traveled light, who bore few arms and less armor, and who could break up into very small groups and move quickly whether advancing or retreating and live off the land when necessary.[63]

On the Baja peninsula, soldiers, both active and retired, managed mission and *presidio* herds, as well as small herds of their own. Some worked for other retired soldiers who had set out to build equity in a cattle ranch. As experienced cattlemen, they adjusted herd sizes according to the uncertain water and forage. However, for the last two centuries in the Western hemisphere, the Spanish Longhorns had demonstrated an ability to survive on their own and under seemingly poor conditions. "These cattle had a quick, alert, and restless manner and moved with a light, elastic gait; they have been likened to wild animals, continually snuffling the air on the lookout for danger."[64] While many observers had described the Longhorn breed as small, the Baja Longhorns likely carried the least weight of all. Jesuit Jacobo Baegert estimated the weight of Baja cattle in the 1760s to be barely 300–400 pounds.[65] Low rainfall meant diminished forage. In the event of unusually good rainfall and forage, the herds increased. Coupled with the knowledge that animals ran wild in the brush country, the soldier-ranchers likely supplemented their workforce with local Natives, as they had done on the Antilles, in north-central Mexico, and in the Pimería Alta. Spanish law forbade American Indians from owning or even riding horses but at some point, chasing down an escaped cow required an Indian ranch hand to hop on horseback and return the stray to the herd.[66]

Esteban Rodríguez, a Portuguese *mayordomo* or foreman at the Jesuit College north of Mexico City, had accepted Padre Salvatierra's invitation to join his new venture in California. Rodríguez landed with him in Loreto in 1697 as one of the padre's "brave party of ten."[67] Salvatierra appointed him to the rank of captain in 1701; however, bureaucrats who resented the Jesuits' power to make military appointments never confirmed Rodríguez's captaincy. By the late 1720s, Rodríguez neared sixty but still had no official rank or pension. To make amends, in 1730 the Jesuits broke their own restrictions against private enterprise and granted Rodríguez grazing rights near Todos Santos in the southern region known as *El Sur de California*. Two soldiers managed the aging and nearly blind captain's cattle. At last, it seemed Rodríguez had a source of wealth on which to retire, but the neophyte insurrection in 1734 disrupted all ranching in the region. For the next five years, the Uchití killed, ate, and dispersed the herds. Their attacks created a population of feral cattle that persisted in the wild for more than a century. Logic dictates that during that century, Indians and various private parties rounded up the wild ones as fair game.[68]

After Captain Esteban Rodríguez died in 1744, the Jesuits appointed his sickly son Bernardo to succeed him, based on Bernardo's malleability to Jesuit direction. Recognizing an opportunity, Bernardo's *Teniente* (lieutenant) and brother-in-law, Pedro de la Riva, openly flouted Bernardo's authority. In command of the sub-*presidio* at La Paz in the Cape region, de la Riva waged a brutal campaign against the Uchití in the far south. In one act of genocide, he took twenty of their children and sent them north to Loreto, to be distributed among other missions in the area. In a second instance, he executed Uchití prisoners. Riva seized a valuable parcel of watered pasturage in the Cape region and built a private herd there, partly to supply beef to his own troop. In a not-unusual custom of the Spanish Empire, the Royal treasury reimbursed the Lieutenant for supplying provisions to himself. The sickly Bernardo Rodríguez passed away at the age of forty, in 1750. His death set the stage for Riva's campaign for the coveted position, and then the unexpected elevation of Private Fernando Rivera y Moncada to Captain, at the age of twenty-five.[69]

Rivera came from Creole gentry in Compostela, province of Nayarit. His father died in 1731, when Fernando was just a boy of nine, causing the family fortunes to decline. In one of the many sacrifices that he made to serve others, Rivera enlisted in the army at the age of eighteen to support his mother. Ironically, his first assignment placed him under the command of *Teniente* de la Riva, stationed with the *escuadra del Sur* at Todos Santos. In that posting, he happened to witness (and later attested to) Riva's appropriation of the ranch land in *El Sur*. Rivera y Moncada's formal appointment as Captain arrived from Spain in 1751. In addition to the command of the *presidio*, he also held civil governing authority and the title of *justicia mayor*, "the crown's judicial representative." As *justicia mayor*, Rivera had the power and responsibility to investigate crimes, apprehend suspects, try them in his court, and mete out sentences.[70]

In the later years of Jesuit tenure (1750–1767) the Baja Indian attacks subsided, due in no small measure to successive waves of smallpox, measles, and syphilis. Then-Private Rivera had witnessed the devastation in the Cape region in the years 1742–1748.[71] But then, energetic new padres like the Bohemian Wenceslao Linck renewed their efforts to push northward and complete the establishment of new missions in the entire peninsula. Jesuits established Santa Gertrudis in the center of Baja in 1751. Further north on the peninsula, Croatian Padre Francisco Consag had found a "large and receptive *ranchería*" in 1746, when he landed a scouting party at the Bahia de Los Angeles. The bay presented a good harbor for re-supply from Loreto with protection from Isla Angel De La Guarda. Consag hoped to dedicate the mission to San Francisco de Borja, an early Jesuit leader of the sixteenth century, who advocated for humane treatment of the Indigenous peoples in the New World. Consag died before he could place a mission there but Linck arrived in 1762 with substantial donations in hand. Captain Rivera moved his headquarters there temporarily to supervise his soldiers and to provide a calming presence for the civilian tradesmen in Native territory. He saw the inadequacy of the water and pasturage in the vicinity of the *cabacera* or mission headquarters and took two soldiers with ranching experience to scout for something better. They unexpectedly found a broad mesa with springs and good forage that they believed would support hundreds of cattle and horses. By 1763, the mesa at "San Borja" supported six hundred head of cattle and eighty mares.[72]

In August 1764, Padre Linck, Captain Rivera, two Germans who had arrived on the Manila *galleon*, and sixteen Cochimí Indians, embarked on a search for the next and what would be the last Jesuit mission site in California. Their survey extended five months but their thorough search resulted in locating Mission Santa María in 1767, initially about sixty miles north of San Borja. In 1769, the mission relocated another thirty miles northward and closer to a Cochimí *ranchería* named Velicatá. Linck had recognized the site's potential in 1764 and took steps to make it a *visita* of Santa María—affiliated with the mission but a village apart from it. Velicatá possessed enough water and forage to support both crops and livestock. The Spanish used Velicatá as their base when they launched their first expeditions into Alta California.[73]

A few entrepreneurial civilians traveled to California from Spain or New Spain for the explicit purpose of building fortunes and raising their social status based on silver mining, pearling, and cattle ranching. When the mines played out and pearl harvests dwindled, these Spaniards turned to herding livestock to build wealth. They sold their animals to feed and clothe all the Spanish subjects on Baja, whether priests, soldiers, neophytes, or civilians who claimed Spanish descent.[74] The Jesuits resisted most efforts at secular economic development, especially those that consumed resources deemed critical to their overall mission to convert and care for the California Indians. Mission cattle suffered when private cattle encroached on mission pastures. The padres also monopolized the Indian labor that had proven essential to the development of all Spanish American colonies. Beyond local religious-secular disputes, the Jesuits' extensive financial support from Europe created a perceived defiance of temporal and religious authority that bred deep resentments among ruling elites. In Baja, the Jesuits paid and appointed military officers, just as Padres Kino and Salvatierra had proposed. The Jesuits' appointive power of this office presented the possibility of a conflict of interest. Manuel de Ocio, a retired soldier-turned-entrepreneur, raised these suspicions in his multiple formal and informal complaints against the Jesuits and Rivera. Stories that the Jesuits had accumulated and hoarded vast treasures in California further inflamed these passions.[75]

On June 25, 1767, King Carlos III of Spain ordered the arrest and forcible expulsion of all Jesuit priests in New Spain. These arrests occurred simultaneously on the mainland, followed by violent crackdowns against anyone who resisted, as directed by *Visitador General* José de Galvéz. California's remoteness proved to be a blessing for the Jesuits there. Catalan Captain Gaspar de Portolá commanded a column of troops marching to Sonora to quell potential uprisings resulting from the expulsions. Instead, a messenger intercepted Portolá with a directive from the viceroy. The communiqué stated his appointment as governor of California and redirected him and his troops to that peninsula. Once there, Portolá had orders to remove the Jesuits, seize all of their property, suppress any resistance, and install Franciscan replacements.[76]

To get to California, Portolá's entire unit traveled to the Spanish port at San Blas, in the modern Mexican state of Nayarit, some five hundred miles south of Loreto. In July 1767, Portolá, fifty soldiers and fourteen Franciscans boarded his small flotilla of three vessels and headed toward Loreto. Their plan to surprise the Jesuits and the garrison ran into summer *chubascos* on the gulf. Storm damage twice forced them back to San Blas. After repairs, they launched a third time in October, and after forty days at sea, Portolá found himself and twenty-five soldiers alone and exhausted, almost three hundred miles south of Loreto. More than five months after the mainland expulsion, they landed near Mission San Jose del Cabo, on November 30, 1767.

Captain Rivera, who had been in the south, met them and made preparations for the march north to Loreto. During the twelve-day march, in the heat, over rocks and thorns, with little water or pasturage, Portolá experienced a sudden awakening to the harsh reality of life on the peninsula. After a month there, he informed the viceroy that half of his dragoons had become incapacitated from the hard work required of men on the frontier and should be returned to the mainland. Rather than relieving its officers and releasing the men from duty, Portolá realized that he could not accomplish any part of his mission without the men of the California *presidio*. Many were sons of soldiers but the land hardened them for duty on Baja. Portolá observed, "It is certain, Sir, that to carry out the service in this country, it is more necessary to have a cowboy than a soldier to care for so much livestock by day and to guard it by night."[77]

When he finally arrived in Loreto, instead of resistance, Portolá found only Jesuit acquiescence and a drought-ravaged populace. He saw that far from a treasure-laden land of pearls and silver, the missions had become destitute after four consecutive years of locust attacks that decimated crops, while drought reduced livestock herds by half. Portolá made Loreto his capital in December but charitably deferred disclosing the formal decree of expulsion until after the holy day of Christmas. On the day before their departure,

February 2, 1768, he allowed the Jesuits to celebrate one final Mass, to share communion with all, and to offer a farewell to the faithful, Indian and Spanish. The outpouring of affection from the people, as the deposed padres made their way to the boats, moved Portolá to tears. Later Jesuit accounts "extolled his kindness, courtesy, and compassion."[78]

Their final embarkation at Loreto ended seventy years of Jesuit work and sacrifice. It also ended their paternalistic and rigid treatment of the Native peoples. Anticipating a delay before their Franciscan replacements arrived, Governor Portolá appointed local soldiers as *comisionados*, tasked with holding the missions together, including their neophyte populations and their assets, especially the livestock herds. *Comisionados* governed without the spiritual power of padres and often under the duress of external forces like the ongoing drought.[79]

Meanwhile, reports had alerted the Spanish Crown to Russian activities and British ambitions on the far northern frontier. These threats to Spanish sovereignty spurred a major reassessment of Spanish colonial strategies. Their next moves shifted imperial energies and resources from the peninsula to the northern territory that came to be known as Alta California.[80]

NOTES

1. Terry G. Jordan, *North American Cattle-Ranching Frontiers: Origins, Diffusion, and Differentiation* (Albuquerque, NM: University of New Mexico Press, 1993).

2. Karl W. Butzer, "Cattle and Sheep from Old World to New Spain: Historical Antecedents," *Annals of the Association of American Geographers* 78, no. 1 (March 1988): 40–47; Carlos Álvarez-Nogal and Leandro Prados De la Escosura, "The Rise and Fall of Spain (1270–1850)," *The Economic History Review* 66, no. 1 (February 2013): 1–2. Christian cattle rustling not only denied economic resources to Muslims, it depressed the population in a sort of frontier region in which the shortage of labor ruled out agriculture on a large scale. The Black Death that struck in 1348 further reduced the population of the *Meseta*-Andalucía region.

3. Álvarez-Nogal and Prados De La Escosura, "The Rise and Fall of Spain," 1–2; Julian Charles Bishko, "The Peninsular Background of Latin American Cattle Ranching," *The Hispanic American Historical Review* 32, no. 4 (November 1952): 494; A. Rodero, J. V. Delgado and E. Rodero, "Primitive Andalusian Livestock and Their Implications in the Discovery of America," *Archivos de Zootecnia* 41, no. 154 (1992): 383–400, 385.

4. Bishko, "Peninsular Background," 507.

5. Butzer, "Cattle and Sheep from Old World to New," 43–44.

6. Jordan, *North American Cattle-Ranching Frontiers*, 93–95.

7. Peggy K. Liss, *Isabel the Queen: Life and Times*, rev. ed. (Philadelphia, PA: University of Pennsylvania Press, 2004), 216–263.

8. Ibid., 316–326.

9. Samuel Eliot Morison, *Admiral of the Ocean Sea: A Life of Christopher Columbus* (Boston, MA: Little, Brown, and Company, 1942), xxxiv–xliii. The phrase "excellence in windward work" refers to sailing toward the wind at an angle and by tacking or "coming about" (zigzagging), making way against headwinds. This maneuverability is also invaluable in tight quarters along a rocky coast or among the islands of an archipelago—in short, exploration. Columbus's caravels only measured about seventy-five feet in length and twenty-five feet abeam (width). They carried few sails on just two masts. The Spanish built their own caravels in Andalucía at the port of Niebla, close to the border with Portugal.

10. Ibid., 327–330.

11. John J. Johnson, "The Introduction of the Horse into the Western Hemisphere," *The Hispanic American Historical Review* 23, no. 4 (November 1943): 587–598; Rodero et al., "Primitive Andalusian Livestock," 390. More than twenty horses began the journey but on this and subsequent voyages, the Spanish suffered significant losses of livestock at sea, often when water ran critically low in extended doldrums near the Equator.

12. Liss, *Isabel the Queen*, 332–335; see also Morrisey, "Colonial Agriculture in New Spain," 24; and Mervyn Ratekin, "The Early Sugar Industry in Española," *The Hispanic American Historical Review* 34, no. 1 (February 1954): 1–19.

13. Jordan, *North American Cattle Ranching Frontiers*, 72–73. See also Herbert E. Bolton, *The Spanish Borderlands: A Chronicle of Old Florida and the Southwest* (New Haven, CT: Yale University Press, 1921), 190; *Encomienda*: the attachment of Indigenous labor to a specific tract of land, by royal grant, from the verb *encomendar* (to entrust). The Crown ended this type of servitude in 1549. See also Herbert E. Bolton, "The Mission as a Frontier Institution in the Spanish-American Colonies," *American Historical Review* 23, no. 1 (October 1917): 43–45.

14. Liss, *Isabel the Queen*, 329–346.

15. Ibid.

16. Johnson, "The Introduction of the Horse," 591.

17. Ibid., 594–596.

18. Ibid., 600–604.

19. Jordan, *North American Cattle-Ranching Frontiers*, 18–55, 65–68.

20. Johnson, "Introduction of the Horse," 608.

21. Ibid., 609–610.

22. Jordan, *North American Cattle Ranching Frontiers*, 72–73. See also Ratekin, "The Early Sugar Industry in Española," 4, 14–15.

23. Jordan, *North American Cattle-Ranching Frontiers,* 23–27, 65–66; see also Bernard Grunberg, "The Origins of the Conquistadores of Mexico City," *The Hispanic American Historical Review* 74, no. 2 (May 1994): 268–271. Andalusians also comprised 34 percent of the known members of the twelve Conquistador expeditions sent to Mexico 1519–1521.

24. Bernal Díaz del Castillo, *The History of the Conquest of New Spain*, trans. and ed. by Davíd Carrasco (Albuquerque, NM: University of New Mexico Press, 2008), 37, 378.

25. Ibid., 24–25, 92, 277–295.

26. Richard J. Morrisey, "The Northward Expansion of Cattle Ranching in New Spain, 1550–1600," *Agricultural History* 25, no. 3 (July 1951): 115–121; Philip Wayne Powell, "Presidios and Towns on the Silver Frontier of New Spain, 1550–1580," *Hispanic American Historical Review* 24, no. 2 (May 1944): 179–200.

27. Bolton, *Spanish Borderlands*, 105–119.

28. Robert H. Jackson, and Edward Castillo, *Indians, Franciscans, and Spanish Colonization: The Impact of the Mission System on California Indians* (Albuquerque, NM: University of New Mexico Press, 1995), 14–15.

29. Morrisey, "Expansion of Cattle Ranching in New Spain," 115–121.

30. Ibid., 115. This line of demarcation runs roughly west-northwesterly from Veracruz, through Mexico City, to the Pacific in the modern state of Nayarit.

31. Powell, "Presidios and Towns on the Silver Frontier of New Spain," fn179–180. The Spanish assigned the generic term Chichimeca to "any nomadic savage on the northern frontier." Of the various nations labeled indiscriminately by this term, the *Huachichiles* of the San Luis Potosi region controlled the largest area and instilled the greatest fear in the Spanish; see also Philip Wayne Powell, "Spanish Warfare Against the Chichimecas in the 1570s," *Hispanic American Historical Review* 24, no. 4 (November 1944): 580–604. See also Donald D. Brand, "The Early History of the Range Cattle Industry in Northern Mexico," *Agricultural History* 35, no. 3 (July 1961): 132–139 and Richard W. Slatta, *Comparing Cowboys and Frontiers* (Norman, OK: University of Oklahoma Press, 1997), 55–59.

32. Morrisey, "Expansion of Cattle Ranching in New Spain," 120.

33. Powell, "Spanish Warfare," 597–598.

34. Ibid., 120–121.

35. Bolton, *The Spanish Borderlands*, 192–201; James E. Officer, "Kino and Agriculture in the Pimeria Alta," *The Journal of Arizona History* 34, no. 3 (Autumn 1993): 288–292.

36. Padre Eusebio Kino's own diaries document his spiritual and scientific work in Eusebio Francisco Kino, S. J., *Kino's Historical Memoir of Pimería Alta: A Contemporary Account of the Beginnings of California, Sonora, and Arizona, By Father Eusebio Francisco Kino, S.J., Pioneer Missionary, Explorer, Cartographer, and Ranchman, 1683–1711*, trans. and ed. by Herbert Eugene Bolton (Berkeley, CA: University of California Press, (1919) 1948). Bolton relied on Kino's diaries in his work entitled *Rim of Christendom: A Biography of Eusebio Francisco Kino Pacific Coast Pioneer* (New York: The MacMillan Company. Reprint, Tucson, AZ: University of Arizona Press, (1936) 1984), 27–36, 39–72.

37. Brian A. Aviles and Robert L. Hoover, "Two Californias, Three Religious Orders, and Fifty Missions: A Comparison of the Missionary Systems of Baja and Alta California," *Pacific Coast Archaeological Society Quarterly* 33, no. 3 (Summer 1997): 11.

38. Harry W. Crosby, *Antigua California: Mission and Colony on the Peninsular Frontier, 1697–1768* (Albuquerque, NM: University of New Mexico Press, 1994), 3; see also Ronald L. Ives, "Kino's Route Across Baja California," *Kiva* 26, no. 4 (April 1961): 28.

39. Crosby, *Antigua California*, 10–13; Officer, "Kino and Agriculture in the Pimeria Alta," 291–294.

40. Ibid., 295.

41. Barnet Pavao-Zuckerman, "Missions, Livestock, and Economic Transformations in the Pimería Alta," in *New Mexico and the Pimería Alta: The Colonial Period in the American Southwest*, eds. John G. Douglas and William M. Graves, 292 (Louisville, CO: University Press of Colorado, 2017). See also Crosby, *Antigua California*, 433fn 6. Regarding the spread of diseases in advance of European arrivals, see William Preston, "Serpent in Eden: Dispersal of Foreign Diseases into Pre-Mission California," *Journal of California and Great Basin Anthropology* 18, no. 1 (1996): 2–37. See also Jared Diamond, *Guns, Germs, and Steel: The Fates of Human Societies* (New York: W. W. Norton, 1999), 87, 92, 164, 195–197; and Robert H. Jackson, "Epidemic Disease and Population Decline in the Baja California Missions, 1697–1834," *Southern California Quarterly* 63, no. 4 (Winter 1981): 308–346.

42. Officer, "Kino and Agriculture," 292–293.

43. Pavao-Zuckerman, "Economic Transformations," 292–293. See also Robert Christian Perez, "Indian Rebellions in Northwestern New Spain: A Comparative Analysis, 1695–1750s" (PhD Dissertation, University of California, Riverside, Riverside, CA, 2003), 132–145. Spanish soldiers like Lieutenant Solís and Opata Indians whom the Spanish had given authority to train Pimas (O'Odham) to herd cattle, undid Kino's good work by violently punishing the Pima. The many incidents of lashings at Tubutama sparked a violent revolt by the Pima in 1695, who killed Father Francisco Seata and destroyed Catholic sacred objects, followed by the retaliatory massacre of fifty unarmed (and likely innocent) Pimas by Spanish troops.

44. Officer, "Kino and Agriculture," 293.

45. Crosby, *Antigua California*, 20–23.

46. Ibid., 42.

47. Ibid., 10, 429n.25. See also Karin Vélez, *The Miraculous Flying House of Loreto: Spreading Catholicism in the Early Modern World* (Princeton, NJ: Princeton University Press, 2019), 3–9.

48. Crosby, *Antigua California*, 22, 28.

49. Ibid., 28–34.

50. Bolton, *Rim of Christendom*, 446–447; Officer, "Kino and Agriculture in the Pimeria Alta," 294.

51. Kino, *Kino's Historical Memoir*, 244–245; Bolton, *Rim of Christendom*, 445–487.

52. Ibid., 434, 445.

53. Peter Masten Dunne, S. J., *Black Robes in Lower California* (Berkeley and Los Angeles, CA: University of California Press, 1968), 26–28. See also Crosby, *Antigua California*, 113–117; Aviles and Hoover, "Two Californias," 3. *Cordonoyos* are fierce summer storms. *Chubascos* are the major tropical storms that form around the Cape.

54. Dunne, *Black Robes in Lower California*, 29–31. Crosby, *Antigua California*, 166. The *Capitana* served under the command of the captain of the Loreto *presidio*.

55. Juan Maria de Salvatierra to Father Ambrosio Odden, "Report on How the First Cattle Came to California," A Missionary Letter. Rivera Library, University of California, Riverside, CA, 1709.

56. Crosby, *Antigua California*, 301.

57. Bolton, *The Spanish Borderlands*, 196–197, 202; Officer, "Kino and Agriculture in the Pimeria Alta," 295.

58. Aviles and Hoover, "Two Californias," 9–10, 22.

59. Ibid., 11–12.

60. Crosby, *Antigua California*, 114–122. An alliance of formerly rival groups rose up against the Spanish, who brought sicknesses that took half of the Indigenous population in just one generation. Warriors killed thirteen members of a landing party from the Manila galleon, and two padres, a soldier, and two servants at missions Santiago and San Jose del Cabo. They destroyed those and two other missions and remained in command of the southern El Sur region until Governor Manuel Bernal de Huidobro of Sinaloa brought troops and some order in 1738.

61. Ibid., 170–171.

62. Odie B. Faulk and Sidney B. Brinckerhoff, *Lancers for the King: A Study of the Frontier Military System of Northern New Spain, With a Translation of the Royal Regulations of 1772* (Phoenix, AZ: Arizona Historical Foundation, 1965), 112–124. During the first half of the Jesuit regime in Baja, twenty-five soldiers shouldered the entire burden of providing security for twelve missions spread over thousands of square miles on the peninsula. Following the rebellion of 1734–1738, the viceroy authorized a new presidio of thirty soldiers for California, distributed among the missions of the *El Sur* region.

63. Ibid., 172–173.

64. L. T. [Lee T.] Burcham, *California Range Land: An Historico-Ecological Study of the Range Resource of California* (Sacramento, CA: Division of Forestry, Department of Natural Resources, State of California, 1957), 53–55.

65. Ibid., 55–57; Crosby, *Antigua California*, 404.

66. Crosby, *Antigua California*, 316.

67. Ibid., 302–303.

68. Ibid., 304–305.

69. Ibid., 312–318, 329–333.

70. Ibid. 335.

71. Ibid., 312, 316, 336; Preston, "Serpent in Eden," 13–14. Preston's data adds dysentery, typhoid fever, and malaria to the list of "Every conceivable Old-World disease . . . [that] raged (often in clusters) up and down the peninsula on the average of about once every four years."

72. Crosby, *Antigua California*, 347–349.

73. Ibid., 391, 393.

74. Ibid., 333–335. 359–363, 367–370. See also John Francis Bannon, "Black-Robe Frontiersman: Pedro Mendez, S. J.," *The Hispanic American Historical Review* 27, no. 1 (February 1947): 75–76.
75. Crosby, *Antigua California*. 380.
76. Ibid., 371–376
77. Crosby, *Gateway to Alta California*, 27–29.
78. Ibid., 371–386.
79. Ibid., 379–380.
80. Ibid., 390–391.

Chapter 2

Marches to New California, 1769–1781

Consistent with northward expansion in New Spain from the time of Cortés's landing in 1519, the Spanish took horses and cattle from Baja California and Sonora and marched them into Alta California two and a half centuries later. Trusted Native neophytes came with them to herd the animals and to train the Indigenous peoples on the new frontier. With horses and cattle, the Spanish asserted control of the land, on which they built the markers of their culture and traditions: mission churches, *ranchos*, *presidios*, and eventually settlements. These institutions changed Native cultures and economies by destroying their traditional food sources and replacing those foods with beef and European crops, and by enlisting Indigenous labor in the hard work of transforming the landscape as *vaqueros* and farmhands.

Through his Council of the Indies, King Carlos III tasked *Visitador-General* José de Gálvez with defending Spain's territorial claims in California and improving the performance of the frontier territories of northern New Spain. Gálvez proposed sweeping changes aimed at generating increased revenues for the Crown, pacifying the Indigenous populations, and drastically altering the relationship between the Catholic Church and its new converts. Gálvez faced multiple challenges and threats along the northern Spanish frontier, including at that moment an uprising by the Serí (Comcaac) people in the coastal region of Sonora, westward of present-day Hermosillo. With limited resources, Gálvez had little choice but to sustain the policy of defensive expansion that had planted missions, *presidios*, and a few *pueblos*, from Texas to California. Once the Spanish planted their flag in the south at San Diego and in the north at Monterrey, they set out to sustain their Alta California settlements with horses, cattle, and people from Sonora. That strategy included bringing *vaqueros* from the settled regions to train the Alta California Indians on the frontier to ride horses, rope, brand, and herd cattle, not only for the benefit of the present mission but also for the next one to be founded in the future, some thirty miles beyond.

In response to Gálvez's plan, Father President Junípero Serra and Governor Gaspar de Portolá planned to make the move into New or Alta California in two separate but supportive groups. Captain Fernando Rivera y Moncada's first group had the tough job of trailblazing and marking a route to San Diego over six hundred miles of forbidding Baja terrain, to be followed by Serra, Portolá, and horses and cattle. Rivera's party's ability to bring most of their horses and mules to San Diego safely proved the availability of water and forage on the trail, which predicted success in driving horses and cattle over that trail soon thereafter.

Portolá and Serra planned to depart Baja a month later to lead the second group that included horses and about two hundred head of Longhorn cattle. Shifting resources to the north literally meant stripping Baja missions in *El Sur* of food, supplies, and equipment to fill the holds of the cargo vessels bound for San Diego Bay.[1] Rivera's overland party commandeered cattle, mules, horses, and supplies from the northern missions as they passed through. Portolá regretted that they had left those "poor missions . . . scantily provided for." They also took scores of Cochimí men away from their homes and families.[2]

Cochimíes lived north of Loreto and occupied about two-thirds of the Baja peninsula, the driest and least hospitable part. Yet, they were the most numerous of all Baja Natives. To hunt and gather, they organized themselves into small groups, possibly fifty to seventy-five people, scaled to match resource availability. They migrated according to the seasons and followed a vertical cycle from mountain to sea and back, dictated always by water availability. In the higher elevations they roasted hearts of *agave* and cactus fruits that had been hydrated only by the marine fog. Seaside, the Cochimí harvested marine resources like fish, shellfish, and sea mammals. As a nomadic people without animals, they possessed only what was portable, limiting trade to a small scale.[3] They made cordage out of agave and yucca fibers and fashioned nets to catch fish or to carry their minimal belongings. Although the Cochimí, and by extension all Baja Natives, lived "precarious" lives by European measures, they achieved an equilibrium within their ecosystems and governed themselves with headmen and councils of elders.[4] Nevertheless, regular meals for their children at the missions appealed to Native women, on whom fell most of the work in gathering traditional foods.[5]

By 1769, some Cochimíes at the northernmost Baja missions of San Francisco de Borja (founded in 1762) and Santa Maria (1767) had begun the process of acculturation to handling cattle, fieldwork, and Christian teachings. The Spanish soldiers and Franciscans needed guides and interpreters to get to Alta California. Once there, the missions required livestock herders, farmers, vineyardists, and foremen to teach the local Natives. Governor Portolá and Captain Rivera y Moncada recruited Cochimíes to fill the crucial role of guides. For the expedition to succeed they also needed Cochimíes to provide backbreaking labor.[6]

On February 26, 1769, forty-two northern Cochimí men joined the first of two parties of the Sacred Expedition at Loreto in southern Baja. Captain Rivera led this first trailblazing party that included Father Juan Crespi, twenty-five *soldados de cuera*, the Cochimíes, *arrieros* or muleteers, horses, and some 150 pack mules. Rivera concentrated on defining a viable route north, meaning one that provided forage for the animals and enough water for all. They reached the northernmost frontier outpost at Velicatá on March 22, took on supplies, and departed on March 24. For several days, they followed the trail taken by the Linck-Rivera journey in 1764–1765 but from then on, they depended on their Spanish scouts and Native guides. They first traversed northeastward on the eastern side of the Sierra de San Pedro Martir into the San Felipe Valley and thereafter, northwesterly toward San Diego.[7]

The Cochimíes knew the trails in their own country well, but soon they led the expedition into unknown territory that compounded the inherent risk of a journey over the harsh Baja terrain and in the dangerous Baja climate. They searched for the way north, guided only by ancient foot trails and information from local Natives. They made their way through mountain passes and around obstacles like *barrancas* or ravines, balancing efficient travel with the critical need for water and forage.[8] Every evening the muleteers, soldiers, and Cochimís unloaded the cargo from the pack animals. Each *aparejo* or packsaddle held 150 pounds of food, tools, armaments, ammunition, and a multitude of other necessities. The men watered all of the animals and hobbled them in forage or fed them with cuttings. The next morning, they again watered the animals (if the supply of water allowed) and carefully reloaded the same packsaddles, balanced for the safety of the load and the animals. Foot trails that allowed humans to pass on foot and in single file, at some points became dangerous for the passage of mules loaded with food and supplies. So Cochimíes and Spanish alike became road builders, hacking through dense chaparral and moving rocks. Under the added duress of scarce water and scant food sources, the men began to break down. In addition to scouting ahead and then doubling back to rejoin the party, the Native guides also bore the litters of sick and weakened members, including their own brothers. Fifty days and over three hundred miles out from Velicatá, the expedition at last came to rest near San Diego Bay on May 13, 1769. Thirty of the Cochimíes who had started the march died or deserted, and only twelve arrived with Crespí and the soldiers. Everyone—soldiers and mariners from the supply ships *San Antonio* and *San Carlos*, and the overland party of soldiers, muleteers,

Cochimíes, and Father Crespí—suffered terribly from scurvy and a host of "broad dietary deficiencies."[9]

Portolá led the second party of the Sacred Expedition with Father Serra. They departed Loreto on March 9 and reached Velicatá in May. Before departing on May 13, Serra consecrated the former *visita* as Mission San Fernando de Velicatá, the only Franciscan Baja mission. They followed the trail broken by Rivera's party and arrived on July 1. Of the 219 original members of both parties and ships, only 126 survived to witness the consecration of Mission San Diego de Alcalá on July 16. By the end of July, the survivors had buried another sixty of their brethren, having suffered a staggering seventy percent casualty rate.[10]

Portolá's original plan included herding some two-hundred head of cattle procured from San Borja to San Diego. Whether on Hispaniola, central Mexico, or Sonora, cattle filled the critical need of food security for new frontier outposts. Crops took time to plant, grow, and be harvested but a slaughtered steer filled empty stomachs right away. Other cattle reproduced and increased the food supply with little care. Soldiers branded forty of those with the Velicatá brand as the seed cattle for what became the newest Baja mission, and they slaughtered four more and jerked (dried) the meat to supply the members of the expedition. Portola had intended to bring the remaining cattle to San Diego with his second party. Soldiers, Cochimíes, and muleteers planned to move those cattle from San Francisco de Borja to Santa Maria de Los Angeles, and then to Alta California. But after discovering that the animals had become footsore and exhausted, the leadership decided to leave those cattle in suitable pastures at Velicatá, and bring them up the following year. This setback illustrated the criticality of cattle to Spanish colonial doctrine by putting the Spanish in the precarious position of surviving on supplies transported by sea, at great risk, or on food they procured from local Indigenous tribes. Their message of the good news of Christianity and Spanish rule looked much less impressive when they could not feed themselves, much less the local Natives. In May 1770, Captain Rivera returned to Velicatá with nineteen soldiers, two muleteers, and a Cochimí named Sebastian Tarabal. This party drove 164 head of cattle from Velicatá to San Diego in July 1770.[11]

The event gave birth to the Alta California cattle herds that fed the missions, soldiers, and the *poblanos* or colonists in the *pueblos* (towns). Cattle brought prosperity to land grant *ranchos* via the hide and tallow trade, and eventually filled the ranges of massive American ranches that flourished from the mid-nineteenth to the mid-twentieth centuries. California Indian *vaqueros* worked on many of those cattle operations and contributed to the success of all.

Simultaneous with the marches into Alta California, Franciscans assumed control of deteriorating missions in Baja and in the Pimería Alta. José de

Galvéz had created more turmoil by attempting to run missions under a new secular policy that subordinated missions to *presidios*, and in which padres provided only spiritual leadership. Partly in reaction to the Jesuit regime and in the interest of reducing administrative costs, Galvéz intended to reduce Church authority by making the *presidio* the primary colonial institution. In their favor, *presidios* exerted direct state power and also brought soldier-tradesmen who trained neophytes in the community. And *presidios* often provided the only employment opportunities for colonists.

Predictably, Franciscans ardently opposed the plan to make citizens out of neophytes that some viewed as "miserable wretches." More importantly, they opposed the plan to re-conceive the mission lands and operations as a tax base.[12] Historically in Spanish America, the mission-*presidio* complex had served as a low-budget mechanism that tenuously secured ever-advancing frontiers against rival empires. But in that system, the padres also controlled the crops and cattle, and by extension, the local Native people.[13]

Franciscan Fray Bartholeme Ximeno's first experiences in the Pimería Alta illustrate the limits of Spanish power on the frontier, whether led by the mission or the *presidio*, and the consequent suffering of the Native people. In 1772, Ximeno reported to his new assignment in the Pimería Alta, at the *Tumacácori* mission. The mission sat about two leagues (roughly five miles) south of the *Tubac* presidio on the Santa Cruz River.[14] Six months later he wrote a status report for his superior at the Franciscan College of Queretaro in central Mexico. His Father-Guardian had asked for input on the results of the Carlos III-Galvéz reforms. Ximeno bluntly stated that Apache attacks had stripped his mission and its *ranchería(s)* of their livestock and crops. He mourned the many lives taken when Apaches attacked the Piman neophytes in their fields and ransacked their homes. Consequently, some of these farmworkers had taken to carrying their belongings out to the fields with them. The Tubac *presidio* garrison had suffered losses themselves and so could do little to stop the rampages. Once, the mission had boasted more than two dozen horse *manadas* or herds, but after Apache attacks, just eight horses remained. The attacks also drastically reduced cattle herds that had provided food security if and when crops failed. From two thousand head at their peak, the herd numbered just forty-six at the time of Ximeno's report.[15] The Apache attacks in Ximeno's precinct exposed the fragility of the mission-*presidio* complex, regardless of which institution held command. Absent a larger military presence that matched the external threat, the Spanish proved unable to protect horse and cattle herds, which doomed the colonial economies and exposed the diffuse neophyte population to the implacable Apaches.

Neither of these opposing concepts considered the impact of Spanish settlements on Native subsistence, especially the damage that Spanish cattle, horses, and mules did by feeding on Indian crops or other traditional plant foods. Franciscans warned against a policy that privileged military forts, manned by soldiers bristling with weapons. However, once the Spanish domesticated animals had degraded traditional Indigenous food sources, and Apaches plundered the new, "invasive" species of horses and cattle, the local neophyte population had no food sources and no protection. They bore the brunt of Spain's failed policy. Franciscans believed that a more dominant military presence did not send a message of friendship, especially in the midst of powerful nations like the *Quechans*, who ruled the region where the Gila River met the Colorado.[16]

Like the Taino on Hispaniola and the Tlaxcalans in Chichimeca country, Christianized Cochimíes herded cattle for the Spanish padres and soldiers and then taught Alta California Indians to do the same. They acted as examples, if not agents, of the new, colonial way of life. The Franciscans valued the Cochimíes for their dependability and described them as possessing a "noble nature."[17] Since the northerly Cochimíes spoke a Yuman dialect, they likely communicated successfully with their fellow Yuman-speaking Kumeyaay in what is now San Diego County. They did less well with the Shoshonean-speaking Luiseño in present-day northern San Diego County.[18]

The Shoshonean-speaking Tongva at Mission San Gabriel did not share their gathered traditional foods, or the produce of the mission, so the Cochimíes grew their own. They longed for a mission community of their own. Head Padre at San Gabriel, Fermín Francisco de Lasuén, made such a request to his superiors in Mexico City but his superiors took no action on behalf of the Cochimíes. Over time, these loyal servants of the Spanish had become stranded in Alta California. The Cochimí had led both Portolá expeditions and taught sustainable agricultural forms and livestock herding to many local Natives. Through intermarriage, they eventually ceased to exist as a distinct ethnicity among Alta California Native peoples.[19] They had played a crucial role in the survival of the missions and in the emergence of Indians as the first *vaqueros* in what became southern California but they have largely been lost to history.[20]

In the first few years after Captain Rivera's party drove 164 head of cattle from Velicatá to San Diego (1770), the demand in Alta California far exceeded the supply. Each mission and *presidio* in Alta California needed to increase their herds but the continual founding of missions demanded livestock donations, as ordered by the Crown. The Franciscans could not count on the Baja missions for more donations—they had none to spare. The Dominicans replaced the Franciscans in Baja in 1772 and inherited the difficulties of drought, pestilence, and hunger that Portolá witnessed when he came to expel the Jesuits in 1768. The Dominicans had to prioritize shoring up their own food supplies, including rebuilding the herds when rainfall and locusts allowed.[21] Additionally, incorrect Alta California mission siting and a shortage of Baja Indian workers (Cochimíes) depressed large-scale crop production in the new province. These factors increased reliance on beef and milk in the diets of neophytes and Spanish colonists, even if that consumption slowed or stopped herd increase.[22]

The importance of proper mission siting cannot be overestimated in its impact on food security, Indigenous receptivity to Spanish culture and religion, and even war and peace. The Franciscans relocated seven of the first ten missions in Alta California due to lack of water, flooding, or to be closer to the *presidio* for security reasons. The padres moved Santa Clara de Asís four times to avoid flooding. Missionaries had to have a reliable food supply in order to attract Indigenous people for religious conversion and to work in the fields. Padres and soldiers relied on milk products and meat from cattle until crops began to feed large numbers at the missions. Lack of proper mission siting that at first led to subpar harvests did not reflect Franciscan negligence. Rather, it revealed the urgency that the Spanish Crown had placed on projecting Spanish imperial sovereignty. The Jesuits before them had self-funded their Baja mission operations and had been able to focus on religious goals instead of territorial ones. But the Crown financed the Franciscan mission ventures and put pressure on them to secure the northern borderlands against rival encroachments. This also explains the urgency with which Portolá and Serra founded the second Alta California mission of San Carlos on Monterrey Bay in 1770. In that accomplishment, Alta California missions truly became outposts of empire. Once Serra established his northern and southern poles at San Carlos and San Diego, he worked to link them together with a chain of self-sufficient missions. The success or failure of that plan hinged on importing cattle. The nearest and most plentiful herds grazed on Sonoran grass.[23]

At that moment, the Spanish had no proven overland supply route from northern New Spain to California, but a priest and a soldier believed it could be done. Padre Francisco Garcés, one of the new Franciscan missionaries in the Pimería Alta, shared Eusebio Kino's urge to explore. Kino had envisioned an overland supply route to the Pacific as a channel for Sonoran goods to the Manila *galleons* as they made port at one or more points along the California coastline. In Kino's vision, the *galleons*, laden with Asian goods and Sonoran supplies, then took their trade goods to ports further south in New Spain, like Acapulco or San Blas, before returning to the Philippine Islands.[24]

Captain Juan Bautista de Anza believed in that vision as strenuously as Kino. Many men had recently lost their lives supporting the Portolá expedition by sea and those who survived the California passage suffered crippling scurvy. The fledgling Alta California missions struggled just to subsist and had experienced "starving times." [25] That suffering underscored the critical need for overland support for the California's. Anza viewed it as the impetus to act but needed the rationale to predict success on land. In 1769, the

Quechans got word of white men traveling up and down the California coast. This information they passed to the Pimas, who informed Anza at his *presidio* in *Tubac*. Since information had traveled eastward from California to the Pimería, it stood to reason that the same route worked in reverse, to transport people, livestock, and goods.[26]

From his newly assigned mission at the neighboring San Xavier del Bac in the Pimería, Garcés ventured three times to the confluence of the Gila and Colorado Rivers and beyond, between 1768 and 1771. In the first two trips, he sought intelligence on local tribes like the Quechans to determine their amenability to religious conversion. On one occasion, he arrived when the confluence had flooded over all banks, so that he believed he had seen only the Gila and needed to continue to the west to find the Colorado. Having not found the Colorado in the California desert, he returned to Bac. But on his third trip, he ventured as far as present-day Calexico, far enough westward to see what he called "The Sierras," probably the Santa Rosa Mountains, and discerned two potential passes through them. His reports on these journeys expressed his confidence in the efficacy of an overland journey to the missions in California. On at least the third trip, he traveled with full knowledge of Anza's plan and in support of it.[27]

De Anza submitted his plan in a letter to Viceroy Antonio Bucareli in May 1772. Bucareli evaluated the plan and sought counsel from all available experts in Mexico City, including Miguel Costansó, a thirty-year-old member of the Royal Corps of Engineers. Costansó had joined Portolá at San Diego by sea and then traveled overland with him to Monterrey Bay and back in 1769–1770. He estimated the distance from Tubac to San Diego at 180 leagues, about 500 miles. He reiterated that Baja had no resources to spare and that the food, cattle, horses, and people to sustain Spain's hold on Alta California must come from Sonora.[28]

Father Junípero Serra also testified before Bucareli's council of war in September 1773 and helped solidify the viceroy's decision to approve the project in late September. Bucareli's instructions reached Anza at Tubac on November 6, 1773. Anza and Garcés announced their intent to depart Tubac on December 15 but the Apaches had their own plans. Just a few days before the planned departure, they drove off 130 of Anza's horses.[29]

Despite this setback, on January 8, 1774, the first Anza Expedition got underway. Anza, Fathers Garcés of *Bac* and Juan Díaz of *Caborca*, twenty-five *soldados de cuera*, five *arrieros*, two of Anza's servants, and a carpenter comprised the human element. They rode and drove something over one hundred horses and sixty-five head of cattle. To avoid any more losses to the Apaches, Anza decided against following the Gila westward to the Colorado River. Instead, he changed course and headed southwest to Caborca in the Altar River valley, also hoping to find replacement horses there. At Altar,

Quechan chief *Olleyquotequiebe*, known to the Spanish as Salvador Palma, delivered a fugitive Native man to Anza—the Cochimí Sebastián Tarabal. Tarabal had struggled north with the Rivera-Crespí party in 1769 and had helped Captain Rivera drive the cattle north from Velicatá to San Diego in 1770. He aptly applied the name Salvador—savior—to *Olleyquotequiebe*.[30]

Retracing Palma's and Tarabal's steps, Anza drove northwesterly through the oasis at Sonoita. Always scouting ahead for the next water or forage source, he at times broke the train into staggered groups to avoid overtaxing rock tanks or *tinajas* and to allow them to refill and slake all thirsts. Some four hundred miles and about a month out from Tubac, men, horses, and cattle rested and recovered near the Gila-Colorado junction, home to the Yuman-speaking Quechans. Success in supplying Sonoran horses, cattle, and colonists to Alta California depended on amicable relations with the Native peoples of the river junction. Palma came to meet Anza in the Spanish camp.[31]

Being satisfied that the chief who brought Tarabal to Altar still had good intentions, Anza then went to a formal meeting with Palma and other Quechan leaders on their home ground. Anza knew that he needed Native help to navigate the unknown territory and peoples ahead. Strategically, the tall Quechans had the power to make the river junction a choke point and prevent any overland transit from Sonora to California. They had the numbers to wipe out Anza's party too, but they also saw benefit in an alliance with the Spanish, particularly in trade goods. As early as the 1690s, the Spanish had raided into Athapaskan territory to the north of the Pimeria Alta (Apaches and Navajo have common Athapaskan roots). From these raids, made ostensibly to suppress "enemies of the province," they forcibly brought back Native individuals to use as laborers in Sonora.[32] Their further willingness to trade for captured Indians with weapons, horses, and raw materials like iron likely stimulated raids made just for the purpose of capturing human beings to be sold into Spanish slavery. Regardless of who the Spanish traded with, their presence destabilized an entire region that already saw a Quechan-led alliance at the Yuma crossing, pitted against the rival Maricopa alliance centered near the bend in the Gila River. The loss of family members to enslavement left wounds in grieving families and created bitter and long-lasting enmities, especially against the Spanish, who bore responsibility for their instigation of the trade.[33]

The Spanish planned to establish hegemony over the Quechans, or "vassalage" but in February 1774, Palma still believed that their presence promised benefits for his people. Palma and Anza met before a large crowd and exchanged speeches and gifts.[34] Although Palma's Quechans had not yet established their own herds, some horses, possibly ones run off from *presidio* herds by the Apaches, circulated westward and northward from Sonora. However, Anza observed in 1774 that the Quechans did not have riding gear. They showed keen interest in the Spanish animals, possibly to gain an understanding of how best to use them. For whatever reason, they helped swim Anza's horses, mules, and cattle across the Colorado River. Some of the Quechans even volunteered to unburden the mules and carry their packs across the big river.[35]

In mid-February 1774, Anza departed the safety of the Colorado River delta and set out for the mountains through which they must pass in order to make Mission San Gabriel. By the tenth day, having gotten lost in the sand dunes, with no water or forage anywhere in sight, they straggled back to the Colorado. They had lost a dozen pack animals and cattle to thirst, hunger, and exhaustion.[36] Anza determined that his train was too big and that he must travel lighter. He placed the majority of the livestock and cargo in the care of three soldiers, three muleteers, and three Sonoran Indian servants, all at least nominally under the protection of Palma until Anza's return from Mission San Gabriel. He made this decision out of desperation but also with some intuitive feeling about their safety with the Quechan chief.[37]

After little more than a week's rest, Anza reconstituted a smaller pathfinding party and made ready to head for the sierras off in the distance. The men pledged to accomplish their mission, on foot if necessary. This group included the two priests, seventeen soldiers, and five "helpers," twenty-four in total. Anza selected his ten strongest mules but left all the cattle with Palma. Without a definite idea of how to get through the desert and what sources of water lay ahead, Anza did not take the chance of losing the cattle. The smaller party started into the desert again on March 2, 1774.[38]

This time, they made certain to avoid the dunes that had so confused and punished them previously. The scouts found water and forage by "skirting" the desert on a more southern route, in line with the present-day Mexicali-Tijuana highway. Having made it to the base of the mountains, they headed north. Within a week, they entered Coyote Canyon and climbed through San Carlos Pass. They descended along the San Jacinto River to wide plains with abundant and varied forage, potable water and, most importantly, the promise of soon arriving at San Gabriel. They traveled through present-day Moreno Valley to Sycamore Canyon in Riverside and camped along the Santa Ana River, not far from an Indigenous village (Cahuillas or Serranos). Two days later, on March 22, 1774, the first Anza Expedition arrived at Mission San Gabriel, populated by Tongva neophytes. Anza had finally opened an overland trail to Alta California and the Pacific Ocean. The Spanish planned to drive large numbers of Sonoran horses and cattle over that trail and fill up the ranges on California mission and *presidio* ranches to feed Spanish and California Indians alike, thereby securing Spain's territorial claims against her rivals.[39] In recognition of this momentous achievement, Viceroy Bucareli sought and gained the approval of the king to reward the explorers. He promoted Bautista de Anza to the rank of Lieutenant Colonel and, for his loyal men, added a bonus to their pay each month for life.[40]

Anza had blazed the trail but the Alta California missions still needed people from Sonora, supplies, horses, and a large number of cattle to accelerate reproduction above the rates of donations for new missions and consumption. In November 1774, Bucareli announced his intention to the Crown to establish a *presidio* and a colony on the Great Bay that came to be known as San Francisco. In that month, Anza had delivered his diary to Bucareli in Mexico and together, they planned the second expedition. Anza proposed to recruit and train twenty soldiers and thirty families from the populace of the Culiacan region in present-day Sinaloa. This journey presented an opportunity for many to make a fresh start and lift themselves out of poverty. Accordingly, Anza required that their pay be made in kind, else they might gamble it away. Anza also selected his officers and Padre Francisco Font as diarist, chaplain, and scientist.[41]

The original train departed San Miguel de Horcasitas on September 29, 1775, and traveled first to Tubac. Sixty-three newcomers joined the party, including Sebastián Tarabal and Fathers Francisco Garcés and Tomás Eixarch, who planned to start a mission among the Quechans at Yuma Crossing. Ten of Anza's Tubac veterans signed on as escorts who later returned with him upon completing the mission. In addition to 240 humans, Anza had assembled 695 pack mules and saddle horses, despite another Apache raid that ran off 500 horses from the Tubac *presidio*. *Vaqueros* drove 355 head of cattle.[42]

This time the caravan headed for the Gila River and followed it to the Colorado, where Anza again met with Chief Palma on November 30. Before heading into the desert, they built housing for Padres Garcés and Eixarch and left servants, muleteers, and interpreters behind to help them, including Tarabal. The huge train rested at the oasis of Santa Olaya before the grueling march through the dunes. In order to survive, the people filled skin water bags and carried extra maize and grass to feed the horses and mules where no forage existed. Cattle fended for themselves. Anza staggered his train in three divisions to allow water sources to refill, and when they reached the wells at Santa Rosa, it took several days for all people and animals to replenish. Heading into the mountains promised more water but scant forage. Day after day, Padre Font's diary reported losses of cattle, horses, and mules that gave out under their burdens or from thirst and hunger. Some fifty of the cattle bolted rearward for water but got mired in mud and struggled to their deaths. Cold and hungry but alive, the colonists celebrated Christmas in the mountain pass. Finally, on December 26, 1775, the train began the descent into the San Jacinto River valley. New Year's Day found them crossing a swollen Santa Ana River, where more animals drowned. On January 4, 1776, the soldiers, colonists, muleteers, *vaqueros*, horses, and the surviving 200 head of cattle arrived at San Gabriel.[43]

Upon his arrival, Anza received reports that some of the Kumeyaay people had attacked the San Diego Mission on November 5, 1775. In the general uprising against forced labor, lashings, and the violation of their women, Kumeyaay gentiles killed Father Luis Jayme, a blacksmith, and mortally wounded a carpenter. Anza and Governor (Captain) Rivera y Moncada, who just arrived from Monterey, traveled to San Diego on January 11 to reinforce the small garrison. After Anza returned to San Gabriel, Rivera conducted an "investigation" of the attack that obtained confessions by torture.[44]

Back at San Gabriel, the seven-week delay fostered impatience, pilfering of supplies, and desertion by five of Anza's recruits, along with horses. Second-in-command Lieutenant Jose Moraga tracked the perpetrators all the way back into the Colorado Desert and caught up with them after 4 days and 250 miles. While Moraga tracked down deserters, Anza returned and got the train underway on February 21, 1776, this time with Monterey as its destination. He led eighteen of the original thirty families, as planned—Sergeant Grijalva had orders to bring the remaining twelve families starting in early May. For the time being, the cattle herd stayed at San Gabriel. Anza first headed westward on what became El Camino Real, the Royal Road or King's Highway. The first night, they camped near present-day Glendale and north of the future site of the Pueblo de La Reina de Los Angeles. Then they passed through the Santa Monica Mountains west of Calabasas. On the third night, Anza's train camped along the Santa Clara River just east of present-day Ventura. The next day they reached the Pacific Ocean, the first sight of which delighted many in the band of pioneers who had never seen it. Now following the Santa Barbara Channel northward, they took note of the plank boats (*tomol*) and steatite pots made by the populous Chumash, as well as many other objects of material culture.[45]

The expedition arrived at Mission San Luis Obispo on March 3, to rousing celebrations, embraces, and a solemn Mass of thanksgiving. After a day's rest, the caravan headed out on the last leg of their journey. North of San Luis Obispo, the rugged Santa Lucia Mountain range stretches northwesterly to Monterey Bay and abruptly meets the Pacific at many points, making passage impossible where no coastal land exists on which to march. So, as Portolá had done in 1769, they headed northeasterly across the Cuesta ridge, then, redirecting northwesterly, descended to the Salinas River and then to the San Antonio River, which watered Mission San Antonio de Padua. There, at the third Franciscan mission established in Alta California, Anza allowed the colony to rest for a day. Back on the move, they regained the Salinas River Valley and followed it to its mouth at Monterey Bay. On March 10, 1776, 162 days out from Horcasitas, the colonial caravan came to rest outside Mission San Carlos.[46]

On March 21, Anza, Font, and several soldiers who knew the area rode up to the large bay that the Spaniards named in honor of the patron saint of the Franciscan friars. They scouted the region surrounding the Bay and selected sites for the San Francisco *presidio* and mission. Colonel Anza marked the site with an implanted cross. At its base, he attached his written message that formalized the claim on behalf of the king of Spain, according to European custom. Before they returned to Monterey on April 8, they had discovered the Sacramento River and had seen the grassy plains of the upper San Joaquin Valley. Anza made ready to depart, while Font made maps of what they had seen and learned. Font had also created a register of the 190 souls who stayed to build San Francisco. On April 13, Anza departed amid tearful farewells to his "colony" and set out for home at Tubac. Anza, Font, the ten troopers from Tubac, a Spanish commissary, and fourteen muleteers, *vaqueros*, and servants headed for San Gabriel to meet again with Captain Rivera before turning south onto the overland trail he had made.[47]

Anza's second expedition (1775–76) delivered 206 head of cattle to Monterey, which turned the tide in establishing self-sustaining herds in the northern part of the mission chain. Thereafter, cattle numbers increased, despite regular slaughtering for their beef, hides, and tallow.[48] Steadily then, missions attracted local Native people to live and work there, crops came in, and bulls, cows, and heifers reproduced at a rate that outpaced consumption. Less than ten years later, the cattle at all of the missions had increased substantially to almost 5,000 head. Combined with horses, sheep, and hogs, total Alta California livestock numbered over 20,000.[49]

Anza's march to San Francisco in 1776 secured the northern missions with soldiers to man the *presidio*, settlers to found the *pueblo*, and hundreds of cattle, horses, and mules to support all. New California *Gobernador* Felipe de Neve arrived in 1777 and saw that the lack of civilian farming forced the presidios to rely on mission food production. He concluded that he must import more settlers from Sonora and Jalisco, the origins of the new San Franciscans. In late 1779, the new *Comandant-General* of the Internal Provinces, Teodoro de Croix, issued orders to Captain Rivera y Moncada to recruit soldiers and settlers for the establishment of a new *presidio* at Santa Barbara and the founding of a *pueblo* to bear the name of La Reina de Los Angeles (The Queen of Angels). Recruiting settlers from the northern frontier dragged on into 1781, despite their state of impoverishment in Sonora and Jalisco. Finally, in the spring of that year, Captain Rivera assembled his own massive migrant train of about 230 soldiers and colonists, and nearly a 1,000 horses, mules, and cattle combined. He gave the order to begin the march northward to the Colorado-Gila junction. They arrived in June and, as had been the case with Anza's expeditions, many animals arrived hungry, thirsty, and used up. Rivera ordered the main body of settlers on to Alta California and remained near the Yuma crossing with a small detachment of about fifteen soldiers to allow some 250 exhausted animals to recover before making the final push.[50]

Unbeknownst to Rivera, the Spanish had begun to build two settlements, "*pueblos* or military colonies," near the river junction in late 1780, intending to control the strategic crossing and the Quechans.[51] The idea of a military *pueblo* came from *Comandant-General* Croix's desire to economize on frontier security and at the same time to deny to the Franciscans the control of neophytes that came from controlling the herds and crops, as in the missions. Croix insisted that the Spaniards not call them missions, although Fathers Garcés and Díaz maintained their missionary purpose. Croix rationalized that a settler militia living in an unfortified village cost only about one-fourth the outlay to build a *presidio* and man it with professional soldiers. However, Croix's plan did not include funding for the many gifts promised to Salvador Palma and eagerly anticipated by his people, like fabric from which to make clothing. In a colossal miscalculation, Croix's hybrid settlement provided little if any armed protection for the Spanish people, gave no authority to the missionaries to engender goodwill by producing and sharing food, and worse, drew a connection between the padres and physical violence. None of the typical colonial institutions functioned.

To make matters worse, by June 1781, the Spaniards had not produced enough food to support themselves, forcing them to purchase Quechan foodstuffs that placed a great strain on the Quechans themselves. Spanish horses and cattle ate Quechan crops, and Spanish soldiers whipped them for livestock thefts. Enter Captain Rivera's hungry animals that grazed on Indian food sources like mesquite tree beans. Salvador Palma had long since lost all faith in the Spanish to benefit his people, as promised by Anza and Viceroy Bucareli, and saw only Spanish insult and injury. He joined with his brother Ygnacio, who had always opposed the alliance, and *Halykwamai* interpreter Francisco Xavier, taken into enslavement at Altar when just a child. Francisco burned for revenge and goaded the Quechans to attack the Spanish.[52]

On July 17, 1781, the Quechans attacked all Spaniards at the two *pueblos* and at Rivera's camp. Over three days, they killed a total of 105 people, including Captain Rivera and all of his soldiers, Padres Francisco Gárces, Juan Diaz, and two other priests, forty-three men and women settlers, and twenty-one children. Spanish sources reported that the Quechans divided up Rivera's horses amongst themselves, killed and ate many of the cattle, and let the rest run wild.[53]

The Quechans spared another seventy-six people that they held as prisoners, possibly to be sold into enslavement. They eventually exchanged most of them for Quechan prisoners when Lieutenant Colonel Pedro Fages led about two hundred soldiers and Pima warriors back to Yuma. As a result of his change of heart toward the Spanish, Salvador Palma regained his people's faith in his leadership through dream power. Despite several retaliatory military campaigns, the Spanish never captured him or Francisco Xavier.[54]

By rising up against the colonists, soldiers, and padres, the Quechans successfully threw off Spanish rule and restored their independence. They had sought an economic and perhaps political and military alliance with the Spanish but the Spanish did not offer partnership. They presumed to rule the Quechans with religion and by force if necessary. The loss of the overland supply route foreclosed any further transfers of cattle from Sonora and slowed the growth of herds in the new California province. Padre Kino had envisioned the shared prosperity of an intra-empire trade network that connected Asian colonies and markets to American ones. Instead, their relative isolation from the rest of New Spain forced the Alta California missions to become self-reliant, if not completely self-sufficient. It had become "in many ways the island that Spaniards in earlier days had believed it to be."[55] Despite the severing of support from Sonora, Alta California mission horse and cattle herds did increase and in time set the stage for trade opportunities far beyond those conjured by Kino.

NOTES

1. John L. Kessell, *Spain in the Southwest: A Narrative History of Colonial New Mexico, Arizona, Texas, and California* (Norman, OK: University of Oklahoma Press, 2002), 263–267.

2. L. T. Burcham, "Cattle and Range Forage in California: 1770–1880," *Agricultural History* 35, no. 3 (July 1961): 140. See also Donald Nuttall, "Gaspar de Portolá: Disenchanted Conquistador of Spanish Upper California," *Southern California Quarterly* 53, no. 3 (September 1971): 186.

3. Aviles and Hoover, "Two Californias," 11. See also Dunne, *Black Robes in Lower California*, 425–427.

4. Crosby, *Antigua California*, 27–28.

5. Ibid., 38.

6. Ibid., 390–391; Richard Street, *Beasts of the Field: A Narrative History of California Farmworkers, 1769 1913* (Stanford, CA: Stanford University Press, 2004), 9. See also George Harwood Phillips, *Vineyards and Vaqueros: Indian Labor and the Economic Expansion of Southern California, 1771–1877* (Norman, OK: University of Oklahoma Press, 2010), 63–64.

7. Street, *Beasts of the Field*, 9–10.

8. Harry W. Crosby, *Gateway to Alta California: The Expedition to San Diego, 1769* (San Diego, CA: Sunbelt Publications, 2003), 73–74.

9. Ibid., 54–60, 104–109; Street, *Beasts of the Field*, 11.

10. Street, *Beasts of the Field*, 10–12; Nuttall, "Disenchanted Conquistador," 186.

11. Hazel Adele Pulling, "A History of California's Range-Cattle Industry 1770–1912," PhD Dissertation, University of Southern California, Los Angeles, CA, 1944, 32–35; Edith Buckland Webb, *Indian Life at the Old Missions* (Los Angeles, CA: Warren F. Lewis, 1952), 168–169; Crosby, *Gateway to California*, 113.

12. John L. Kessell and Fray Bartholeme Ximeno, "San José De Tumacácori-1773: A Franciscan Reports, from Arizona," *Arizona and the West* 6, no. 4 (Winter 1964): 308.

13. José Refugio De La Torre Curiel, "Franciscan Missionaries in Late Colonial Sonora: Five Decades of Change and Conflict," in *Alta California: Peoples in Motion, Identities in Formation, 1769–1850*, ed. Steven W. Hackel (Berkeley, CA: University of California Press and San Marino: Huntington Library, 2010), 50–51. See also John L. Kessell, "Friars Versus Bureaucrats: The Mission as a Threatened Institution on the Arizona-Sonora Frontier, 1767–1842," *Western Historical Quarterly* 5, no. 2 (April 1974): 151–162; Mark Santiago, *Massacre at the Yuma Crossing: Spanish Relations with the Quechans, 1779–1782* (Tucson, AZ: University of Arizona Press, 1998), 1–10.

14. Miguel Carrera Stampa, "The Evolution of Weights and Measures in New Spain," *The Hispanic American Historical Review* 29, no. 1 (February 1949): 10. One Spanish league is equivalent to 2.6 miles.

15. Kessell and Ximeno, "San Jose de Tumacacori-1773," 307–310. Neophyte villagers of Tumacacori, the provisional *cabecera* or headquarters, fortunately lived close to their fields and pastures but in the outlying *ranchería(s)*, the farmworkers had to travel an average of about two leagues from home (more than five miles), just to get to their fields. Consequently, they lived with the constant threat of Apaches plundering their homes while they worked in the fields.

16. Kessell, "Friars Versus Bureaucrats," 151–162. See also Santiago, *Massacre at the Yuma Crossing*, 12–26; and Nicole Mathwich and Barnet Pavao-Zuckerman, "Bureaucratic Reforms on the Frontier: Zooarchaeological and Historical Perspectives on the 1767 Jesuit Expulsion in the Pimería Alta," *Journal of Anthropological Archaeology* 52 (2018): 156–166. Archaeological evidence using the bones of cattle in the Pimería revealed that as imperial policy deemphasized large-scale crops grown at missions, cattle herds increased to fill the gap in food production. However, repeated Apache depredations rendered any policy moot.

17. Street, *Beasts in the Field*, 9.

18. Ibid., 9.

19. Ibid., 16–17, 21–22.

20. Ibid.,17–19.

21. Aviles and Hoover, "Two Californias," 10–11, 14–17, 20. Between 1774 and 1834, the Dominicans founded nine more Baja missions and endowed each with livestock from the neighboring missions.

22. Pulling, "California's Range-Cattle Industry," 35–39; Aviles and Hoover, "Two Californias," 11–14, 22–25; Webb, *Indian Life*, 169–171.

23. Aviles and Hoover, "Two Californias," 11–12.

24. Kino, S. J., *Kino's Historical Memoir of Pimería Alta*, 195–196, 204–213. See also Harlan Hague, "The Search for a Southern Overland Route to California," *California Historical Quarterly* 55, no. 2 (Summer 1976): 150–153.

25. Herbert Eugene Bolton, *Anza's California Expeditions, Vol. I: An Outpost of Empire* (Berkeley, CA: University of California Press, 1930), 36–41; see also John L. Kessell, *Friars, Soldiers, and Reformers: Hispanic Arizona and the Sonoran Mission Frontier, 1767–1856* (Tucson, AZ: University of Arizona Press, 1976), 91–96.

26. Bolton, *Anza's California Expeditions*, 44; Kessell, *Friars, Soldiers, and Reformers*, 91–96.

27. Clifford E. Trafzer, *Yuma: Frontier Crossing of the Far Southwest* (Wichita, KS: Western Heritage Books, 1980), 15–17; Bolton, *Anza's California Expeditions*, 43–48.

28. Ibid., 50–51. Webb, *Indian Life*, 170. In 1773, Father Francisco Palou reported a total of 319 head of cattle on the five existing missions of San Diego, San Carlos, San Antonio, San Gabriel, and San Luis Obispo, including fifty-four being held for the planned missions at San Francisco, Santa Clara, and San Buenaventura.

29. Bolton, *Anza's California Expeditions*, 63–65.

30. Street, *Beasts in the Field*, 17–19; Bolton, *Anza's California Expeditions*, 65–80; Kessell, *Spain in the Southwest*, 285. In 1773, Tarabal and his family had fled the San Gabriel mission, hoping to return to their home mission at Santa Gertrudis in Baja. Keeping far to the east to avoid recapture, the Mojave Desert took the lives of his wife and child. Quechan Indians rescued Tarabal near the conjunction of the Colorado and Gila Rivers and delivered him to Anza in the Altar Valley. Anza impressed Tarabal into service as his guide and Pima interpreter. Street claims that Tarabal first met up with Anza at Tubac, while Bolton asserts that Chief Palma brought him south from Colorado-Gila to Altar over a known trail. In any event, the unsung Cochimí hero played a key role in Anza's success. Tarabal possibly perished in the 1781 Quechan attacks on the two Colorado River outposts that killed many soldiers, including Captain Rivera y Moncada, Padre Francisco Garcés, and three other missionaries.

31. Bolton, *Anza's California Expeditions*, 86–93.

32. Jack D. Forbes, *Warriors of the Colorado: The Yumas of the Quechan Nation and Their Neighbors* (Norman, OK: University of Oklahoma Press, 1965), 112–140.

33. Santiago, *Massacre at the Yuma Crossing*, 12–15; Forbes, *Warriors of the Colorado*, 112–140. The Maricopa alliance also included Halchidomas situated on the California side and north of the river junction, and Cahuillas farther to the west in the California Desert.

34. Bolton, *Anza's California Expeditions*, 94–101.

35. Ibid., 102–105; Forbes, *Warriors of the Colorado*, 172.

36. Ibid., 118–127.

37. Ibid., 105–111, 128; Hubert Howe Bancroft, *History of California, Vol. I, 1542–1800* (Santa Barbara, CA: Wallace Hebberd, 1963), 220–223.

38. Ibid., 134–135.

39. Ibid., 144–153. Known to the Spanish at that time as the Philippine Sea.

40. Ibid., 196–197.

41. Ibid., 204–229; Herbert Eugene Bolton, The *Spanish Borderlands: A Chronicle of Old Florida and the Southwest* (New Haven CT: Yale University Press, 1921), 272–273.

42. Bolton, *Anza's California Expeditions*, 244–246.

43. Trafzer, *Yuma: Frontier Crossing of the Far Southwest*, 1980, 17–18; Bolton, Anza's California Expeditions, 278–286, 284, 304–336.

44. Claudio Saunt, "My Medicine is Punishment: A Case of Torture in Early California, 1775–1776," *Ethnohistory* 57, no. 4 (Fall 2010): 679–683; Bolton, *Anza's California Expeditions*, 343–348.

45. Mary Null Boulé, *California Native American Tribes: Chumash Tribe* (Vashon, WA: Merryant, 1992), 34–36. Bolton, *Anza's California Expeditions*, 359–361. Padre Font estimated the Chumash population at between ten and twenty thousand, entirely sustained by the bounty of the sea and animals hunted on land with bows and arrows. The Chumash obtained the steatite (also called soapstone) from Catalina Island, transported onboard their hand-crafted plank boats that they sealed with asphaltum or tar that naturally bubbled up from the ground.

46. Bolton, *Anza's California Expeditions*, 349–394, 417–320.

47. Ibid.

48. Ibid., 172–173.

49. Webb, *Indian Life*, 173; Bancroft, *History of California, Vol. I, 1542–1800*, 387–398; and Hubert Howe Bancroft, *California Pastoral, 1769–1848* (San Francisco, CA: History Company, 1888), 170–172.

50. Bancroft, *History of California, Vol. I, 1542–1800*, 333–344; Forbes, *Warriors of the Colorado*, 195–200.

51. Forbes, *Warriors of the Colorado*, 185.

52. Forbes, *Warriors of the Colorado*, 185–199; Santiago, *Massacre at the Yuma Crossing*, 12, 76–111, 124. Southward of the Quechans on the Colorado, lived in succession, the Kohuanas, Halykwamais, and Cocopas.

53. Trafzer, *Yuma: Frontier Crossing of the Far Southwest*, 19–20; Forbes, *Warriors of the Colorado*, 201–203.

54. Forbes, *Warriors of the Colorado*, 200–214; Santiago, *Massacre at the Yuma Crossing*, 112–126.

55. Steven W. Hackel, *Children of Coyote, Missionaries of Saint Francis: Indian-Spanish Relations in Colonial California, 1769–1850* (Chapel Hill, NC: University of North Carolina Press, 2005), 55–59; Forbes, *Warriors of the Colorado*, 204–205.

Chapter 3

California Mission Cattle and Native American *Vaqueros* 1769–1833

Consistent with Spanish practices throughout northern New Spain, horses and cattle played a critical role in the success of the new province of Alta California. Spanish Longhorns on the range bolstered the survivability of missions, *presidios*, and *pueblos* and thereby ensured that the foundational values of Spanish colonial strategies remained intact and in force: the assertion of Spanish territorial sovereignty, religious conversion of the Indigenous peoples, and wealth for the Crown. Longhorns grazing on grass in view of San Francisco Bay or along the San Gabriel River embodied that continuity, but Alta California's remoteness from the centers of authority and support of New Spain also augured a unique experience within the Spanish Empire. Lush Alta California ranges fed ever-increasing herds of horses and cattle that within a very few decades made the province an international center of trade in cattle hides and tallow. Missions provided safe spaces for the gestation of that market supply and then the emergence of a new class of worker, also essential to the success of the colonial ventures—the California Indian *vaquero*.

Spanish mission *ranchos* played a large role in the success of the missions. As part of the mission whole, the functioning of the *rancho* required communal cooperation in the *rodeo* or roundup and in the *matanza* or slaughtering. *Ranchos* also demonstrated a persisting Spanish presence that controlled the surrounding spaces through the thousands of cattle and horses that grazed on Sonoran, Texan, and California grass. Not insignificantly, each mission donated cattle and horses to populate the next missions. So, the mission herds not only asserted present control of their immediate locality, but they foretold future control of new and distant Indigenous spaces.

Presidio garrisons, smaller versions of medieval fortresses in Spain, always accompanied missions in the Spanish borderlands and controlled spaces that were formerly the exclusive domain of Indigenous peoples. This military detachment presented a show of force and control to foreign powers, and enforced Spanish order in the colony. Attached to the *presidios, ranchos del rey* or the king's ranches,[1] maintained herds of cattle and horses that belonged to the Spanish Crown, for the use of the garrison. American Indians had no desire to become subjects of the king of Spain but their labor contributed greatly to the success of the Spanish outpost. The semi-arid landscapes of the northern borderlands of New Spain dictated that most crops grown were for local subsistence and that cattle ranching offered the best economic use of the land. Additionally, Spanish Longhorn stock required little care and often went feral.[2] Unlike the Aztecs in the sixteenth century, California and Texas Indians did not readily convert to working on a Spanish *rancho*. Still, rounding up and roping cattle touched the primal nerve of the chase and hunt, and played a central role in acculturating the Natives. *Ranchos* also created new local economies by supplying mounts for soldiers, and beef for Spanish and Indian consumption.[3]

Cattle and horses thrived on the virgin grasses and other herbaceous plant forms of the California range and required little care, save to keep them out of mission crops. In their extensive grazing, the animals destroyed much of the native grasses and also consumed traditional foods. This started a crippling cycle in which the reduction of traditional foods increased Native dependence on crops and cattle as food sources. And, as these herds increased in an "animal population explosion," the cattle foraged farther from the missions, consuming an ever-increasing amount of traditional Indian foods, increasing dependence on crops, and so on.[4] The animals also increased in numbers greater than the mission personnel themselves could control. Eventually, the padres had no choice but to allow soldiers, Spanish *vaqueros*, or Indians like the Cochimíes to train southern California Indians to ride and to handle cattle. Based on armed resistance such as the Chichimecas waged in the sixteenth century, Spanish law prohibited American Indians from owning or riding a horse but necessity overruled legalities, especially so far from Mexico City. At San Gabriel, Father Lasuén communicated this need to Governor Pedro Fages in 1787, simply stating that he must employ Indians "for there are no others." Fages forbade the practice in writing but clearly could not enforce the law on the widely dispersed and vast ranges of the mission *ranchos*.[5]

The padres chose Native workers who learned quickly, were dependable, and were certainly good Christians. Once elevated from fieldwork, the California Indian *vaquero* donned *pantalones* and boots, and the distinctive *chaquetas de cuera*, the leather jackets of soldiers. His status had changed too. Despite the relatively low socioeconomic status of herders, the mounted Indian *vaqueros* "shared the formidability of warriors."[6] Soldiers, herders brought up from neighboring provinces, and some padres like Eusebio Kino taught the local Indians how to rope, saddle, and use the *jaquima* or halter, before the Spanish bits became available.[7] Sometime between 1769 and Father Lasuén's letter to Governor Fages in 1787, an Alta California Indian first mounted his horse and returned an errant steer to the herd or roped a calf for branding. Cochimíes helped to herd the first cattle onto Alta California soil but likely they herded on foot. From no later than 1787, Indian *vaqueros* mounted up and began to earn the reputation in California as expert riders and ropers. Their reputation preceded them among other cattlemen, even into the twentieth century, such that those cattlemen often referred to an especially skilled cowboy as having been "raised among the Indians."[8]

California Indian *vaquero* skills at riding and roping made a major contribution to mission economies, especially once the Mexican government authorized trade for cattle products. The Spanish established the missions with the knowledge that California's desert barriers and the Pacific currents rendered the province difficult to reach by land or sea. They expected that each Alta California community of padres, soldiers, and Indians would achieve as much self-sufficiency as the resources of the surrounding country allowed. Many of the Franciscan fathers who came to California had worked among the Indigenous peoples of the Sierra Gorda in central Mexico, and they operated according to a set of rules for the spiritual and temporal guidance of the Indian neophytes. Father Pedro Pérez de Mezquía, first president of the College of San Fernando, codified those rules in a manual based on his own mission experiences in Texas.[9] Missionaries understood the connection between well-fed Indians and the receptivity of their spiritual message reflected in the cattle herds attached to each and every mission. They also brought seeds and cuttings with them to plant fruits and vegetables as well as grains. The padres possessed their own practical cultivation knowledge. Some had access to old volumes like *Secretos de Agricultura*, written by Father Miguel Agustín in 1617 and reprinted in 1781, or *Agricultura General*, published in 1777.[10] Under the supervision of the padres at first, California Indians planted wheat, corn, barley, beans, peas, potatoes, squash, grapevines, and melons, among numerous other useful crops. They also planted the first citrus trees in the province.[11]

Eventually, the many agricultural and infrastructural requirements of the mission enterprise grew beyond the control of the padres, such that they appointed one of the soldiers of the guard as *mayordomo* or foreman.[12] After Father Serra traveled to Mexico City in 1773 to secure greater support, the government also assigned from four to six young tradesmen to each mission, who trained Natives in farming, carpentry, muleteering, and cattle ranching. As the mission economy expanded in scope and complexity, functions like soap and candle making, weaving, and hide tanning required their own *mayordomos*, positions often filled by neophytes.[13]

Journals of numerous foreign visitors and the padres' own correspondence document that, beyond grain crops and livestock herds, the missionaries planted numerous vegetable gardens, fruit orchards, and even shade and ornamental trees. Captain George Vancouver visited Mission San Buenaventura and several northern missions in 1792–1793 and saw oranges, pears, peaches, figs, and vegetables and herbs, all in abundance. In 1829, Alfred Robinson arrived in California as the agent for New England trade company Bryant and Sturgis. He visited Mission San Gabriel and saw orange, citron, lime, peach, pear, and pomegranate trees among the more than two thousand trees planted at San Gabriel.[14] With this produce and the cattle herds, the missions did achieve a measure of self-sufficiency. Such abundance afforded the Spanish colonists the ability to trade for household goods, like tools, cooking pots and utensils, fine fabrics, clothing, shoes, and many other ordinary items that their relative isolation denied them, such as writing paper, pins, sewing needles, and tableware. Trading cowhides and tallow gave the missions access to these goods.

Before the early 1820s, the Spanish Crown considered any trading that missions conducted with Yankee merchants as illicit but in 1823, Alta California Governor Don Luís Antonio Arguello legalized the cowhide and tallow trade with foreign agents.[15] Foreign merchants made port in Alta California from distant points of origin: the Sandwich Islands, South America, and especially New England. They came to buy the most plentiful produce of the missions and later the *ranchos*— cowhides and tallow. In exchange for the hides, nicknamed "California bank notes,"[16] the Yankee traders imported all manner of manufactured goods at highly inflated prices. The success of this economic activity depended upon skilled California Indian *vaqueros* who rounded up the cattle for slaughter.

Governor Arguello's opening of trade with foreign merchants did not guarantee prosperity for all missions. Missions experienced a fluctuating and limited California Indian labor supply due to desertions and diseases. Continuous planting exhausted the soils and reduced crop yields, and the lack of Indian laborers forestalled the clearing and plowing of fresh fields. Droughts and floods also put crop yields at risk; extended droughts reduced the natural range forage on which the cattle and horse herds fed. All the while, gentile Indians raided the missions for horses to both ride and eat. These raids depleted this valuable resource so essential to mission cattle roundups. The combination of these factors limited the numbers of hides and the bags of tallow that the missions (and later *ranchos*) could produce as tradable wealth.[17] Despite these deficiencies, the southern missions at San Juan Capistrano, San Luis Rey, and San Gabriel held two-thirds of all California mission cattle in 1834,emphasizing the indispensability of Indian *vaqueros* and their horses to mission economies.[18]

Missions provided each *vaquero* with a saddle. Through adaptations of the Moorish, Persian, and Mexican saddles over the course of centuries, the California *vaquero's* saddle emerged with a high pommel in the front to secure the braided leather rope called *a reata*, and the animal controlled by it, and with a high cantle in the back. The high cantle design kept the rider on the horse and well forward so that his weight would not create kidney sores from sliding too far rearward. The California saddle used a single cinch, centered on the wooden saddle tree (frame), to keep the cinch behind the horse's forelegs but forward of the belly. When the rider roped an animal and tied the *reata* to the horn, the center cinch and the tree distributed the pull on the horn more evenly.[19] Mixed-blood and full-blood Indian *vaqueros* from Mexico taught California Indians the art of cowboying, including how to make and use *reatas*, quirts, and chaps, among others.

The California *vaquero's* equipment consisted of a *reata*, with a loop at the end of it, and a long lance-like prod called a *garrocha*, both of which herdsmen had employed to control cattle on the Iberian Peninsula before Columbus's voyages.[20] In later years, Anglo-American cowboys corrupted *la reata* into lariat and *lazo* into lasso. With this thrown loop or lasso, the *vaquero* caught individual cattle to be branded and marked, or for slaughter. He also threw the lasso to catch a horse out of his *caballada* (his own band of trained mounts) or to capture wild horses. "To lasso" also describes the act of catching an animal with a thrown loop.[21]

Herdsmen on the southwestern coast of Spain resorted to using the *garrocha* to drive cattle that could not be led by salt licks. In the salt marshes of southwestern Spain, known as *Las Marismas*, the vegetation is salt-tolerant and therefore salt-containing. The cattle fed on these plants all spring and summer. When the summer dry heat gave way to fall and winter rains, herdsmen moved the cattle from the coastal marshes to higher elevations and hilly woodlands, not by leading them with salt licks but by prodding them from behind with *garrochas*. Those herdsmen also pulled floundering animals out of the mire by throwing the lasso around the neck of the animal and securing it to the tail of their horse. *Vaqueros* in the Americas used both the *garrocha* and the lasso, but used them differently according to their needs and surroundings.[22]

California Indian *vaqueros* began learning to ride and rope as early as four or five years of age. They wore spurs over their boots, with big Spanish rowels that held sharp points an inch long.[23] In the thorny thickets of Baja, *vaqueros* wore heavy leather *armas,* draped over the saddletree like an apron and folded back over the *vaquero's* legs, for protection.[24] Alta California *vaqueros* also wore deerskin *armitas*, a lighter and shorter version of the *armas* that came to just below the knee. They used the *armitas* when vegetation in the coastal ranges did not pose the same threat of cutting into the *vaquero's* legs and his mount's breast, as in Baja. *Vaqueros* also favored this form of protection in hot weather. *Chapareras* (or *chaparejos*), commonly called "chaps," covered the front and sides of the vaquero's entire leg. *Vaqueros* tied them in the back with rawhide thongs. The name derives from the rough and sometimes cutting brush called chaparral that *vaqueros* often found cattle hiding in and from which they must be rousted out. *Armitas* and chaps also protected the rider's legs from rope burns from the *reata*, fence splinters, and animal bites. If the *vaquero* needed to protect his legs in the thorny thickets, he also needed to protect his feet in the stirrups. Two large circular pieces of "very stout leather" formed *tapaderas* when tied together with strips of deerskin called *gamuza* that also attached the *tapaderas* to his stirrups.[25]

In the matter of dress, they inherited the *charro* tradition transplanted from Sonora and Jalisco in Mexico. This included decorated shirts, medium-length pants, a red sash around the waist, leggings called *botas*, and a high-crowned and wide-brimmed sombrero. Californios also wore a low-crowned and wide-brimmed hat secured with a neck string that seemed more appropriate to the colorful and fearless riding that these sons of the Dons displayed when chasing wild horses. During the period from 1770 to 1846, *vaquero* clothing, accouterments, and even the shortening length of hair went through a "transition from colonial to modern dress."[26] Consistent with the *charro* influence, saddle makers hand-tooled ornate designs into saddle leather and other riding equipment, possibly embellished with silver (See Figure 4.1, page 68).[27]

Vaqueros worked the *rodeos* or roundups under the supervision of a *mayordomo* or ranch foreman. In the early mission days, a single roundup inventoried all of the cattle for the entire mission but as the herds expanded, missions established multiple ranches to diffuse the consumption of the range forage and to keep livestock away from crops. Each week, the *vaqueros* rounded up a number of cattle for slaughter, sufficient to supply the mission or *rancho* with beef. During the dry summer months, *vaqueros* rounded up a larger number of animals that they slaughtered to make jerky. The largest roundups took place in spring or fall, depending on the local climate; however, the *rancheros* preferred to round up in the spring when the calves were sure to still be following their mothers.[28] San Jose in the colder north had permission to wait until August and September when the calves had grown and could be counted, marked, and branded as required by Spanish and Mexican law.[29]

Without fences between ranges, the cattle from the multiples of mission ranches wandered when not closely watched and mixed with those of another, as well as with cattle from the *ranchos del rey* (king's ranches) and the *pueblos*. These conditions necessitated *rodeos* presided over by a *Juez de Campo*, a Judge of the Plains. *Vaqueros* and the *mayordomo* from each ranch separated their animals from the rest and held them until the judge verified or denied their assertion of ownership. Judges discerned ownership by reading the brand. Spanish law required that each and every calf be branded on the flank or hip at their first *rodeo*, and when sold, the new owner placed their brand on the animal's shoulder. When the judge made his decision, the owner drove his herd off and the judge moved on to the next herd. These proceedings transpired without any documentation. "No documents were given. None were necessary; and furthermore, in those days there were very few who could write."[30] All abided by the decisions and went back to business. This tradition persisted into the American period.[31]

Each Alta California mission created and registered a unique brand, and their Indian *vaqueros* learned how to heat up the irons and apply the brand. The branding iron, or *fierro*, must not be too hot, and it must not be pressed too hard, lest it burn through the skin into the flesh, inflicting unnecessary pain or even debilitating the animal and damaging what later became the hide. In the early years of the missions, before blacksmiths and other tradesmen came north to train the Indians, blacksmiths in the more settled provinces to the south made the first irons according to the designs specified by California padres.[32]

Similar to the practice in Baja California, military authorities often stationed soldiers at the Alta California missions who possessed useful trades, from carpentry and masonry to blacksmithing, saddle-making, and hide tanning. These soldier-tradesmen taught neophytes how to build and maintain the buildings, make tools, plant crops, build irrigation ditches, and slaughter cattle and process the cowhides. Mission *vaqueros* slaughtered animals weekly to provide beef for domestic consumption. They held these smaller-scale *matanzas* mainly for meat and consumed most of the carcass.[33] The annual commercial killing season that began in late spring when the cattle had time to fatten up on green grasses lasted about three months and prioritized volume production. Mission workers produced the hides and tallow as rapidly as they could, so an "enormous amount" of meat went to waste, even though Spanish Longhorn cattle, often described as "'leggy' and slim-bodied," ran only between 600 and 800 pounds.[34]

In both cases, vaqueros began the *matanza* by controlling the steer. The first *vaquero* threw his lasso over the horns of the animal. A second *vaquero* then roped one of the hind legs, throwing the animal to the ground. The heeler or *vaquero* who had caught the hind leg, dismounted and then tied all four legs together. Having done this, he then plunged his knife into the animal's neck to sever its artery and waited until it died.[35] William Davis preferred this Californian method of *matanza* with the animal lying flat because it preserved more blood in the meat, keeping the meat juicy, giving it a sweeter taste, and making it more nutritious than the beef produced by the American method of draining all the blood.[36]

As soon as the animal died, skinners dragged the body away from the slaughtering space and, with their razor-sharp knives, deftly skinned the carcass in about thirty minutes. They then handed the bloody hide to other Indian ranch workers who cut small holes around the outside edges and staked the hide on the ground to dry. Properly staked, the hide did not shrink. For mission consumption, the workers then took at least two hundred pounds of meat and large quantities of tallow: big pieces of fresh meat for immediate cooking and consumption, and long strips of lean meat, cut from the sides and back for *carne seca* or jerky.[37] To make jerky, Indians first cut the strips about an inch thick, a few inches wide and from one to three feet in length, then dipped the strips in brine and hung them like stockings on a clothesline to be dried by the sun. By continually turning the brine-soaked strips, the meat dried before it could spoil and was then bundled up with rawhide thongs and stored for later use.[38]

California Indians also learned to extract large quantities of fat from the butchered steer, from 100 to 150 pounds per animal.[39] They took the best quality *sebo*, and the most plentiful, from the interior, around the kidneys and other organs. Yankee merchants and missions alike prized this tallow. From it, they made candles and soap. Cooks liked to use the fat closest to the hide, the *manteca*, instead of hog's lard for frying or baking. By heating the fat in large pots, mission workers tried or rendered creamy white tallow. Once they strained out the impurities and bits of meat, they sent some of this tallow to the candle and soap makers. For trade, they packaged the tallow in very large hide bags called *botas,* that presumably held as much as 25–40 *arrobas* (an *arroba* is 25 pounds).[40] Workers first placed the bag in a hole that had been dug and staked it around the top edge so that when they poured in the hot tallow, the *bota* stayed in place and held its shape as a container. Once cooled, ranch workers transported the tallow to the ship landing sites. The mission *vaqueros* slaughtered about one-third of the mission's cattle each year to help feed the mission and to satisfy the need for the multitude of products traded in exchange for hides and tallow.[41]

For the trade in hides, mission workers performed a preliminary scraping, followed by stretching and drying. Once the hides dried, workers released them from the stakes, folded them lengthwise with the skin side out and transported them to the landing site. At that point, the ship's company put the hides "in soak" in seawater to soften them. They closely scraped them clean of meat and fat particles. Dry salting for two days and then brining the hides for two more killed the bacteria that would decompose them so whether ranch or merchant workers performed this first step, time was of the essence.[42] The brining solution consisted of seawater and much added salt loaded into large wooden vats.[43] At this point, the raw hide still retained its hair. Tanners, at first Spanish and then Indian, supervised the work of salting and brining, followed by soaking the hide in limewater to loosen the hair, which the tannery workers scraped off.[44]

Depending on the greater needs of the mission, leather craftsmen worked the hide raw or used tanned hides for the most flexibility. Rawhide performed many functions in the missions and the ranchos. Leather workers tightly stretched rawhide across a frame in a latticework to make a comfortable cot or a single piece for a door or even the hinges of the door. They tied fence rails together with strips of it to build corrals. Large rawhide *botas* carried tallow and smaller ones carried water. Builders employed rawhide straps to join timbers and much thinner thongs to attach handles to tools and weapons. Rawhide served many purposes as a universal and handy mending material. An old bell in the Santa Barbara mission, bound by very old rawhide, survived the 1925 earthquake.[45]

Mission ranch workers also tanned rawhide to make it supple for clothing and shoes. To soften it, tanners layered rawhide and ground oak bark in vats and then added water to draw out the tannic acid from the bark and soften the rawhide over time. Once set up, they left the hides in the solution for a minimum of three to six months. After repeated rinses, the tanned leather now needed one last treatment. Workers rubbed oil or even tallow back into the leather to restore the moisture that tanning removed. At last, workers hung the salted, brined, limed, tanned, rinsed, and rubbed leather in a building where it would gently dry, ready for use by the artisans to create the many tools and accouterments of mission and *rancho* life.[46]

A *vaquero* without a *reata* is just a horseman. With his *reata*, the *vaquero* lassoed and branded calves, held a cow for doctoring, and when it was time, brought them under control for slaughtering. The *reata*, thrown by a skilled *vaquero*, made a profitable cattle economy possible. Leather artisans made *reatas* for the California *vaquero* but in the absence of an artisan, *vaqueros* also made their own and taught others. In what is now San Diego County, Mexican *vaqueros* taught the sons of a widowed Kumeyaay Indian woman how to make *reatas* and reins for use on their ranch, among many other skills of the *vaquero*.[47]

To make a *reata*, the *reatero* began by cutting a narrow strip along the outer edge of a cowhide, and then carefully and in a long, spiral pattern continued this technique until they made one long, continuous strip of hide. The skilled *reatero* controlled the length of the strip by its width. A narrower strip is a longer but weaker strip. He then shaved off the hair, an easier task than scraping it off the entire hide. The *reatero* stretched the strips and soaked them in water to make them more pliable for the braiding. Having tied one end of from four to eight strands to a post or a tree, he set about braiding the individual strands into a single strong rope, and then, oiling to soften and a final stretching to finish it. The finished product would hold when the *vaquero* looped the end and threw it over the horns of an eight-hundred-pound steer and made the other end fast around his saddle horn. *Reateros* or *vaqueros* made most *reatas* at about sixty feet in length because "that was and is about as far as a man can throw a lasso, 35 feet is considered good, with the average throw about 25 feet."[48] *Reateros* or *vaqueros* also crafted reins out of those same strips.

California Indian *vaqueros* collected their own *caballada* to have fresh mounts available as each horse wore out from hard riding.[49] These California horses, like their progenitors in Mexico, had ultimately descended from Moorish Arabian stock. They possessed great agility and endurance. Like the cattle, they grazed on the open range and some went wild. Eventually, *rancheros* made the hard decision to reduce these wild herds by slaughtering them in order to save the pasturage for ranch cattle. Numerous foreign visitors attested to the vaquero's daring and prowess on horseback. In 1838, American immigrant William Heath Davis witnessed an extraordinary technique employed by a *vaquero* attempting to retrieve a runaway steer that had bolted from the herd during a roundup. The alert *vaquero* gave chase and when he came up even with the runaway, reached down to grab the tail. When he had hold of it, he spurred his mount to accelerate, which produced a sudden lurch, and then released the tail, causing the animal to roll over and over. When it recovered and got to its feet, the stunned animal tamely rejoined the herd. The trick "was highly enjoyed by the *vaquero* and was a feat requiring no little skill, strength, nerve, and horsemanship on his part."[50]

Davis reported in the 1830s that as many as 20,000 wild horses roamed the San Joaquin Valley. Davis connected this huge resource with the endless demand for horses to do ranch work and described how the sons of the Dons rode out after wild horses at breakneck speed, for sport. First, they removed their saddles and tied their *reatas* around the horses like a cinch but left enough slack to wedge their knees under the *reata*. This freed the rider's hands to throw the lasso around the neck of a wild horse in full flight. "If a rider found himself in the midst of a band of wild horses there was danger that he and his horse might be overridden and trampled to death. This sometimes occurred."[51] If they did not die in the attempt, they returned with dozens of high-spirited and powerful new mounts for their *ranchos*.

The rapid expansion of horse and cattle herds on California rangeland prompted the decision taken by mission padres to train their Indian neophytes as *vaqueros*. The burgeoning herds represented prosperity but they also degraded the range. The first Spanish to set foot on California grasslands saw the ideal setting in which to continue the Spanish cattle economies that had come from Andalucía in Spain, transplanted to the Antilles, central Mexico, Sonora, and finally to Alta California. From the 4,000 head of cattle on mission ranges at the time of Father Serra's death in 1784, mission herds increased to approximately 67,000 in 1800.[52] The cattle had no major predators, and loss to theft or the wild had little effect.[53] With no real plan to conserve the range by systematic pasture rotation, Spanish, Mexican, and American cattle increased the pressure on the native flora. Droughts forced livestock to go farther afield and to chew plants down to the roots. Ultimately, the ever-expanding herds consumed Indian vegetative food sources and the forage of Indians' sources of hunted meat, and forced all California Indians, neophyte and gentile, to adopt cattle as a survival strategy.[54]

The decimation of bunch grasses illustrates this process. Bunch grasses possess a delicate root system of fine fibers that function more to feed moisture to the slender stems than to anchor them into the soil. As cows or horses feed on the bunch, they tear it out of the ground. Their hooves also act as spades that can pry the grass out of the soil and thereby disrupt the reproduction and renewal of the grass.[55] After domesticated animals consumed native grasses to the point of extinction, invasive and non-native species like mustard filled the voids.[56]

Once the missions established multiple remote cattle ranches, this process of using up native plants, followed by the fill-in of foreign ones, expanded across multiple ecosystems and wide geographic areas. Mission San Luis Rey owned a total of twenty ranches; Mission San Gabriel had seventeen ranches for cattle and horses, plus others for goats, pigs, and sheep. San Gabriel established an *Asistencia*, a sort of branch mission, at Rancho San Bernardino some forty miles east of the mission. The San Gorgonio Pass lies thirty miles further eastward, fully seventy miles from the mission. But San Gabriel also established a site there, in the vicinity of present-day Beaumont, to grow grain and herd mission cattle.[57] Local Cahuilla Indians worked cattle there, along with Tongva employed by San Gabriel.[58]

Before the secularization of the missions in the 1830s, the California mission ranches dominated the landscape. The boundaries of one mission coincided with the next closest mission, so that missions could claim control, though not ownership, of most of the lands close to the coast, from San Diego to Sonoma, north of San Francisco. But missions did not own nor control all of the cattle and horses in California. Soldiers at *presidios* and settlers in *pueblos* like Los Angeles started herds that also multiplied on whatever California grass they resided on. When the small herds outgrew *presidio* lands, several soldiers petitioned Governor Pedro Fages in 1784 for the use of tracts of land beyond *presidios* and *pueblos*, in order to build their own herds. These three soldier-petitioners, Manuel Nieto, Juan José Domínguez, and José María Verdugo, had served under then-Captain Fages in his old command at the San Diego *presidio* in 1769, Verdugo just eighteen at that time.[59]

The original Spanish pattern of colonization of northern New Spain contemplated only *ranchos* that served the missions, *presidios*, and *pueblos*, on temporary land concessions from the Spanish king. The fact that Fages needed guidance from his superiors on the authority to make such grants to veterans, lends credence to the contention that the idea of individually owned *ranchos* originated in Alta California.[60]

Two years after they filed their petitions, Fages received approval from Mexico City to make the grants, contingent upon certain performance requirements: the tracts could not encroach upon mission, pueblo, or Indian *ranchería* lands and water sources, and the grantee must build a stone house. The grant further stipulated stocking the ranch with at least 2,000 head of cattle and employing enough *vaqueros* and sheepherders to prevent livestock trespass on neighboring ranches.[61] Spanish colonists had established the *pueblo* of Los Angeles just three years earlier and started their own herds. It is possible then, that the new *rancheros* filled their labor needs by employing *poblanos,* or citizens of the *pueblos,* to work the cattle and horses on their ranges. It is also likely that some full-blood Indian or *mestizo vaqueros* (mixed blood) relocated from mission *ranchería(s)* to help build up the new Nieto, Domínguez, and Verdugo herds.[62]

Fages granted Nieto approximately 150,000 acres, bounded by the San Gabriel River on the west and the Santa Ana River on the east. Nieto's Rancho Santa Gertrudes occupied land on which Californians later built the cities of Long Beach and Huntington Beach, and tapped the oil fields on Signal Hill. The Spanish in California employed crude means of marking boundaries by landmarks, along *zanjas* (irrigation ditches), individual trees, or piles of stones; therefore, all parties accepted sizes of the *ranchos* as approximations. Nieto retired from the army in 1795 and lived only eleven more years but at his death, his heirs claimed the greatest individual wealth in California. Cattle on the Domínguez grant, known as Rancho San Pedro, foraged on some 75,000 acres. Disputes between Domínguez's heirs and a creditor resulted in a settlement that severed the entire Palos Verdes peninsula from the original grant. Appropriately, the city of Rancho Domínguez is situated on Rancho San Pedro land. Fages granted José Verdugo, the third of his former *soldados de cuera,* lands roughly northwest of the San Gabriel Mission and eastward of Mission San Fernando, including the Arroyo Seco, site of the present-day Rose Bowl. Although the histories of these *ranchos* focus on the Spanish subjects that obtained title from the Crown, most of the credit for their successes belongs to the California Indian *vaqueros* who herded, birthed, marked and branded, and slaughtered the cattle that produced the wealth. They also broke and trained the horses required to get the job done.[63]

Under the Spanish Crown, Alta California missions, *presidios*, and *pueblos* fulfilled the limited purposes of the empire to ward off Russian and British encroachment. Thus, development proceeded at a languid pace. Governors made about twenty-seven land concessions during the entire Spanish and early Mexican periods (1782–1833),[64] primarily due to mission control of large tracts of southern California land and their jurisdiction over the San Gabriel and Santa Ana rivers. In 1821, the people of New Spain threw off Spanish rule and reconstituted their nation as the Republic of Mexico, assuming all of the powers formerly vested in the Crown. Because successive appointed governors made no attempts to nullify the original mission authorizations, the missions maintained their hold on Alta California land, blocking the economic development of the state. Secular leaders demanded legislative change.

Spanish colonization of the Americas relied on strategies forged during the *Reconquista* and honed to the challenges presented in the Antilles and in New Spain. Horses and cattle for subsistence, the spiritual message of the Catholic faith, and military power combined to effectuate the appropriation of lands and resources belonging to the Indigenous peoples of the New World. The Spanish hoped to pacify Indigenous peoples with the Catholic faith in order to employ them in the hard labor of building colonial institutions and economies that justified the invasion of their homelands. The Spanish mission system adjusted to local conditions and with the help of fellow *Indigenes* as change agents, produced an Indian workforce that when combined with domesticated European animals provided subsistence that replaced traditional foods and tied the workers to the mission complex.

Spanish missions marched steadily northward in New Spain, and each outpost of empire supplied the people and animals to found the next one, a process they repeated for two centuries until missionaries and soldiers landed on the "island" of California. Toward the end of the eighteenth century, soldiers and missionaries from California, along with converted or neophyte Indians, marched north into Alta California. As they did on every American frontier, the Spanish drove along cattle and rode horses for that first mission at San Diego in 1769. Cattle, and horses to control them, filled the critical role of providing food security for colonizers and Indigenous alike. When mission herd sizes reached a point of self-sustainability, it also likely meant that the padres could no longer control them without help. That help came from California Indians—Kumeyaay, Luiseño, Cahuilla, Serrano, Tongva, and others—elevated to the role of herder on horseback, the *vaquero*. The accouterments of the job, the saddle, the spurs, and other material cultural markers set the Indian *vaquero* apart from other neophytes.

The mission economies relied on cattle and other livestock until crops began to yield, while Spanish tradesmen and Indians constructed churches and dwellings. Slaughtered cattle provided food, hides, and tallow for the mission's needs, as well as tradable goods for supplies and other manufactured products that the missions could not make for themselves. The budding but limited trade in Spanish California hides and tallow hinted at the economic potential of the remote colony and stimulated the ambition of Mexican Californios to realize that potential. That required the privatization of all mission land.

The ready-made market of consumers for California hides and tallow facilitated the transition of the *rancho* from religious to secular and accelerated that change by its gravitational pull on both the producers and consumers of California commodities. Increased demand enticed more Californios to seek land grants for *ranchos*. They soon filled up their ranges with great numbers of cattle, which brought traders from around the world, their ships filled with all manner of made goods to trade, including shoes made from the same California hides filling up the holds of their ships.

NOTES

1. Hubert Howe Bancroft, *California History, Vol. II 1801–1824, California History Vol. III 1825–1840* (Santa Barbara, CA: Wallace Hebberd, 1963) and Bancroft, *California Pastoral*; Jordan, *North American Cattle-Ranching Frontiers*, 165. The Spanish herded cattle onto Texas ranges several generations before they accomplished the feat in Alta California. Southwestern historians reveal commonalities of Texas and California colonial strategies in Sandra L. Myres, "The Ranching Frontier: Spanish Institutional Backgrounds of the Plains Cattle Industry," in *The Walter Prescott Webb Memorial Lectures: Essays on the American West*, eds. Harold M. Hollingsworth and Sandra L. Myres, 19–39 (Austin, TX: University of Texas Press, 1969) and Odie B. Faulk, "Ranching in Spanish Texas," *The Hispanic American Historical Review* 45, no. 2 (May 1965): 257–266.

2. Myres, "The Ranching Frontier," 31.

3. Ibid., 35–36; Faulk, "Ranching in Spanish Texas," 257–266.

4. Burcham, "Cattle and Range Forage in California," 140–149 and Burcham, *California Range Land*, 185–187; Hackel, *Children of Coyote*, 68–75.

5. Phillips, *Vineyards and Vaqueros*, 71–72; Jose Del Carmen Lugo, "Life of a Rancher," *Historical Society of Southern California Quarterly* 32, no. 3 (September 1950): 226–227.

6. Jordan, *Cattle-Ranching Frontiers*, 8.

7. David Dary, *Cowboy Culture: A Saga of Five Centuries* (New York: Alfred A. Knopf, 1981), 47–48.

8. Arnold Rojas, *The Vaquero* (Santa Barbara, CA: McNally and Loftin, 1964), 24.

9. Webb, *Indian Life*, 52–53.

10. Ibid., 54.

11. Walter Reuther, Herbert John Webber, and Leon Dexter Batchelor, eds., *The Citrus Industry, Vol. 1: History, World Distribution, Botany and Varieties*, Rev. ed. (Berkeley, CA: University of California Press, 1967), 26. In 1841, former Kentucky trapper William Wolfskill obtained sweet orange cuttings from Mission San Gabriel,

and "set out" the first commercial grove of citrus in California. Seven years later, just as Wolfskill's trees began to bear fruit in Los Angeles, James Marshall found some gold nuggets near Sutter's Mill in the north. Gold Rush demand made fortunes in wheat and cattle, along with many specialty crops like oranges.

12. Webb, *Indian Life*, 54.
13. Ibid., 84–88; Lugo, "Life of a Rancher," 225–226.
14. Webb, *Indian Life*, 84–88. See also Alfred Robinson, *Life in California During a Residence in that Territory, Comprising a Description of the Country and the Missionary Establishments* (New York: Da Capo Press, 1969), 31–34.
15. William Heath Davis, *Seventy-Five Years in California: Recollections and Remarks by One Who Visited These Shores in 1831, and Again in 1833, and Except When Absent on Business Was a Resident From 1838 Until the End of a Long Life in 1909*, ed. Harold A. Small (San Francisco, CA: John Howell--Books, 1967), 26, 229–230.
16. Richard Henry Dana, *Two Years Before the Mast and Twenty-Four Years After* (New York: P. F. Collier and Son, 1937), 77–86.
17. Jackson and Castillo, *Indians, Franciscans, and Spanish Colonization*, 14–26; Jordan, *North American Cattle Ranching Frontiers*, 159.
18. Jordan, *North American Cattle Ranching Frontiers*, 163.
19. Rojas, *The Vaquero*, 29–33; Phillips, *Vineyards and Vaqueros*, 219–220.
20. Butzer, "Cattle and Sheep from Old to New," 48.
21. Dary, *Cowboy Culture*, 20.
22. Jordan, *Cattle-Ranching Frontiers*, 20–25.
23. Bancroft, *California Pastoral*, 290.
24. Rojas, *The Vaquero*, 93–94.
25. Lugo, "Life of a Rancher," 223; Richard W. Slatta, *The Cowboy Encyclopedia* (Norman, OK: University of Oklahoma Press, 1997), 64–66; Russell Freedman, *In the Days of the Vaqueros: America's First True Cowboys* (New York: Clarion Books, 2001), 29–30; Clifford E. Trafzer, *American Indians as Cowboys* (Newcastle, CA: Sierra Oaks Publishing, 1992), 48–53.
26. Jo Mora, *Californios: The Saga of the Hard-Riding Vaqueros, America's First Cowboys* (Garden City, NJ: Doubleday, 1949), 98–112.
27. Trafzer, *American Indians as Cowboys*, 48–53; Jordan, *Cattle-Ranching Frontiers*, 167–168; Rojas, *The Vaquero*, 93.
28. Charles Nordhoff, *California for Health, Pleasure, and Residence: A Book for Travellers and Settlers* (New York: Harper and Brothers, 1882),188.
29. Webb, *Indian Life*, 176, 178.
30. Lugo, "Life of a Rancher," 230.
31. Robert Glass Cleland, *The Cattle on a Thousand Hills: Southern California 1850–1880* (San Marino, CA: The Huntington Library, 1951), 55.
32. Webb, *Indian Life*, 177–179.
33. Davis, *Seventy-Five Years in California*, 31–32.
34. Webb, *Indian Life*, 174, 176.
35. Davis, *Seventy-Five Years in California*, 30–31.
36. Ibid., 31.

37. Ibid., 26.
38. Webb, *Indian Life*, 198; Cleland, *The Cattle on a Thousand Hills*, 63.
39. Davis, *Seventy-Five Years in California*, 26.
40. Ibid., 26; Stampa, "The Evolution of Weights and Measures in New Spain," 13.
41. Webb, *Indian Life*, 174.
42. David Prescott Barrows, *The Ethno-Botany of the Coahuilla Indians of Southern California.* (Chicago, IL: University of Chicago Press, 1900), 30. Desert Cahuilla people used the salty lagoon commonly known as the Salton Sea as a source of salt for their diet and for trade with other southern California tribes. It is possible but unlikely that they provided enough salt to preserve cowhides, because the traders brined hundreds of thousands of hides right at the landing sites on the Pacific shore with large quantities of salt.
43. Dana, *Two Years Before the Mast*, 187–189; Robinson, *Life in California*, 51.
44. Webb, *Indian Life*, 190–193.
45. Ibid., 195.
46. Ibid., 188–195.
47. Trafzer, *American Indians as Cowboys*, 33, 36–38.
48. Dary, *Cowboy Culture*, 33–35; Webb, *Indian Life*, 195–196.
49. Phillips, *Vineyards and Vaqueros*, 220.
50. Davis, *Seventy-Five Years in California*, 28–29.
51. Ibid., 27–28.
52. Bancroft, *California Pastoral*, 191.
53. Jordan, *Cattle-Ranching Frontiers*, 162.
54. Florence Connelly Shipek, "Saints or Oppressors: The Franciscan Missionaries of California," in *The Missions of California: A Legacy of Genocide*, eds. Rupert Costo and Jeannette Henry Costo, 29–47 (San Francisco, CA: Indian Historian Press, 1987); Pulling, "A History of California's Range-Cattle Industry," 201–207.
55. Pulling, "A History of California's Range-Cattle Industry," 200–202.
56. Ibid., 202.
57. Webb, *Indian Life*, 92; Burcham, *California Range Land*, 134–135; Cleland, *The Cattle on a Thousand Hills*, 21–22.
58. Richard A. Hanks, *This War is for a Whole Life: The Culture of Resistance Among Southern California Indians, 1850–1966* (Banning, CA: Ushkana Press, 2012), 11–12.
59. Burcham, *California Range Land*, 134; Cleland, *The Cattle on a Thousand Hills*, 7–12.
60. David Hornbeck, "Land Tenure and Rancho Expansion in Alta California, 1784–1846," *Journal of Historical Geography* 4, no. 4 (1978): 372.
61. Cleland, *The Cattle on a Thousand Hills*, 7.
62. Ibid., 6, 30.
63. Ibid., 7–18.
64. Hornbeck, "Land Tenure and Rancho Expansion in Alta California," 376. Hornbeck claims that twenty-seven grants were issued 1784–1846; Cleland, *The Cattle on a Thousand Hills*, 19. Cleland believes that the governors made fewer than twenty.

Chapter 4

Hides and Tallow

Native American Labor and the Rise of Californio Society, 1833–1848

In 1808, Napoleon Bonaparte invaded Spain, dethroned King Fernando VII, and provoked the Spanish people to mount a national insurgency against the French occupation. The insurgency ignited republican idealism in Spain and in her colonies. In the years 1810–1820, few Spanish supply ships made port in Alta California, and the frontier province suffered from neglect and lack of resources. Missions sustained themselves and provided destitute *presidios* with beef, grains, and other supplies provided by California Indian labor. Indian *vaqueros* still rode herd on California ranges. Their ease in the saddle and facility with the lasso sustained the province's primary economic asset—its tens of thousands of Spanish Longhorns that they and their fellow Indian ranch workers turned into tradeable hides and tallow. In desperate need, the governors traded for supplies from Lima merchants, American smugglers, and even the Russians at Fort Ross, north of San Francisco Bay.

In 1824, an independent Republic of Mexico emerged. To populate the northern frontiers, the Mexican Congress passed the Colonization Act of 1824, further clarified by Supplemental Regulations in 1828. These laws set a framework for land grants in Alta California but resisted the colonization of mission lands. Finally, the Secularization Act of 1833 fundamentally changed land tenure in California by releasing all mission lands for private development. Prospective *rancheros* had only to map out a parcel to gain a land grant, since the value of the land resided in its capacity to carry horses and cattle. The numerous and widespread mission herds of horses and cattle formed the economic base of Mexican California. Governors had legalized the trade with foreign merchants from the early 1820s and set in motion the rapid and symbiotic expansion of land grant ranchos and markets that consumed their growing supply of hides and tallow, typified by Yankee merchants. The new laws also put a legal veneer on the plunder of mission lands and assets, especially cattle.

Establishing the new *ranchero* class as semi-feudal lords required a source of cheap labor. Someone had to process the hides and tallow for trade. Distributing mission lands among the Native converts of the missions might have fulfilled the stated goals of missions: conversion, acculturation, and citizenship, but that ideal would have denied Indian labor to the *rancheros*. So, by law and custom, Californios kept Indian labor on the *ranchos* and institutionalized their status at the bottom of Californio society. Eventually, American imperialism overshadowed the prosperity and the injustices of the *rancheros* but the romantic ideal of that brief period persisted in reality under American rule and in fantasy, down to the present day.

In June 1822, eleven years before Secularization, the British ship *John Begg*, of the enterprise McCulloch, Hartnell and Company, landed at Monterey and requested a meeting with Alta California Governor (and Lieutenant Colonel) Pablo Vicente de Sola. Their representative sought legal sanction to trade their manufactured goods and commodities for California hides and tallow. The representative concluded a three-year contract with the governor in 1822, effective January 1823. The contract gave McCulloch, Hartnell and Company exclusive rights to trade for the hides and tallow from any mission that agreed to participate in the arrangements, at the price of 1 peso per hide and 2 pesos per arroba (25 pounds) of tallow.[1]

For the most part, the mission padres welcomed the opportunity to trade mission cattle for household goods like carpets and window panes, cooking vessels and utensils, farm and agricultural tools (including knives for the *matanza*), luxury food items like sugar, cocoa, tea and coffee, clothing articles of all kinds, and even musical instruments. At times, the missions provided hides that were not completely scraped clean and therefore not truly preserved, which ruined some of the cargo. These instances prompted the extensive salting and soaking of hides discussed in chapter 3. However, by the time that McCulloch, Hartnell and Company's contract expired in early 1826, the venture had proved unprofitable for them. American Yankee traders like Bryant and Sturgis and others out of Lima, Peru, had eaten into the California supply of hides and tallow by paying higher prices. Hides from Brazilian and other sources flooded the market and lowered the prices that McCulloch, Hartnell and Company cargoes fetched in England.[2]

McCulloch, Hartnell and Company suspended operations in 1827, but they had stimulated demand in California for goods from the wider world and set the stage for the boom that made private ranches profitable and prestigious, and that filled California ranges with even more Longhorn cattle.[3] Behind the complexities of the California hide trade—supply and demand, local customs, and cultural factors—lay the simple facts that California ranges had produced hundreds of thousands of cattle, and that foreign merchants came from afar to buy the hides and tallow derived from them. Furthermore, both missionaries and Californios loved the wonderful array of goods put on display on the decks of the Yankee ships.[4]

Bryant and Sturgis claimed the honor of being the first of the Boston merchants to legally trade in California. Prior to their entry into the cattle parts business, they clubbed seals to death on the Farallon Islands off the coast of San Francisco. But when they arrived in 1822 for the purpose of trading with the missions, they found that McCulloch, Hartnell and Company had beaten them to the punch. They had secured a contract endorsed by Governor Sola and Prefect Father Mariano Payeras, who coordinated mission policies with the civil government. Despite offering to buy hides at twice the price that McCulloch, Hartnell and Company contracted for, Bryant and Sturgis's supercargo (commercial operations manager) William Gale found that the padres who had signed contracts with the British company honored their word.[5]

In 1828, Bryant and Sturgis stepped in to fill the void in demand left by the British withdrawal. They plied California waters profitably for another fifteen years. Smaller Bryant and Sturgis vessels carried ten thousand hides but the *California* packed fully forty thousand hides in her hold. At 25 pounds per hide (500 tons), it was "loaded to its chain plates." Bryant and Sturgis regularly dispatched a large vessel like *California* or the *Alert,* with forty thousand hide capacity, tended by a smaller sister ship such as the *Pilgrim*, that moved up and down the coast, collecting hides at San Francisco, Monterey, and Santa Barbara, then delivering them to the large ship, berthed at San Pedro. Among the many other New Englander crewmembers, author Richard Henry Dana served on the *Pilgrim* in 1835. When a large freighter like the *Alert* sat low in the water, it meant that she had been fully loaded and was ready to unfurl her sails and head for Boston. Bryant and Sturgis ceased their California operations in 1842 but not before they had exported approximately five hundred thousand hides from California to Boston during the period 1822–1842. They did about 80 percent of that volume from 1830 to 1840.[6] For Bryant and Sturgis alone, California *vaqueros* rounded up, roped, threw, and then slaughtered over forty thousand head of cattle per year in that boom decade. Over the entirety of their California venture, they needed California Indian *vaqueros* and ranch workers to kill, skin, and clean the tallow from an average of about five hundred animals every single week for twenty years.[7]

Boston Native Alfred Robinson arrived at Monterey in February 1829 on board the Bryant and Sturgis ship *Brookline*. By mastering Spanish and converting to Catholicism, the twenty-two-year-old clerk integrated into Californio society and earned handsome commissions from Bryant and Sturgis's profitable business over the next nine years.[8]

Figure 4.1 Californio *Ranchero* with Roped Steer. Source: The Picture Art Collection/Alamy Stock Photo.

From Monterey, Robinson traveled southward overland to Mission San Buenaventura to make rough estimates of his raw material supply (cattle) at the northern missions and to observe this strange new country. His first surveys of the missions included estimates of the herds. Santa Ynez, north of Santa Barbara, had about nine thousand head of cattle and San Buenaventura six thousand. Further north, La Purisima had cattle in abundance but the mission had fallen into disrepair owing to the loss of support after Mexican independence. Likewise, San Luis Obispo had degraded although it had many good horses, some of which had strayed from the mission to "mix with the wild cattle of the mountains." At the La Purisima ranch named "Guadeloupe," Robinson witnessed "Indians busy at their annual '*matanzas*' or cattle killing." Two *vaqueros* worked in concert to catch and throw the cow or steer to the ground. The header threw his looped *reata* or lasso over the horns and his partner or heeler caught one or both hind legs with his own lasso. Once on the ground, another Indian sliced the animal's throat. Robinson had traveled to California to buy large numbers of cattle hides but may not have been prepared to see the mass slaughter that produced them.[9]

When he finished his tour of the northern ranches, Robinson began the return journey to Monterey and, like De Anza, traveled over El Camino Real. North of San Luis Obispo, his party topped off on the formidable

Cuesta Grade that afforded stunning views of the Pacific, the coastal range, and inland valleys dotted with oaks and lush grasslands. Spanish Longhorn cattle grazed there, as they had been doing since Anza's *vaqueros* bolstered the northern missions with their two hundred head of Sonoran cattle in 1776. The Robinson party eventually descended into the Salinas River Valley and on to Monterey. They embarked and sailed south to Santa Barbara, where they offloaded the Bryant and Sturgis goods for display and where Robinson established himself as a *comerciante*, a licensed trader or merchant.[10]

Then, the *Brookline* sailed south and landed first at San Diego, where the venerable Father Antonio Peyri of the Mission San Luis Rey had come to meet them. He boarded their ship as the crew saluted him with thundering guns. Peyri came to shop at the Bryant and Sturgis trading store, and he left, bearing many items for the mission. The *Brookline* disembarked to sail up to San Pedro but without Robinson and the ship's supercargo William Gale. Accompanied by Gale's brother-in-law Don Manuel Domíngues[z], the small group undertook a rapid tour of the southern missions. Beginning at San Luis Rey, their itinerary included stops at Missions San Juan Capistrano, San Gabriel, San Fernando, the *pueblo* of Los Angeles, and through Rancho Domínguez to the port of San Pedro. Intending to survey its ranches, the group headed first for Mission San Luis Rey.

Father Antonio Peyri had founded the largest of the missions in 1798 and remained in charge. Robinson noted that about three thousand Indians were affiliated with the mission, although many returned to their home villages once indoctrinated and baptized in the Catholic faith. Those neophytes who stayed had been trained in various trades. Some of the most trusted men learned the arts of herding and roping cattle on horseback. According to Robinson, the San Luis ranches controlled sixty thousand head of cattle held among the mission's several large ranches. Three leagues to the east, cattle grazed on pastures at a locale called San Juan. In succession northeasterly, the group saw Pala, Temecula, and San Jacinto. Robinson's party also passed through Rancho de Las Flores as they headed northwesterly to San Juan Capistrano on the coast.[11]

After visiting the missionary at San Juan, the Bryant and Sturgis party rode up to see Rancho Santa Ana and its proprietor Don Tomás Yorba. Tomás's father, Don José Antonio Yorba, had founded the *rancho* in 1810 at the end of a long military career. As a Catalonian Volunteer, he served under Gaspar de Portolá in an unsuccessful invasion of Portugal during the Seven Years War and came with him to New Spain to expel the Jesuits from Antigua or Lower California in 1767–1768. He then marched north with Portolá into Alta California and over forty years had attained the rank of Sergeant. Upon his retirement in 1810, *Gobernador* José Joaquin de Arrillaga granted Sergeant Yorba and his wife's nephew, Don Pablo Peralta, 62,000 acres along the southeasterly bank of the Santa Ana River in what is now Orange County. They built adobe homes, planted crops, grape vines, and fruit trees, and Yorba raised four sons, including Tomás and Bernardo. The ranch had many horses and cattle when the elder Yorba died in 1825, followed by Peralta in 1829.[12]

The Bryant and Sturgis visitors dined with Yorba and then took their leave. Don Tomás accompanied the party northward to the Santa Ana River and guided them to a safe place where they forded the river. Crossing there, they thanked Don Tomás for his concern for their safety and marveled at the thousands of heads of cattle and herds of wild horses that roamed and grazed on the grassy plains that eventually led them on to San Gabriel. Robinson described the fourth Alta California mission, founded in 1771, as "flourishing," headed by the "generous . . . and . . . lively" Father José Bernardo Sanchez. He knew that the mission also had a large ranch far to the east, named after Saint Bernardine, but since it lay many leagues away, they did not divert from their itinerary. Not mentioned and possibly unbeknownst to Robinson and Gale, Mission San Gabriel ran multiple cattle ranches east of the mission. Located northeasterly from their fording of the Santa Ana River and near Indian *rancherías* or villages lay Jurupit along the northwest bank of the Santa Ana River, west of present-day downtown Riverside; San Bernardino as previously mentioned, at the base of the Cajon Pass; Yucaipat where Live Oak Canyon meets San Timoteo Canyon in southeastern Redlands; and the large and loosely defined San Gorgonio Rancho, situated in the pass between Mount San Gorgonio and Mount San Jacinto in the present-day Beaumont-Banning area.[13]

Mission San Fernando lies westward of the prosperous Mission San Gabriel. Robinson saw that the mission padre there had hoarded many hides and stone vats of tallow, out of his distrust of traders like Bryant and Sturgis. Consequently, many hides had rotted in the storehouse, no doubt considered a travesty to a businessman like Robinson. Robinson estimated that the amount of tallow at San Fernando would fill the holds of several ships. The group's journey to San Pedro then resumed, first heading through the pass of "Cowwanga" (Cahuenga) to the Pueblo de Los Angeles, where the group rested one more night. The next day, they turned south, rode through the famous "Rancho Domínguez," owned by Don Manuel's family, reached the port of San Pedro and rendezvoused with the *Brookline*.[14]

The Colonization Act of 1824 restricted grants to native-born and naturalized Mexican citizens, including American and other foreign-born immigrants. According to the Supplemental Regulations of 1828, petitions must include the personal history of the petitioner, their citizenship status, a description of the land desired, and a *diseño* or map of it. Grantees further promised to occupy the land along with several hundred head of cattle. The Mexican Congress passed the Secularization Act of 1833 and set the maximum size of a grant at eleven square leagues, or approximately 48,000 acres.

The California provincial assembly reinforced the specific cattle requirement by decree in 1835, in which "150 head of cattle are needed to entitle the owner to a brand." [15]

Mission padres did not see secularization as a boon to the California economy. Rather, they saw it as the destruction, often, of their life's work and as detrimental to the lives of Indians. While some neophytes stayed at their mission, others exited but stayed in nearby pueblos or even came together in sort of ad hoc refugee camps. Still others drifted to *pueblos* like Los Angeles and descended into drunkenness and destitution. Across all of these re-shuffled living arrangements, former mission Indians wanted land and livestock—not as a reward but as just compensation. They especially felt betrayed when they saw former mission cattle and horses migrate over to the administrator's land, or perhaps sold on the hoof, or even slaughtered for the animal's hide and tallow.[16] Then too, mission padres determined that "If the property were to be destroyed, they resolved that the *natives of the country* should reap its benefits as long as it lasted, and from this time the work of destruction went on."[17] Destruction in Robinson's words meant mass *matanzas* of mission cattle herds before the administrators got their hands on them. For these various reasons, *mission* cattle numbers dropped by 90 percent from 1834 to 1842.[18]

California governors issued some seven hundred concessions between 1833 and 1846 when Americans invaded California.[19] The sheer number of grants awarded indicates that a gold rush mentality had taken hold, in which prospective *rancheros* could envision rapidly increasing herds that produced thousands of hides and *botas* of tallow for trade.[20] What had been part of mission subsistence and normal operations soon emerged as the principal economic engine for *ranchos*. Ranch cattle required no feeding and little care beyond branding but *rancheros* had to have reliable labor. They needed southern California Indian *vaqueros*.[21]

For California Indians, secularization meant change and uncertainty. Despite promises of land on which they might gather to sustain the Native community, the government granted almost all the lands to the *gente de razon* (people of reason), citizens of mixed Spanish and Indian blood who called themselves Californios, perhaps to deny the Indian part of their heritage.[22] In their narrowly defined intentions to save the souls of Indians, the missionaries had forcefully repressed Indian culture and religious practices. With crops and domestic animal meat, the padres intended to make Indians dependent on mission provisions, and in doing so, wean them from their traditional economies and maintain control over them. Neophytes had indeed learned to feed and clothe themselves the Spanish way, and in the process, they became indispensable to the stability and sustainability of the entire mission system and the economy of Alta California.[23]

However, in 1826 the first Mexican governor of Alta California decreed that the missions should emancipate those neophytes whom the padres believed were capable of living free of mission restraints and of supporting themselves. Outside of their tribal social norms, strictly enforced by their family and lineage members, the rules and surveillance of the missions provided structure. Without either of these supports, many of the released Indians struggled to become the shining examples of Christian conversion that their padres desired. Some gambled away their personal and real property and had to return to the mission; authorities made others do so by force.[24]

Secularization of the missions opened their vast lands to new arrangements in which profits from large-scale private cattle operations now superseded the religious and social imperatives of the missions. Personal enrichment of the few replaced mission communality, all at the expense of Indian welfare. In 1834, Governor José Figueroa published the *Manifiesto a la República Mejicana*. Through this collection of documents, he sought to establish a distinct Californio social and political identity within the Mexican Republic based on their shared experience of California's mission history. The *Manifiesto* also argued that Indians had rights to some of the mission lands to be allotted to male heads of families and single adult males. Despite this egalitarian gesture, California remained stratified along racial lines. Those Californians who claimed Spanish blood (of any quantum) referred to themselves as the *gente de razón* (people of reason) and more deserving of the land than Indians, whom they referred to as *gente sin razón* (people without reason). Indians undeniably occupied the lowest social status in Spanish and Mexican society. The same Indigenous people who had met and often saved the lives of the Spanish as they staggered half-starved onto their territory in the late eighteenth century, faced a new sort of indenture, the economic shackles of peonage. The California territorial government sought to keep mission Indian labor on mission land and cleared the way for members of the *gente de razón* to administer former mission lands and any Indians living thereon.[25]

In the same year that Figueroa issued his *Manifiesto*, which at least had acknowledged Indian land rights, another son of Don José Antonio Yorba petitioned the city council of Los Angeles for a large grant. Bernardo Yorba wanted a large tract of former Mission San Gabriel land that adjoined his father's Rancho Santiago de Santa Ana.[26] A San Gabriel padre, likely Father Tomás Esténaga, appealed to the council to reserve that land for the mission's Indian *vaqueros* and their families, according to Figueroa's *Manifiesto*.[27] Despite the intent of the *Manifiesto*, the council decided in Yorba's favor. They decided for Yorba over the Indians on racial grounds, couched in their description of him as an "exemplary citizen." Though Indian *vaqueros* had contributed to the Yorba family fortunes for decades, they received little consideration in the form of real property for their hard work and loyalty.[28]

The story of the "friends of the mission" at San Gabriel is an exception to the rule and offers an example of loyalty rewarded in secularized California. In 1834, sixty-three-year-old Juan Mariné petitioned the authorities for that portion of the mission lands known as Rancho San Pasqual, three square leagues in size (over 13,000 acres). Mariné, a Spaniard, had retired from the army with the rank of lieutenant. He married the widow Eulalia Perez, a Native woman who had worked her entire life at San Gabriel as a midwife and nurse. Former mission priest, the warm-hearted Father José Sanchez had suggested this marriage so that Mariné's accession to the land would reward Eulalia for her selfless service. Rancho Santa Anita, among a dozen other small ranches, also went to friends of the mission. "These friends were men who had married Mission women (like Hugo Reid and Michael White) or certain Indians who had worked for the Mission (like Victoria Reid, Prospero and Simeon), to the *mayordomo*, to the *zanjero*, and to others." Father Sanchez's successor Fr. Tomás Esténaga, who had advocated for justice for the San Gabriel Indians in the Bernardo Yorba petition, succeeded in obtaining these dozen grants for those most deserving. Mariné received his (and Eulalia's) grant in 1835 by approval of the mayor and council of Los Angeles, and by the state assembly and governor. Sadly, Mariné and several successors failed to cultivate the rancho and fulfill the requirements and opened the grant to denouncement. Manuel Garfías held the grant at the time that the American Land Commission upheld its validity. President Abraham Lincoln signed his patent (title) in 1863. Ultimately, though, Garfías fell on hard times and sold the ranch to one-time Office of Indian Affairs sub-agent Benjamin Davis Wilson. Beyond Wilson's repute for service in the Office of Indian Affairs, Wilson's grandson, Lieutenant General George S. Patton Jr. achieved the greatest family glory.[29]

Indian *Ranchería(s)*, situated within the sphere of the mission, frequently fell under the control of ambitious Californios, as actual grantees or as appointed *administradores*. Many of these administrators enriched themselves at the expense of the Indians and then petitioned the governor to be granted ownership of those same mission lands.[30] Others simply milked what income could be derived from mission herds (hides and tallow) and Indian produce and left the mission destitute. Future Governor Pío Pico's reign as administrator at San Luis Rey stands out as one of greed and abuse of authority, if not outright brutality. He found excuses to siphon off mission livestock to add to his own herds and when former *alcalde* Pablo Apis led a group of neophytes to petition for his removal, the government officials jailed Apis and his men. At the end of his time there, Pico left San Luis Rey and its neophytes destitute.[31]

California territorial law also subverted emancipation by requiring Indians to provide "indispensable common labor" on undistributed lands for the public good, reminiscent of the Spanish labor usage custom of *repartimiento*.[32]

Moreover, administrators or new *rancho* owners had the power to punish disobedient Indians with forced labor, sometimes in shackles, for minor violations such as leaving the rancho without a pass or for drunkenness. This suggests routine surveillance of *rancho* Indians and that the threat of coercion had a salutary effect on all Indian workers. The repression prompted resistance and violence to the point that Mexicans in some localities required military escorts to move about.[33]

In the unsettled aftermath of secularization, Indians often continued to tend mission herds and crops, and gather and eat traditional foods. A few mission Indians petitioned for their own small plots of land on which to grow their own food and to care only for their families. The governors or regional prefects honored some of these requests that turned mission *ranchos* into Indian *pueblos*, as happened at San Pascual and Rancho Temecula.[34]

In 1835, Mission San Diego established the *pueblo* of San Pascual to resettle eighty-one of their neophytes. They situated the *pueblo* in a mountain valley fed by Santa Ysabel Creek, an area upon which mission cattle had once grazed. To ensure a solid foundation, the new community included skilled tradesmen like herdsmen, muleteers, carpenters, blacksmiths, farmers, leather workers, and weavers. Although not the original leader, by 1837 a shaman named José Panto had taken control and assumed the title of Captain.[35]

The Kumeyaay of San Pascual made the most of their limited arable land. When the rain and snow predicted a good creek flow, they planted and irrigated wheat, corn, and beans. In drier years, they grew small domestic gardens and relied on their herds of cattle and sheep for meat, hides, and wool. By 1845, their community numbered sixty-one Christians and forty-four gentiles.[36]

In 1846, a U.S. Army column led by General Stephen W. Kearny clashed with Californio Lancers led by Andres Pico and encamped at San Pascual. The Californios inflicted serious losses on the Americans and had them surrounded on a hill. Kearny himself had been wounded. Without relief, they faced surrender or annihilation. In that pivotal moment, José Panto came to the aid of the Americans. In an interview published in 1917, Panto's daughter Felicita remembered that he or one of his men led Kit Carson and Lieutenant Edward F. Beale through the Mexican lines under cover of darkness to return with American reinforcements from San Diego.[37]

The story of the Temecula Rancho in what is now southern Riverside County followed a narrative similar to that of San Pascual. The Indians who settled at Rancho Temecula proved Indian capability to form and sustain communities based on a cattle economy. In 1843, the governor granted former Army officer Felix Valdéz the six square league Rancho Temecula—over 26,000 acres and encompassing present-day Temecula and Murrieta. In view of this, in 1843, Father José Zalvidea carved out a small, half-square league parcel of land in the Temecula Valley for the benefit of Luiseño headman Pablo Apis and his family.[38] Apis's erstwhile enemy, Governor Pío Pico, confirmed the grant in 1845. Apis was born in 1792 in the vicinity of Mission San Luis Rey, where he learned to read and write and was baptized at age six. His appointment to the position of *alcalde* indicates that the young man possessed superior intellect and leadership qualities. He demonstrated these traits in his long campaign of civil disobedience to oust Pío Pico from his administrator position at San Luis Rey 1835–1840.[39] At what came to be known as Little Temecula, the former mission *alcalde* organized the planting of corn, wheat, and beans, an orchard and vineyard, and owned three hundred head of cattle and one hundred horses. Within three years, visitors observed that the Indians irrigated their crops from springs, and sold grain, vegetables, and fresh beef to immigrants. Visitors also noted that thirty thatched lodges had been constructed, as well as adobe buildings. The Indian "settlers" built homes for families, their hard work produced food for all, and the residents enjoyed peaceful interactions with their neighbors.[40]

Californios and Mexican governors restricted the grants made to individual Indians to only a few but they could not prevent the creation of tribal herds. Cahuilla Paramount Chief Juan Antonio (*Cusuhatna*) saw a convergence of interests in allying his people with the powerful Lugo family, owners of Rancho San Bernardino, who desperately needed protection from Indian stock raiders. At that time, the Cajon Pass served as a conduit to the Lugo ranch and others, for Utes of the Great Basin and Chemehuevi from the Colorado River, and provided an escape route back to the Colorado River and beyond with their stolen stock.[41]

Don Jose Del Carmen Lugo lived in all three periods of California history—mission, Rancho, and American. Born in 1813 and the son of a Spanish soldier, Don Jose claimed that from the age of sixteen, all he knew was ranching. He had little formal education but had earned respect as a man of his word and a good cattleman. Having been born in Los Angeles, he grew up and came of age in the society and company of *rancheros*, in which his father Don Antonio María Lugo held a prominent place.[42] Don Jose acquired title to the former San Gabriel ranch called San Bernardino in 1841.

The Lugo family members knew that they and a few *vaqueros* alone could not resist the continual loss of their capital to the raiders. After a group of New Mexican immigrants left the Lugos for the promise of their own land elsewhere, the Lugos held a meeting between local *rancheros* and the Mountain Cahuilla. Juan Antonio agreed to the new arrangement, possibly in 1844 and settled with some of his people in Politana, now Colton. For such an offer to be made or accepted, the Cahuilla had to be good horsemen.[43]

The alliance with the Cahuilla remained strong after the war that made California a U.S. territory in 1848. In 1851, however, a band of American outlaws, led by a John "Red" Irving, targeted Lugo's home in San Bernardino to settle a personal dispute. Lugo asked for immediate help from the small U.S. Army detachment on his land but they refused. Lugo then sent for Juan Antonio. He and some one hundred men came together from three villages to hunt down the robbers, who had already sacked Lugo's home for anything of worth. In the chase, the Cahuillas struggled to get within arrow range of the Irvings. They chased the gang to where present-day Live Oak Canyon dead-ends into San Timoteo Canyon. There, trapped in dense chaparral, the Cahuilla warriors killed all of them with arrows and blows to the head, and claimed their victims' weapons, horses, and clothing.[44]

Despite their crime spree on innocent people, killing the outlaw gang aroused the white Americans in the region, including the soldiers who had refused Lugo's plea for help. Indians had killed thirteen white men and that act demanded a response. Lugo defended Juan Antonio in court and a full investigation exonerated the Indians, but the resentments and threats led Lugo and his cowboys to be fully armed at all times, even during roundup. Finally, out of fear for his family's safety, Lugo sold Rancho San Bernardino to a group of Mormons in 1851 and retired to Los Angeles where he lived out his days.[45]

During the seven-year alliance with the Lugos, the Cahuilla gained considerable knowledge and experience in managing a large cattle operation. Because of this alliance with the Lugos, Juan Antonio's family and many other Mountain Cahuilla became cattlemen. The Lugos may have shown their gratitude or made payment for the Cahuilla protection in the form of cattle, either founding or adding to a tribal herd. When the arrangement ended, Juan Antonio withdrew to the village of *Sahatpa* in what is now San Timoteo (*Tukwet*) Canyon, just west of Beaumont. Cattle constantly strayed in search of forage and consumed Indian plant foods. Rancho San Gorgonio cattle likely behaved in the same way and, as in other areas, some went feral. The Cahuillas learned how to run herds on the Lugo Ranch at San Bernardino, on the Yucaipat ranch, and at San Gorgonio.[46] Cattle remained the most liquid form of wealth in Spanish and Mexican California and a reliable food source. Juan Antonio possessed considerable wealth that he controlled for his people that likely included cattle in his villages.[47]

Like the *hacendados* of northern Mexico, the Californio *Dons* kept Indian and *mestizo vaqueros* in debt. The *ranchero* exerted this sort of economic power to ensure that an Indian *vaquero*, especially a highly skilled and reliable one, remained in his employ and in a virtual state of peonage. Keeping and supplying alcoholic beverages on the *rancho* meant that Indian workers stayed at home, instead of riding off to Los Angeles, where drunken brawls landed both good and bad employees in jail.[48] Further, California law prohibited the movement of indebted Indian laborers from one employer to another until they discharged the debt and had obtained a document to prove it. "The *rancheros* ruled as lords on their great landed estates, and the Indian workers who tended the fields and herds were their serfs." [49]

The lack of hard money in the *rancho* economy also meant that the *rancheros* paid their Indian workers with goods from the equivalent of company stores that most of the *rancheros* operated.[50] Indian workers purchased basic supplies, clothing, alcohol, and even the means to celebrate a wedding or a religious holiday, and credited all to their personal and family accounts against future wages. They paid off the debts with their most valuable and tradable asset, their labor.[51]

Tomás Yorba perhaps embodied the ideal Californio *ranchero*, known for his hospitality, gentlemanly comportment, and devotion to his Catholic faith. He also kept strict accounts of transactions at his company store. His account book offers a glimpse into the debt that his employees took on when they needed all manner of goods. Yorba's accounts, if read closely, show the central place of cattle in Alta California life at a granular level, in the matter-of-fact appearance of cattle, cow hides, horses, and other livestock in records concerned with ordinary economic life in the province.

Rancheros commonly paid their workers 8 pesos per month, "sometimes with soap and a bullock added."[52] Jose Antonio Ruiz went to work for Tomás in October 1843 at 3 pesos per month, to pay the debt that his father Martin owed Yorba. The record does not tell the fate of Martin but he had left the scene, likely by death. Young Ruiz further ran up the family debt for basics like *pantalones*, shoes, and cotton cloth. To help amortize the balance owed, his mother, Catarina Lisalde de Ruiz, brought twelve cowhides in to the store in July 1844. At 14 reales each (and 8 reales to a peso), the hides reduced the balance by 21 pesos. The record did not report how Señora Ruiz came by those hides but someone had slaughtered twelve animals, skinned them, and preserved the hides for trade.[53]

Gabriel Garcia also appears on the books and presents intriguing possibilities. His Yorba account reveals that he worked as a *serviente* for Yorba but without details about his duties. His pay did include "one young beef" per month, as well as soap and 8 pesos of money. By taking the young beef per month, he had the option of consuming it, adding it to a small herd if he had grazing rights on Yorba land or elsewhere, or trading it for other purposes. Some of his purchases invite speculation as to his activities outside the ranch. He bought one whole barrel of *aguardiente* (brandy) plus 40 pints and 1 liter of the drink, possibly for resale. His record includes a notation "Owes for two horses of the store and two mares which I loan to the *Indian*," perhaps identifying Garcia as a full-blood Indian *vaquero* or as a *mestizo*.[54]

Gabriel Garcia also rode south with General Andrés Pico to confront the invading American force under Stephen Kearney at San Pascual in 1846.

Accounts of the battle reveal that Garcia and other lancers attacked American artillerymen who manned a howitzer. They lanced three Americans; the soldier whom Garcia lanced died of his wound. Garcia was forty-three at that time and had to have been an excellent horseman to do so. Whether Garcia worked mostly as a ranch hand for Yorba, or made his way with entrepreneurial ventures, or both, his being paid in livestock underlines the centrality of the cattle economy to life in California then—a significance that lasted for generations.[55]

Although the former mission lands had almost completely shifted from Spanish imperial strategies to private Mexican ambitions, the Spanish cultural impact of some eighty years persisted in southern California life, and the mission as an organizing principle continued to shape Indian work and life. Keeping in mind the harsh punishments inflicted upon Indians by the padres and their surrogates, the devastating losses to disease, and the separation of children from their parents, the communality of the Catholic missions more closely aligned with Indian values than did the individuality of American liberalism. Even life on the secular rancho resembled mission life more than its American free enterprise counterpart. The big house took the place of the mission church as the central gathering point and the Don replaced the padre as the central male authority. The vast southern California grasslands still supported great herds of cattle, horses, and other livestock, and California Indian *vaqueros* still formed the backbone of the ranching workforce.[56]

In 1821, the Spanish subjects of New Spain achieved independence from the mother country and founded the Republic of Mexico. The small landed class and those who wanted to join them were determined to develop the province of California by secularization and agitated for the release of mission land holdings to private ownership. The new grant holders rapidly filled up the rangelands with their cattle and horses, and expected to trade the hides and tallow from their cattle for the manufactured goods carried by foreign merchants. The new prosperity established an oligarchy of *rancheros* that called themselves Californios and *gente de razon*.

California Native peoples rarely benefited in the new system in which their roles had not changed, only their new masters. For Indian *vaqueros,* the work on *ranchos* differed little from mission cattle work. In both places, they had little or no autonomy, and yet their skills with the lasso and in the saddle remained absolutely critical to the California cattle economy. Indian people had no political power that the Euro-American recognized, and secularization took a heavy economic and social toll on them. Although a few Indians actually received small grants, they were the exception and not the rule. Loosed from the moorings of the predictable and somewhat secure life of the mission by emancipation, many of the neophytes struggled to survive outside the *rancho* life. Many stayed in their *ranchería(s)*, situated on the same lands claimed by missionaries, now under new ownership. Where soldiers had enforced control by the mission padres, debt kept many Indians in peonage to the Don. As long as demand for hides and tallow stayed strong, those who worked on the ranches had a place in which to live, though, according to the dominant society, they could not claim it as their own.

By the 1840s, though, economic and political factors threatened the trade. An oversupply of hides caused prices to drop to the point where merchants broke even or took losses. As tensions rose between Mexico and the United States, merchants also feared the plundering of their ships by privateers flying Mexican colors. The United States declared a war of territorial conquest against Mexico in 1846, and in 1848, gained great territories called the Mexican Cession that became the American Southwest, including California. What had been a trickle of American immigrants to the province became a steady stream. American sovereignty destabilized California *ranchero* society and soon brought a flood of land-hungry immigrants that threatened Indian life ways and homelands.

NOTES

1. Adele Ogden, "Hides and Tallow: McCulloch, Hartnell and Company 1822–1828," *California Historical Society Quarterly* 6, no. 3 (September 1927): 255–256. For Spanish or Mexican peso-American dollar conversions see William J. Barger, "Merchants of Los Angeles: Economics and Commerce in Mexican California," *Southern California Quarterly* 82, no. 2 (Summer 2000): 135–136. Both the peso and the dollar contained 1 ounce of silver and merchants accepted either for payment, so that McCulloch, Hartnell and Company paid a dollar per hide.
2. Ogden, "Hides and Tallow," 259.
3. Ibid., 259–264.
4. Ibid., 256–257.
5. Adele Ogden, "Boston Hide Droghers Along California Shores," *California Historical Quarterly* 8, no. 4 (December 1929): 289–290.
6. Ogden, "Boston Hide Droghers," 289–298.
7. Ibid., 294–296.
8. Robinson, *Life in California*, v–vi.
9. Robinson, *Life in California*, 84–86.
10. Ibid., 86–87.
11. Ibid., 24–25; Phil Brigandi, "The Outposts of Mission San Luis Rey," *San Diego Historical Society Quarterly* 45, no. 2 (Spring 1999): 106–112.
12. Terry E. Stephenson, "Tomás Yorba, His Wife Vicenta, and His Account Book," *Historical Society of Southern California Quarterly* 23, no. 3/4 (September–December 1941): 127–131; Nuttall, "Gaspar de Portolá," 185–186. Cleland, *The Cattle on a Thousand Hills*, 19. Cleland's foundational work addresses the transitions of Mexican-granted land to American-patented titles, or the denial thereof and for a map showing

the various Yorba family *ranchos,* see Lisbeth Haas, *Conquests and Historical Identities in California, 1769–1936* (Berkeley, CA: University of California Press, 1995), 7.

13. Robinson, *Life in California,* 29–34. John W. Robinson and Doody and Meltzer's works flesh out the inland landscapes of colonial and Mexican Southern California in John W. Robinson, *The San Bernardinos: The Mountain Country from Cajon Pass to Oak Glen, Two Centuries of Changing Use* (Arcadia, CA: Big Santa Anita Historical Society, 1989), 9; and Louis Doody and Betty Kikumi Meltzer, *Losing Ground: The Displacement of San Gorgonio Pass Cahuilla People in the 19th. Century* (Banning, CA: Malki-Ballena Press, 2007), 16–19. See also Cleland, *The Cattle on a Thousand Hills,* 21–22.

14. Robinson, *Life in California,* 29–36. See also Cleland, *The Cattle on a Thousand Hills,* 10–12. The ranch land that Robinson called "Rancho Domínguez" originally bore the name Rancho San Pedro, one of the three original Land Concessions of 1784, granted by then-Governor Pedro Fages. In litigation that finally was resolved in 1834, Governor Figueroa detached and awarded the Palos Verdes Peninsula to the Sepulveda family, leaving a still-massive Rancho Domínguez (San Pedro) of 38,000 acres.

15. Bancroft, *California Pastoral,* 343; Hornbeck, "Land Tenure and Rancho Expansion in Alta California," 378; Cleland, *The Cattle on a Thousand Hills,* 23.

16. Jackson and Castillo, *Indians, Franciscans, and Spanish Colonization,* 87–101.

17. Robinson, *Life in California,* 160.

18. Bancroft, *California Pastoral,* 339. Italics mine. Just how many cattle moved to private *ranchos* remains unknown. From about 400,000 head in 1834, missions held only about 30,000 head in total, in 1842.

19. Cleland, *The Cattle on a Thousand Hills,* 22–23.

20. Hornbeck, "Land Tenure and Rancho Expansion in Alta California," 383.

21. Ibid., 385.

22. Haas, *Conquests and Historical Identities in California,* 37.

23. George Harwood Phillips, *Chiefs and Challengers: Indian Resistance and Cooperation in Southern California, 1769–1906,* 2nd ed. (Norman, OK: University of Oklahoma Press, 2014), 51.

24. Ibid., 50–53.

25. Haas, *Conquests and Historical Identities in California,* 29–38.

26. Phillips, *Vineyards and Vaqueros,* 92–93.

27. W. W. Robinson, "The Story of Rancho San Pasqual," *Historical Society of Southern California Quarterly* 37, no. 4 (December 1955): 348–349. The good Padre Esténaga played some undocumented role in the transference of some Mission San Gabriel land to "friends of the mission." Some of these friends were men who had married Mission women and others, Indians who had worked for years at the mission as *mayordomos.*

28. Haas, *Conquests and Historical Identities in California,* 36, 48–49.

29. Robinson, "The Story of Rancho San Pasqual," 347–353.

30. Florence Connolly Shipek, *Pushed Into the Rocks: Southern California Indian Land Tenure, 1769–1986* (Lincoln, NE: University of Nebraska Press, 1987), 25–28.

See also Douglas Monroy, *Thrown Among Strangers: The Making of Mexican Culture in Frontier California* (Berkeley, CA: University of California Press, 1990). Monroy describes the combination of administrator corruption and the easy cheating of the few Indians who received grants of former mission lands, owing to their lack of understanding of the Euro-American concept of real property.

31. Monroy, *Thrown Among Strangers*, 125–127; see also Phil Brigandi, *Temecula: At the Crossroads of History* (Encinitas, CA: Heritage Media, 1998), 20–22.

32. Haas, *Conquests and Historical Identities in California*, 35–36; James J. Rawls, *Indians of California: The Changing Image* (Norman, OK: University of Oklahoma Press, 1984), 3–4. In the Spanish system of *repartimiento*, landowners or *mayordomos* petitioned for Indian labor. When granted, villages sent a certain rotating quota of their male population to work for a fixed period. Even before the Viceroy of New Spain repealed this practice in 1633, the *hacienda* and debt peonage had begun to replace *repartimiento* and persisted through the *rancho* period.

33. Shipek, *Pushed Into the Rocks*, 26.

34. Phillips, *Vineyards and Vaqueros*, 40–43, 60–62.

35. Richard Carrico, *Strangers in a Stolen Land: Indians of San Diego County from Prehistory to the New Deal*, 2nd ed. (San Diego, CA: Sunbelt Publications, 2008), 118–120; Glenn J. Farris, "Jose Panto, 'Capitan' of the Indian Pueblo of San Pascual, San Diego County," *Journal of California and Great Basin Anthropology* 16, no. 2 (1994): 149–161.

36. Farris, "Jose Panto," 153.

37. Farris, "Jose Panto," 154; Elizabeth Judson Roberts, *Indian Stories of the Southwest* (San Francisco, CA: Harr Wagner Publishing, 1917), 221–228; Carrico, *Strangers in a Stolen Land*, 44.

38. Phillips, *Chiefs and Challengers*, 62. Half of a (square) league is about 2,200 acres.

39. Leland Bibb, "Pablo Apis and Temecula," *Journal of San Diego History* 37, no. 4 (Fall 1991): 256–271; Brigandi, *Temecula*, 30–33.

40. Brigandi, *Temecula*, 30–33; Phillips, *Chiefs and Challengers*, 180–181.

41. Hanks, *This War is for a Whole Life*, 20–22.

42. Lugo, "Life of a Rancher," 187–188.

43. Phillips, *Chiefs and Challengers*, 74.

44. Richard A. Hanks, "Vicissitudes of Justice: Massacre at San Timoteo Canyon," *Southern California Quarterly* 82, no. 3 (Fall 2000): 233–253. Juan Antonio did not petition for a land grant, but he advanced his people's fortunes by establishing a tribal herd and by running and protecting the Lugo-owned Rancho San Bernardino 1844–1851; Lugo, "Life of a Rancher," 213–214; Phillips, *Chiefs and Challengers*, 93–96.

45. Lugo, "Life of a Rancher," 214–215; Hanks, *This War is for a Whole Life*, 22–24.

46. Phillips, *Chiefs and Challengers*, 96; Doody and Kikumi Meltzer, *Losing Ground*, 30–31.

47. Doody and Kikumi Meltzer, *Losing Ground*, 175.

48. Phillips, *Vineyards and Vaqueros*, 231; Dary, *Cowboy Culture*, 29, 56; see also Davis, *Seventy-Five Years in California*, 91–92. According to Davis, the wine

"was made from the old mission grapes," and could have been *aguardiente*, a heavy brandy-like wine that appeared colorless when first produced, but that took on an amber hue with age.

49. Rawls, *Indians of California*, 21; Bancroft, *California Pastoral*, 438
50. Phillips, *Vineyards and Vaqueros*, 230–232.
51. Cleland, *The Cattle on a Thousand Hills*, 30.
52. Stephenson, "Tomás Yorba," 138.
53. Ibid., 138. If young José Antonio made no more purchases, he could retire the debt within three months.
54. Ibid., 140. Italics mine. Since Garcia was listed in the 1836 census as born in Los Angeles, mixed blood seems more likely and Yorba's reference to him as the "Indian" could be based on appearance.
55. Stephenson, "Tomás Yorba," 127–156.
56. Cleland, *The Cattle on a Thousand Hills*, 33. In 1845–1846, Alta California exported 80,000 hides and 1.5 million pounds of tallow, 1 million board feet of lumber, and a 1,000 barrels of wine and brandy.

Chapter 5

The Early American Period, 1848–1890

American rule in Alta California officially began with the ratification of the Treaty of Guadalupe Hidalgo in 1848, between the United States of America and the Republic of Mexico. American rule brought new political and land tenure systems, the entry of a new majority ethnicity and culture, and the transformation of the California cattle industry. Predictably, turmoil and conflict accompanied such rapid and fundamental change though cattle remained central to the California economy. Californios continued to run large herds on land grant ranges, and California Indian and Mexican cowboys continued to rope, brand, and slaughter cows and steers for their beef, hides, and tallow. Native groups also kept their own modest herds—some on their few land grants, like those led by Pablo Apis and Jose Panto. Others, like Juan Antonio's Cahuillas, built tribal herds. After partnering with the Lugo family at Rancho San Bernardino, the Cahuilla brought their own cattle with them to the San Gorgonio Pass area.

The invasion of California by the U.S. military and the steady flow of immigrants that followed did not diminish the importance of cattle. Instead, the gold strike in the north generated an unprecedented demand for beef to feed the flood of humanity. These events initiated the eventual displacement of Spanish culture, the state religion of Catholicism, and the Mexican *rancho* way of life. From 1846, just before the U.S. Congress declared war, through the cataclysmic Gold Rush that began in 1849, to the Land Act of 1851, California's political, economic, and cultural status changed from a Mexican *rancho* feudal society to American capitalism and statehood.

Over the next forty years, Americans and other immigrants gained control of most of the Mexican land grant *ranchos* in southern California, although Californians of all ethnic origins continued to run cattle and horses on many smaller ranches, scattered across the state.[1] Cattle ranching remained important in a diversifying economy and ranchers continued to value the work of Native American and Mexican cowboys though they occupied the lowest rung on the social ladder. Instead of emancipating California Indians from peonage to *rancheros,* Americans institutionalized it through indenture in the *Act for the Government and Protection of Indians of 1850.* Despite the law's benevolent title, this third wave of Euro-American rule posed the greatest threat to Native Californians and forced them to navigate treacherous new currents and find ways to adapt and survive.

Rationalizing that traditional California Indian lands and water sources belonged in the public domain, American settlers claimed them for their own homesteads. They fenced off Native access to traditional sources of foods, medicines, tools, weapons, and water. Smallpox, measles, influenza, venereal diseases, and other epidemics took a terrible toll on families and tribal units. Executive Order reservations in the 1860s and 1870s offered the promise of recognized Indian land ownership but without enforceable titles. Agents of the Office of Indian Affairs witnessed and reported these violations of sovereignty but had little authority to stop the bleeding. By the 1880s, under these unrelenting pressures, Indian societies had reached a breaking point. In the face of these threats, they pressed their cases for sovereignty over some portion of their ancient domains. Indians held on and continued hiring out as cowboys as well as running their own cattle wherever possible. They learned to use the tools available to them. They petitioned local courts for recognition of their chosen leadership and appealed to federal officers to protect their lands. They made shows of force, and used non-violent assemblies. Finally, in 1891, after years of bitter disappointments and numerous studies and reports, the U.S. Congress passed *An Act for the Relief of the Mission Indians in the State of California* (1891). Southern California Indians at last had a legal relationship with the federal government. They used the law as a base on which to regenerate their communities and to fight for recognition of their sovereign status and an evolving identity still rooted in the land.

The successful hide and tallow trade that had dominated Alta California's economic life roughly from 1824 to 1849 incentivized local cattle ranchers to grow their herds. More steers and cows meant more trade goods from Yankee merchants. The continuing economic and social importance of the cattle trade also amplified the importance of Native American cowboys and ranch workers, who also represented the territory's majority ethnicity in 1848. California's example of successful cattle markets further encouraged ranchers in other territories to drive beef cattle herds west from the United States, other American territories, and Sonora. Immigrants also rode hundreds and thousands of wagons into California, pulled by teams of oxen. These trends of building and transforming California herds with new breeding stock accelerated during the Gold Rush and in early statehood. Despite the twin shocks of flood and drought, immigrants continued to pour into the state, driven by gold and land fever. For California's Native peoples, however, the sweeping changes that came with American rule threatened their very survival.

The arrival of Spanish cattle and horses in Alta California in 1769 had doomed traditional Native economies but also provided a lifeline of survival. Mexican *ranchos*, if anything, reinforced and deepened the connections between California Indians and horses and cattle. As long as the hide, tallow, and possibly horns predominated as the main tradable assets of a steer or cow, California ranchers prioritized reproduction and paid little attention to breeding for more tender and juicy meat. Males remained uncastrated and the herds roamed with greater freedom than they did on the mission ranges. Mission *mayordomos* had kept them on ranches far from crops and took care not to over-graze the range. They had also rotated herds to allow forage to recover. But then the surge of land grant ranches rapidly filled the spaces that the padres left open in the mission landscape. The Spanish Longhorn cattle, however, remained a constant across the mission and Rancho periods. In the 1840s, ranchers and visitors to Alta California described the Longhorns with much the same language used by earlier explorers, missionaries, and visitors throughout New Spain: semi-wild, tough and stringy flesh, hardy, fleet-footed, and able to fend for themselves against other wild animals. "The cows are small, do not fatten readily, and produce little milk." Pre-Gold Rush Californio Dons, including naturalized American immigrants, thus prioritized quantities of animals for their tradeable hides and tallow over the quality of the beef. The demand for Indian cowboys and ranch workers thus remained high.[2] Before flood, drought, and the American system overwhelmed their lands and culture, the *rancheros* enjoyed one last golden moment—the unexpected windfall of demand for beef created by the Gold Rush of 1849.[3]

At the signing of the Treaty of Guadalupe Hidalgo in February 1848, the non-Indian population of the entire territory of California hovered at about fifteen thousand. Of this total, Hispanic Californians numbered seven thousand, U.S. citizens six thousand, and the remainder a mix of various other immigrants. In his 1853 report to the Secretary of the Interior, the Commissioner of Indian Affairs, George W. Manypenny, reported the California Indigenous population at that moment was approximately one hundred thousand.[4] A special state census taken in 1852 revealed more than 255,000 non-Indian people in the new state, the product of gold fever. Most newcomers coalesced around the gold fields and cities like San Francisco, which grew rapidly as a portal for imported food to feed the throngs of gold-seekers and assorted opportunists. New settlements closer to the action also sprang up to do the same. Merchants made fortunes selling supplies, tools, and clothing to the miners. Other newcomers saw the fortunes to be made by producing food locally, and extensively grew wheat and barley.[5] Southern California's *ranchero* class made fortunes by driving their cattle to the north, primarily for beef.[6]

Even before the Gold Rush, Californians had been moving their cattle to help establish the viability of settlements outside California, even in non-Spanish territories. For their own early outposts in the Pacific Northwest, the Spanish loaded California cattle onboard ships bound for the Olympic Peninsula and Vancouver Island in 1792. The British Hudson's Bay Company also purchased the beginnings of their own herd for Fort Vancouver, on the Columbia River in the vicinity of present-day Vancouver, Washington. This herd grew from seventeen head in 1824 to 450 in 1836. In 1837, former fur trapper Ewing Young collected 800 Longhorns from herds in the area between Monterrey and San Jose. He and his cowboys drove them north into Oregon's Willamette Valley, where a group of American settlers awaited. And, in 1848, Mormons acquired a herd of California cattle for their new settlement near the Great Salt Lake.[7]

Before the Gold Rush of 1848, cattle in southern California sold for $4 a head and hides brought about $2 . Gold prospectors willingly paid ten to twenty times that price and higher. In San Francisco, the price hit $75 a head. Practically overnight, new economic flows saw herds of a thousand animals or more heading north and gold returning southward to the ranchers. Their cowhands—mostly Native and Mexican—performed the hard labor of driving herds over four hundred miles. They ran the risks of ambush by rustlers and marauding Indians, and natural hazards like swimming cattle across rain-swollen rivers. Cattle thieves also caught on quickly to the bonanza and often attacked northbound herds even before they left southern California.[8]

Drive bosses had two routes north from which to choose: inland, up through the San Joaquin Valley, and the coastal route, essentially following El Camino Real, first used to drive cattle by Juan Bautista de Anza in the 1770s. In 1847, a year before gold was discovered and five years before he accepted the appointment as sub-agent for Indian Affairs in southern California, Benjamin Davis Wilson drove approximately two thousand head of cattle up to Sacramento over the interior route.[9] He started his herd northward from Los Angeles on an ancient trail that passed between the Santa Susana Mountains to the west and the San Gabriel Mountains to the east. The trail led through the mountains and reached an elevation of over four thousand feet. During Spanish, Mexican, and early American rule, travelers called it El Camino Viejo (The Old Road). Wilson and his cowboys pushed the cattle through that pass and a canyon choked with wild grapevines. Present-day Interstate 5 approximately traverses Wilson's route out of the Los Angeles Basin.[10]

Down on the floor of the lower San Joaquin Valley, the route necessarily veered northwesterly around the Tulare Lake and Basin. Many small rivers and streams channeled Sierra Nevada snowmelt into a marshy basin that had once supported about 18,000 Yokut people at the outset of Spanish colonization.[11] As they trailed northward, the drovers kept to the western bank of the San Joaquin to avoid crossing the multiplicity of that river's tributaries on the eastern side. Having avoided many small crossings, the cowboys faced their last and biggest obstacle, crossing the San Joaquin closer to its mouth. Even in early summer, herds often backed up waiting for the water level to drop.[12]

In May 1852, San Diego County rancher and former Army officer Cave Johnson Couts brought a mixed herd (in ages and brands) of about a thousand head north by the coastal route. The coastal route followed El Camino Real and included heading inland northeast of San Luis Obispo and crossing the Cuesta Grade. The route then switched back northwesterly down the Salinas River valley to Monterey and on to San Francisco, Stockton, or Sacramento. Upon arriving at the mouth of the San Joaquin River, Couts found that his cattle joined some 12,000–15,000 head already waiting to cross. He and his crew finally swam their animals across the San Joaquin River some twenty-five miles upstream, near Stockton. The entire journey from southern California took less than two months but waiting to cross the San Joaquin and finalizing the sale of the herd consumed another month. During that month, Couts had the problem of finding forage and water for his living inventory. On August 14, Couts sold all 943 head about 30 miles southeast of Stockton in the vicinity of the Stanislaus River. At $20 a head, he and his partners grossed $18,860.[13] A scion of a slave-holding family in Tennessee, "Couts had no qualms about using brute force to impose his will on those who labored for him."[14] Furthermore, many in San Diego believed that Couts bore responsibility for the deaths of two Indians by mortally brutal punishments.[15] But he also rated California Indians as skilled cowboys. Therefore, the likelihood exists that Indian cowboys from San Diego County helped drive Couts' cattle up to Stockton in 1852.[16] By extension, Indian cowboys from all points in southern California took part in drives to the Gold Rush camps.

With Gold Rush demand persisting and even increasing, Midwestern and Texan ranchers saw their main chance and headed cattle for California. Even large herds of sheep came from New Mexico.[17] Immigrant farmers, cattle speculators, and their hired hands pushed at least a half-million head of cattle into California in the decades before and after California entered the Union in 1850. The most consequential livestock migration, though, began in 1849 when herds of beef cattle came from Texas, Missouri, or Illinois to satisfy the rapidly increasing demand for beef by the gold seekers. Based only on census data and points of entry records, a half-million head of migrant cattle entered California from 1840 to 1860.[18] Herders that evaded detection for a variety of reasons drove in substantial but uncounted numbers of animals. Despite the large number of cattle consumed, cattlemen also managed to upgrade the local herds with breeding stock like Black Angus or Herefords. Like the Spanish Longhorns, these imports produced hides and tallow but the quality and quantity of meat per animal far surpassed their Spanish predecessors.[19]

Notably, American Indian cowboys from other regions helped drive those better breeds of cattle to California. Delaware Indians helped drive a herd from Oregon to northern California in 1844, led by John C. Fremont. Cherokee cowboys drove a herd from the Canadian River in Texas to California. Yaqui and O'odham Indians helped drive Sonoran cattle through the Yuma crossing and into California. During the 1850s, the Quechans still reigned over the vital Colorado River crossing, although the U.S. Army understood the strategic significance of the site and built Fort Yuma on the hill overlooking the Colorado River in the early 1850s.[20] The names of these Native American wranglers and cowboys may only live on in the oral traditions of their tribes. Nonetheless, their participation in these movements in the supply chain of American rule demonstrated agile adaptations to a rapidly changing world. In an adaptation considered criminal by Euro-Americans, Great Basin Indians continually raided into California for horses, beef, and other plunder. Their adaptation operated on the demand side of the market.[21]

Simultaneous with the political, economic, social, and cultural turmoil that came with American rule, the U.S. government struggled to understand the exact nature of the new territory, its vast resources, and its Native inhabitants. For the Indigenous peoples of California, the land had always been and remained their mother—an unbreakable physical and spiritual connection. In the *Annual Report of the Commissioner of Indian Affairs for 1848*, Commissioner William Medill acknowledged that the Indian Office had scant knowledge of the Native peoples in the territories ceded by Mexico. Medill proposed shifting administrative districts from elsewhere in the country to superintend the new departments of Oregon, New Mexico, and California. The as-yet unnamed California appointee had much research ahead of him before making policy recommendations regarding California Indians.[22] In 1849, the Department of the Interior assumed control of the Office of Indian Affairs from the War Department. In 1850, California sub-agent Adam Johnston described the mounting tragedies perpetrated against California Indian people and their resources. Attacks by gold-seeking whites had scattered, decimated, or starved out many of the northern tribes. Johnston undoubtedly had his hands full in the north and did not mention conditions in southern California.[23]

Then, in 1851, three federal Indian commissioners embarked on a statewide effort to negotiate peace with California Indians and a peaceful transition to American rule. In a matter of months, the American Commissioners signed eighteen treaties with approximately twenty-five thousand Natives to create eighteen large reservations for all the Indigenous people of California. The three men, Oliver M. Wozencraft, George W. Barbour, and Redick McKee, divided California into three jurisdictions. Barbour assumed responsibility for the southern third of the state but spent much of his time treating with Indians in the Tulare and southern San Joaquin Valleys. After concluding a treaty with the southernmost of these tribes at the Tahone [Tejon] Pass, he set out for Los Angeles. He intended to continue his work with all the Native groups living southward to the border with Mexico and eastward to the Colorado River but their money had run out. Barbour witnessed the suffering caused by waves of gold-seekers, land-hungry settlers, diseases, and physical violence. He conveyed his shame and sadness in his report. "I feel less fear of danger in travelling the country from Indians than from white men."[24]

All three commissioners held the firm belief that no treaty had the power to maintain peace with starving people. California's plentiful cattle offered one source of food, and a mobile one at that. Depending on supply, demand, and the size of the animal (600–800 pounds), cattle prices ran from $48 to $120 a head in the northern part of the state and from $18 to $40 a head in southern California.[25] Commissioner Wozencraft reported that most of the lands proposed for Indian resettlement would not produce enough crops alone to support them but that the native vegetation would sustain beef cattle and horses. Successful fulfillment of the treaties utterly depended on it: "They must have food."[26]

The Commissioners held the two final treaty councils in southern California, at Temecula in present-day Riverside County and at Santa Ysabel in present-day San Diego County. On January 5, 1852, Luiseño leader Pablo Apis hosted the ceremonial signing of the Treaty of Temecula at his rancho known as Little Temecula. Wozencraft had negotiated the treaty. Chiefs and captains of the Cahuilla, Luiseño, and Serrano peoples attended.[27] Sadly, sometime after the treaty signing in 1852, possibly late 1853, Pablo Apis died. The lack of any public notice precluded formal tributes from the whites who felt the loss of a good friend and a mediator for peace among the races.[28]

San Pascual Kumeyaay headman Jose Panto attended the Treaty of Santa Ysabel ceremony on January 6, 1852, expecting a fair compromise with the people who now occupied Kumeyaay land. In addition to the questionable authority of McKee, Wozencraft, and Barbour to negotiate binding treaties with the Native American peoples of California, the Commissioners usually met with leaders representing only a minority of all Indians of the region. Additionally, not all of the Native leaders had the full backing of their people, further diminishing the legitimacy of the proceedings from the standpoint of Indians. Even if all *ranchería(s)* or villages in San Diego and Riverside counties had democratically vested their representatives with treaty-making authority, the majority of American Californians vehemently opposed any such agreement that removed prime farming, ranching, and gold-mining lands from their full exploitation by white Americans. Prior to the ratification of the Seventeenth Amendment to the U.S. Constitution in 1913, state legislatures chose their United States Senators. The California legislature in 1852 overwhelmingly voted to direct their Senators to quash the proposed treaties, leaving the Indigenous people of California with no legal relationship with the United States, and no legal framework within which to fight for their basic human rights. Instead, "they were simply to be 'invited to assemble' on government lands." Settlers encroached upon tribal lands at will and local government officials often imposed taxes on people whose rights they otherwise did not recognize. Despite the Senate's refusal to ratify the treaties, Jose Panto tirelessly petitioned American government officials to formally affirm their land rights, as the Mexican government had done in 1835.[29]

In place of treaties, the federal government appointed agents tasked with maintaining the peace and facilitating Indian self-sufficiency without the level of funding that might make their efforts effective. In October 1852, Superintendent Edward Fitzgerald Beale offered Benjamin Davis Wilson an appointment as sub-agent for southern California Indians. The native Tennessean had migrated to the mountains of New Mexico in 1833 to trap and trade furs in Santa Fe. His familiarity with the Spanish language and customs aided his integration into Californio society to which he immigrated in 1841. The former mountain man married Bernardo Yorba's daughter, Ramona, and became a *ranchero* by purchasing a ranch near present-day Riverside from Juan Bandini. In California *ranchero* society, cattle provided tangible proof of wealth and an entrée to a higher class. Henceforth, Californios referred to B.D. Wilson as Don Benito.[30]

Sub-agent Wilson made an inspection tour of the numerous Native villages and reported his observations and recommendations in *The Indians of Southern California in 1852*. Wilson expressed compassion for the Indians, whom the state and federal governments had neglected during the Gold Rush. In his view, their perceived docility required paternalistic guidance so that they could achieve some level of self-sustenance and a slow but steady advancement toward civilization. In light of the violence that fortune hunters inflicted on them, Wilson made a case for deploying financial resources to help Native peoples support themselves by raising crops and herding cattle and sheep. Indeed, he saw that some southern California Indians had already incorporated small stocks of horses and cattle into their survival strategies. He asserted that this way offered a peaceful and more financially efficient alternative to extermination. However, Wilson misplaced his compassion by recommending a secular version of the missions that he believed had come so close to a "glorious accomplishment" and that Indians supposedly recalled with nostalgia.[31] As they had done during the mission and *rancho* periods, Indians continued to provide the indispensable source of labor for the creation of wealth in the early American period. Unlike those earlier periods, in which familial units of Indian labor attached to a specific place, the fluidity of job opportunities increased the importance of mobility for Indian wage workers, both male and female. Indian mothers and daughters also took work as domestic servants in white households, which separated them from their families. Their absences also removed them from the reproductive pool or at least made it more difficult for them to have children. The new regime, however, did not expand Indian access to wealth derived from the land; Euro-American control of land tenure foreclosed real Indian benefit from the new and diversifying economy.[32]

As the boom in cattle prices continued, *rancheros* depleted their breeding stock and spent their riches on extravagant clothing, decorated saddles, and home furnishings. Many put up their *ranchos* as collateral for borrowed money. They had not foreseen an end to the boom and the concurrent bust of their fortunes but just as surely as prices had spiked, they plummeted. By 1855, demand for beef had been met and because ranchers in Texas, Sonora, and elsewhere continued to drive in cattle, prices dropped to $10–$15 a head by the end of the decade.[33]

The depressed market forced some of the largest southern California ranchers, like Abel Stearns, to cut their losses. Stearns slaughtered fifteen thousand head and sold them for whatever price he could get, like in the old days of hides and tallow. Many *rancheros* lived too well on their windfalls of gold and incurred debts with rapacious interest rates of from 3 percent to 8 percent per month. Once-prominent *rancho* families became as landless as their Indian *vaqueros*. The scarcity of capital in an isolated region, the non-existence of a banking system, and shady dealings by opportunists contributed to the market bust and the loss of Californio family estates. Still, on the *ranchos*, Indian *vaqueros*, who likely shared little in the soaring profits, entered a new time of uncertainty. At least in their poverty, they had very little to lose.[34]

Not all Californio *rancheros* lost their ranches and fortunes to conspicuous consumption and reckless borrowing from unscrupulous lenders. Don José Lugo did not succumb to either of these vices, yet he did not escape the rampant financial ruin of his class. He had sold Rancho San Bernardino in 1851, not under financial duress but to escape the ethnic hatred of white Americans, after his Cahuilla friends dispatched the Irving gang. The Red Irving gang were a pack of predators who tried to extort money from Lugo, and having failed, sacked his home in San Bernardino. Lugo called for help from his friend Juan Antonio. The Cahuilla Paramount Chief and his men hunted down and killed the Irvings, which sparked a racial backlash from white Americans. Having sold his ranch to avoid the backlash, Lugo should have been free and clear, but for unnamed friends or family members who had asked him to co-sign their loans. As a good family man, he did co-sign, to his own ultimate ruin. He sacrificed his entire fortune and even his home, to pay the debts of others, as promised. As a good cattleman and a man of his word, Don José Del Carmen Lugo could do no less.[35]

These underlying scandals of racial hate and violence landed upon all nonwhites, from the Indigenous to former Mexican citizens to African-descent Americans and Chinese immigrants.[36] And in the 1850s, even California's geographical distance from the rest of the states did not shield it from the impending crisis of the Union. Despite the sectional rancor over slavery in the East, members of the U.S. Congress, North and South, found consensus in continued funding for large surveying and road improvement expeditions out west. These projects forged foundational transportation corridors into California that helped immigrants and livestock flow into the state. For the Native peoples of California, however, these developments put even more pressure on already threatened sources of traditional foods, forage, and arable land and water. In a cruel twist of irony, the so-called new roads often followed ancient trading networks used by Native peoples to exchange goods, build alliances, and fulfill cultural and spiritual requirements.[37]

Edward F. Beale led two road surveys in the late 1850s. The former naval officer, veteran of the Battle of San Pascual, and the founder of California's first reservations, laid out the route along the Thirty-Fifth Parallel. His first journey connected Santa Fe, New Mexico to the Colorado River (well north of the Yuma Crossing), and then crossed the Mojave Desert to present-day Barstow and San Bernardino. His large parties included American Indian guides and hunters, as well as topographical engineers and construction crews. From 1857 to 1859, Beale surveyed and partially built the road along the Thirty-Fifth Parallel. He lobbied for it as the best wagon road from Fort Smith, Arkansas to the Pacific, and soon, the best railroad route. Surveys led to wagon roads that became railroads (in this case the Santa Fe Railroad), and then, interstate highways. In the twentieth century, Beale's route became the legendary Route 66.[38]

Bigger and stronger oxen also made a significant contribution to the upgrading of California livestock, including for the Indians. Immigrants in wagon trains drove teams of trained oxen, their primary mode of transportation. Some of the immigrants continued to use the oxen as motive power for carrying freight or plowing fields. At the Mendocino Agency, sub-agent H. L. Ford reported that his charges employed five yoke or ten of his forty-four oxen to break the land with a plow for the first time. They plowed only one acre per day but Ford believed that plowing would go much easier and quicker the next year.[39] Out of necessity, others consumed their oxen for beef. Since the Spanish Longhorn oxen tended to be smaller and therefore less powerful, bigger American oxen helped transform and stimulate the California economy. They pulled more freight in heavier wagons and moved all manner of goods on new roads. Increased mobility of goods and services decreased isolation and smoothed out wide fluctuations in supply and demand.[40]

Although economic principles of cattle supply, demand, and prices tend to dominate discussions of the 1850s California, the heavy hand of nature struck in the form of a drought in that decade, too, in 1857. Faced with major crop failures, agent J. R. Vineyard at the Tejon reservation wisely released a number of the Native residents from tending dying crops to forage for traditional food sources in hopes of surviving the winter. Vineyard proposed to supplement the meager crops and traditionally gathered foods with beef, likely purchased from neighboring *ranchos*. In an example of backward priorities, California Superintendent T. J. Henley worried that the Tejon reservation Indians might slaughter some of their neighbors' cattle to feed their families in a time of want. Starting or increasing even small tribal herds had the potential to provide some food security and preclude any need to steal. Remarkably, Indian Office reports suggest that the government had not as yet decided to establish reservation herds, this in a vast land of cattle ranches, where beef had served generations as an emergency food source in times of drought. Additionally, by 1857, the price per head had dropped into the $10 range, a small price to pay to care for Indigenous peoples already struggling to survive while being dispossessed of their lands.[41]

With or without a federal government policy to buy cattle for reservations, southern California Indians knew to keep small herds for food security wherever possible, including the Kumeyaay people at San Pascual. The Census of 1860 revealed that José Panto had built up a productive farm of one hundred acres where he lived with his wife María, his son Juan, and daughter María de Jesus. With horses, cattle, sheep, and farm equipment, José Panto numbered among the wealthiest men in San Diego County.[42]

Even without direct testimony from Juan Antonio or his successor Manuel Largo on the sources of the Cahuilla cattle, conditions on the ground offer several plausible sources. Cattle regularly drifted away from mission and *rancho* herds and became feral. Cattle often served as payment for services rendered, such as the protection that Juan Antonio's men provided to the Lugo family and their Rancho San Bernardino livestock. Cattle naturally increased on Cahuilla pastures, regardless of their origin.[43]

However, for non-Native cattlemen who raised cattle for profit, prices for California cattle had bottomed out because the supply far outweighed demand in 1860. To illustrate the glutted California market in 1860: California's non-dairy cattle numbered about 948,000 head, representing 6.4 percent of the entire U.S. herd of 14,700,000. Meanwhile, the human population had reached 380,000, or just 1.2 percent of the national total. Put another way, California ranges held 2.49 head of cattle for every man, woman, and child in California, about five times the national average.[44] In the context of this huge surplus of beef, any hunger that California Indian children, women, and men suffered indicates the willful withholding of food based on race, with intent to decrease that population.

The entry of "American" breed animals foretold higher-quality herds in the coming decade, once supply reached a rough equilibrium with demand.[45] Then, an abrupt market correction arrived sooner than anyone expected, and neither Indian, Californio, nor Anglo-American possessed the resources to defend against fickle nature. Following close on the heels of social and economic disruptions, natural disasters struck in rapid succession. The floods of 1862 submerged the state capital for three months, created an inland sea in the San Joaquin Valley, and wiped out crops and as many as two hundred thousand head of cattle. The over-abundance of rain in the winter and spring of 1862 also produced "luxuriant pasturage" in the summer, which fattened surplus animals in a glutted market. Lack of rain during the next two seasons condemned many of the fattened cattle to waste away and die of thirst.[46]

The smallpox epidemic of 1862–1863 further depleted the Indian ranch workforce. The epidemic hit the Mountain Cahuilla hard, as Paramount Chief Juan Antonio succumbed to the disease in early 1863 along with as many as three-quarters of his people, in an epidemic that raged from Los Angeles all the way to the Colorado River.[47] A newspaper report in February of that year claimed that he died at Sahatpa village (in *Tukwet* or San Timoteo Canyon, just west of Beaumont), although Judge Benjamin Hayes believed that he died in San Jacinto. Regardless, the loss of so many Cahuilla and their imposing chief weakened the countervailing force that Cahuilla numbers had exerted against onrushing white settlers. Most of the Mountain Cahuilla abandoned the village and returned to San Jacinto Mountain with their cattle and horses.[48] Subsequently, settlers claimed Cahuilla land in San Timoteo Canyon and the San Gorgonio Pass area.[49]

As a shrewd politician, Juan Antonio had hoped to gain favor with the American government, which he hoped would benefit his people like his former allies, the Lugos had done.[50] The great chief had hoped to secure a future wherein his people coexisted alongside the Americans in peace and freedom. As an important and visible leader, Juan Antonio's actions drew the notice of newspapers like the *Los Angeles Star*.[51] By extension, other southern California Indians, without Juan Antonio's notoriety, likely worked first as *vaqueros* on the missions and *ranchos* and then started and tended their own tribal herds of horses and cattle.

In the years 1863–1865, drought forced the slaughter of cattle for the paltry value of their hides and horns. In 1867, all of the reservations within the California Superintendency held just 94 horses and 498 head of cattle, in total.[52] The 1870 Federal Census revealed a 46 percent decline in cattle numbers from the more than 1.2 million head counted in 1860. In southern California, the count in Los Angeles, San Bernardino, and San Diego counties combined amounted to just 43,000 head.[53]

The big "die-ups" of cattle caused by flood and drought did not put an end to the California cattle industry but added to the weight of change pressing on the old ways of doing things.[54] Absent the strong external demand for hides and tallow, and without a Gold Rush-size demand for beef, California cattle ranchers shifted to an intensive approach to supply, to get more meat and milk per animal by cross-breeding shorthorn American animals to the Spanish. Large landowners subdivided the old *ranchos* and found a ready market for smaller parcels, set up as family-worked farms and ranches. The steady increase in farmed acreage forced the end of open-range ranching as fences went up—at the expense of the ranchers. Simultaneous with macro climatic events, a steady stream of immigrants drove in small numbers of cattle that diffused the livestock populations among the more numerous small spreads.[55]

The flood of 1862 and the drought of 1863–1864 killed off half the cattle herd and ruined many ranchers. Domesticated animals consumed traditional Native foods and American fences restricted access to what remained. By these events and practices, southern California Indians had become much more vulnerable to external market forces than ever before. The floods and drought that hit their own subsistence efforts hard also meant that opportunities to earn wages on ranches and farms literally dried up. In addition to climatic and economic trauma, California Natives suffered incalculable losses to smallpox, venereal disease, alcoholism, kidnapping, and murder. They felt especially hard the losses of their leaders and keepers of the culture. The loss of both elders and their young proteges left irreparable gaps in the continuity of tribal knowledge and a decrease in the reproductive pool. These many losses emboldened settlers to exploit the perceived weakness. The Office of Indian Affairs did little more than report on the losses. Under these compounded threats to Indigenous sovereignty and identity, survival itself represented resistance.[56]

At the start of the decade, the Luiseño *ranchería* called Little Temecula, founded by Pablo Apis, Jose Panto's San Pascual, and Juan Antonio's Cahuilla people, still held small herds of cattle and horses. In May 1865, Agents J. Q. A. Stanley and W. E. Lovett called an assembly of local villages in the Temecula area to distribute food and conduct a census. Stanley's report indicated that under Apis's successor, José Antonio, conditions on the Little Temecula ranch had degraded, socially and economically. Antonio allowed liquor to be sold on the rancho and some of Apis's heirs had mortgaged their share of their birthright, putting the future of the community in jeopardy, should the mortgage holders foreclose on any portion of the title. Nevertheless, 196 men and 192 women and children still tended 225 head of cattle, 150 horses, and 163 sheep. The *rancho's* orchards and vineyards had stopped producing or had died, likely victims of the drought of 1863–1865. Despite weak leadership and negative external influences like alcohol, the Luiseños persisted on the land for twenty-two years, a testament to Pablo Apis's vision and to his people's determination to adhere to that vision.[57]

Over time, Apis's heirs sold off their individual shares of the ranch. A white man named Isaac Williams bought up half the ranch, while Apis's widow, Casilda Coyote de Apis, still held the other half. Williams had married into the Lugo family and eventually owned Rancho del Chino. Other white men tried unsuccessfully to squat on the land. However, in 1872, a Louis Wolf acquired Casilda's share of the Little Temecula, putting a final end to Luiseño ownership or occupancy of this last piece of Indian land in the Temecula Valley.[58]

In the 1870s, the trends already established in the first two decades of American rule continued: cattle ranchers continued to upgrade the breeding quality of their herds, immigrants claimed and squatted on more California Indian lands, and southern California Native leaders refused to accept a permanent dispossession of their ancestral homes. The California economy continued to evolve into a more diversified one, in which farming rivaled cattle ranching in political power. The subdivision of large ranches and farms redistributed land among a greater number of smaller ranchers and farmers. This diffusion reduced large-scale demand for Indian cowboys and ranch workers. Aside from the loss of the big *ranchos*, new sources of labor entered the market. Unemployed Chinese railroad workers and whites who went broke digging for gold competed with Indians for work. Nonetheless, Indian workers, mounted or not, continued to play a significant role in the survival and prospering of new ranches, farms, towns, and households across southern California, provided they had the ability and willingness to travel far and wide to support their families.[59]

As early as 1860, the ethnic makeup of cattle ranchers had also diversified, to the point where the majority of the roughly 1,700 stock raisers claimed non-Hispanic descent.[60] Nevertheless, Spanish traditions, practices, and terminology had been imprinted on California life and endured. Yet another visitor to the state described and affirmed this cultural persistence into the 1870s.

Prussian immigrant, East Coast newspaperman, and author of books on the sea, Charles Nordhoff wrote his 1873 guidebook to stimulate travel to and settlement in California. Besides providing migrants with travel logistics and sights to see, Nordhoff described the economic potential of California, including its cattle ranching. New fence laws fundamentally changed cattle ranching but twenty-five years after California became an American territory, ranchers still largely followed Spanish laws and customs, and used terminology brought to Alta California in 1769 by Franciscan padres and soldiers of the *presidio*.[61]

A notice promulgated by the San Diego County Board of Supervisors on January 5, 1872, announced the appointments of that year's Judges of the Plains and directed those named to schedule roundups for all the cattle in the county. *Rodeos* necessarily started in the south of the state and worked northward as the weather warmed. Whether decided by state law or by the local government, ranchers in San Diego County held four separate *rodeos* that year, one for each of the designated ranges: Coast Range, Temecula Range, Agua Caliente (Warner's Ranch) Range, and Southern District. Rancher Cave Couts served as one of the *Jueces de Campo* (Judges of the Plains) for the Coast Range, joined by an F. P. Forster, likely Francisco, the second son of Don Juan Forster and Isadora Pico Forster (1842–1880). Juan Forster owned a ranch named Rancho De La Nación with San Diego Bay as its western boundary, hence the likelihood that F. P. Forster saw to the interests of his father's ranch as Judge on that range. The ranch's 27,000 acres encompassed most of present-day Chula Vista, National City, Bonita, Sunnyside, and western Sweetwater Valley.[62] Two members of the Estudillo family served as Judges for the Temecula Range, consistent with their family's original grant of Rancho San Jacinto Viejo. Three Judges at Large had the duty to schedule the regional roundups, in time and place. This distinction indicates that they held administrative if not supervisorial roles.[63]

According to the law empowering these officials,[64] Judges of the Plains had the duty to enforce the laws requiring proper brands and other markings on all cattle and other livestock traveling through the country. The owner of the traveling livestock had to present proof of sale in type and quantity to the local Judge of the Plains, who then accompanied said livestock through his district and, theoretically, handed them off to the Judge of the next district. Judges of the Plains had the duty to arrest any drover who failed to produce the legal papers and take them before a magistrate. They also served warrants and arrested anyone suspected of stealing, hiding, or killing cattle.[65] These coercive powers notwithstanding, large roundups provided spectacles of the magnitude of California cattle herds and the community of ranchers, foremen, and cowboys.

In the days of the big ranches in southern California (Mexican or American), roundups commonly included twelve to twenty ranchers and their foremen, and from six to fifteen cowboys from each ranch. Each of the cowboys brought their own string of six to eight horses. According to these estimates, a roundup might entail as many as three-hundred humans and two-thousand horses. In so large a gathering, the cattle easily numbered twenty-thousand heads. The processes of gathering, sorting, and branding each and every calf took days to accomplish. By custom, the hosting rancher fed all of his guests for as many days as it took to complete the work. Then, once they had finished the job and before they returned all the herds to their home ranges, the cowboys put on informal displays of great feats of horsemanship and roping. With Judges of the Plains present at roundups to ensure fairness and honest dealings all around, gatherings of this sort by nature engendered a sense of community among the ranchers and the cowboys.[66]

Of the informal skill competitions, Nordhoff singled out the team roping for high praise. He wondered at the skill employed by *vaqueros* to catch and throw a calf, especially the throw by the heeler, accomplished from what he described as an intuitive feel for the animal's next movements, formed by a lifetime of ranch work. He marveled at the intrinsic partnership formed between a cowboy and his horse in this work. Once the cowboy succeeded with his throw of the lasso, the horse kept the steer at bay by maintaining tension on the rope. Nordhoff also witnessed trust and courtesy in the relations between the *Padrone* of the *rancho* and his Indian *vaqueros*.[67]

Those California Indians still residing on the great ranches performed many tasks, including milking cows, tanning leather and sheepskins, making shoes, and raising grapes and grain. The women had many roles of their own, such as sewing, making candles from tallow, milling flour, and making wine from the grapes. The Indian men also constructed large vats of cement and stone, if the ranch did not own metal ones, in which they melted the tallow for soap and candles, and for sale.[68]

Like Nordhoff, Special Agent John G. Ames visited southern California but as a "special commissioner to inquire into the condition and necessities of the Mission Indians in Southern California." His report appeared within the *Annual Report of the Commissioner of Indian Affairs of 1873*. Having heard of his arrival in Los Angeles, Luiseño headman Olegario Calac and ten of his captains traveled there and met with Ames on three separate days to communicate their grievances regarding unabated encroachments onto Luiseño land, including burial grounds, and usurpation of their water by settlers.[69]

Ames also met with Cabezon, the great and venerable leader of the Desert Cahuilla, in the San Gorgonio Pass. Said to be more than ninety years old, Cabezon arrived at the head of a company of horsemen, like a "marshal in uniform." Cabezon's people numbered more than a thousand at that time and, because of their labor on farms and ranches, deserved great credit for the prosperity enjoyed by settlers in the Pass area. Beyond economic benefit, Ames honored Cabezon as a man of peace and wondered what the fate of American immigrants might have been at the hands of a warlike chief of the Desert Cahuilla.[70]

One of Ames's assistants visited three *ranchería(s)* in San Diego County, including San Pascual. He met with the Captain of the village, "Panto Lion," and asked him to summon his people for a meeting. The Kumeyaay people of these locales recited the all-too-familiar litany of grievances: settlers preempted the lands upon which the villagers actually resided, some cheated Indians out of wages for their labor, and, astonishingly, some settlers even confiscated Native-owned cattle and horses for "trespassing" on preempted lands. Whites considered Indians an obstacle but one small ranch owner near Temecula differed. He presented his cynical ideas of the best use of Indians to Ames's assistant. One Indian family resided on a corner of his ranch.

> His wise and humane (?) conclusion was that the owners of large ranches should not drive "their Indians" away, but should keep them as workers, and set apart certain portions of the ranch for them. "There is worthless land enough upon every ranch," he said, "for Indians to live on." [71]

Ames's entreaties did not result in surveyed and patented reservations immediately, but in historical hindsight, his thorough report and open tour of many *ranchería(s)* added to the movement building in support of justice for all Native peoples of southern California.

In 1874, San Pascual Captain Jose Panto continued his quest to establish legal title to his beleaguered pueblo. To that end, he planned to travel with Luiseño leader Olegario Calac to Washington, DC, to make their case directly to President Ulysses S. Grant. Before Panto could make the journey, his horse threw him and he died at San Pascual on April 27, 1874.[72]

Whites held Luiseño Pablo Apis and Kumeyaay José Panto in high regard as men of peace. When they died, their visions of sovereign Indian communities, established on traditional lands and living peacefully alongside Californios and American settlers, eventually died as well. Romantic images of men on horseback aside, cattle ranching is at bottom a business. Ranchers and their customers valued cattle for their meat, hide, and tallow. Cattle also served as a symbol of wealth and prestige, but for the Indians of San Pascual, Little Temecula, and Sahatpa, cattle meant survival and sustained them on land over which they had a modicum of sovereignty. Though short-lived, cattle enabled them to continue to express their Native identities, including the identity of successful cattle ranchers.

In a just world, historians might categorize the stories of Little Temecula ranch and the village of San Pascual as typical of the experiences of the former neophytes of secularized missions. By extension, their experiences applied to all Indians of southern California. Their hands and backs made the mission and *rancho* economies go, and they rightly deserved some benefit from land redistribution, even in the form of smaller grants like the ones discussed above. Instead, these exceptional stories tell of gallant but doomed Indian resistance to what became a flood of immigrants seeking to farm or ranch on traditional Kumeyaay, Cupeño, Luiseño, Cahuilla, and Serrano lands.

Charles A. Wetmore's 1875 report built on the many local visits made by Reverend Ames and his assistants. The illegal confiscation of the Indians' stock reaffirmed their need for cattle as food security. His plan, though paternalistic, posed the stark choice of either clearing patented land exclusively for southern California Native people or of witnessing the death of their societies. Based on the continuing demographic decline, Wetmore strongly recommended that they receive only enough land to serve their present numbers. "Experience shows that larger reservations always invite encroachments with impunity by the whites." Wetmore realistically considered the potential for white political resistance in his plan. Sixteen years later, the same specter of white backlash hovered over the Smiley Commission.[73]

Acknowledging that Congress took no action on the remedies recommended in the Ames Report, Commissioner of Indian Affairs Edward P. Smith reiterated the need for early action, even based solely on saving money. The longer the government waited, the higher the prices to buy or trade land claimed by settlers. In 1874, the government passed on the opportunity to secure tracts for all the southern California Natives, including Pablo Apis's Luiseños, for the total expenditure of $100,000. In 1875, Smith requested $150,000 for the same purpose, all to no avail.[74]

California Indians had little to encourage them in the decade of the 1870s. President Ulysses S. Grant's Executive Order reservations at first offered hope to Indians but did not deter the settlers from claiming the land on which Indians scraped out a living. About six months after President Ulysses S. Grant issued an executive order to establish two reservations in San Diego County, captains of the Luiseño, Cupeño, and Mountain Cahuilla elected Olegario Calac as General or Paramount Chief in July, 1870. Olegario stood out among nineteenth-century Native American leaders for his willingness to brave the fire of racial hatred while using American legal institutions to resist forced removal from Luiseño homes. The offered reservation had no secure title and was of poorer land quality. Amid Native and white anxieties, Grant rescinded the executive order in February 1871, justifying the Luiseño fears of living on land with no title.[75]

In a face-to-face meeting with the U.S. president in November 1875, Olegario explained to President Grant the cause for self-determination by his people, on a secure homeland. In December 1875 and in May 1876, President Grant established or enlarged fifteen reservations in southern California by executive order, including Cahuilla, Cabazon, Potrero (Morongo), and Agua Caliente (Palm Springs).[76] President Grant's Executive Orders did not deter whites from encroaching; neither did they deter Indians from resisting the encroachments. In June 1877, Luiseños led by Olegario blocked a non-Native cattleman's herd from trespassing on traditional Luiseño land near Warner's Springs, to prevent the trampling or consuming of traditional sources of food, medicine, and cultivated gardens.[77] About a month later, the local sheriff tried to carry out a court-ordered eviction, when Olegario and about 150 men surrounded him. They allowed him to leave unharmed but such defiance from an Indian certainly drew the attention and resentment of local whites. Nonetheless, Olegario sought a legal and non-violent solution, and planned to appeal the order in court. Before he could do so, Olegario Calac died in his sleep on July 31, 1877. The coroner's report concluded natural causes but some of his followers believed that foul play took the great leader's life.[78]

A story told by a Luiseño to agent Samuel Lawson in 1879 confirms that the Luiseños also held tribal cattle herds and could not tolerate trespass cattle. Olegario believed in using the American judicial system to address the many injustices of his people, perpetrated by land-grabbing whites. He perceived that under American rule, wherever land disputes arose, the side holding a piece of paper on which government authorities conferred ownership always won the dispute. Therefore, Olegario hired American attorneys to represent his people in an American court. When they ran out of currency to pay the fees, they sent one attorney thirty-one head of cattle to settle the debt.[79]

Toward the end of the decade, California superintendents reported on the horse and cattle holdings of the Native Californians, estimating between 800 and 1,000 horses and only 300–400 head of cattle.[80] California Indian cowboys had been herding cattle for a century and surely had not forgotten how to ride and rope, so perhaps these low numbers represent the impact of the drought of 1880, if it forced the culling of herds to conserve water and forage. The low numbers may also derive from the cumulative impacts of encroachments, livestock thefts, hostile settlers who just wanted the Indians gone, and a federal government that did a poor job of protecting them. Such conditions likely discouraged Indians from risking precious resources to build herds, houses, and corrals, only to have them taken away on the slightest pretense. Congress also failed to authorize even the smallest of sums to help the embattled Indigenous people to farm like Americans or to run cattle on their own exclusive ranges, not ones that had been grazed over by trespassing cattle.[81]

In a river of bad news, an island of relief occasionally forms, as did one reported by Agent Samuel Lawson in 1882. In June of that year, Lawson visited a landless and homeless group of Luiseño families, recently ejected from Little Temecula. They settled on some dry hills that land-hungry settlers had passed over, dug wells (possibly of the walk-in type built by southern California Natives), and developed a domestic water supply for drinking and to cultivate small gardens. In the previous winter months, they had planted wheat and barley for dry farming and in June, harvested 500 sacks of barley, with a substantial surplus to sell. Lawson noted that the

Luiseños' success attracted the attention of "the ubiquitous 'land grabber,'" which motivated him to immediately write to the Commissioner for help in securing the land for the Indians. Lawson reported that "with commendable promptness" he received an executive order that set the land aside for that village. "It was the most gratifying event of the year." However uplifting the story, this outcome represented a rare exception to the norm and also the great good that decisive action might have accomplished. Lawson's story does not mention whether the Luiseños had cattle. In 1865, the community at Little Temecula held 225 head of cattle and 150 horses. But in 1882, without land, water, and grass to call their own, this vagabond group likely saw livestock as a luxury.[82]

Less than one-fourth of the state's estimated twenty thousand Indians lived in the sphere of the four agencies in 1881.[83] If the reported numbers of three hundred to four hundred head of cattle apply only to "agency Indians," the actual numbers of cattle might be higher. From 1882 to 1890, the annual reports of horses averaged 1,444 and cattle at 933 head, but these are totals for all four agencies in the state. Even if southern California Indians held one-fourth of these tallies—361 horses and 233 head of cattle—such paltry numbers suggest poverty and hunger. Indian Service officer for the Mission Agency, John S. Ward, reported in 1886 that squatters had overrun the Morongo reservation and had claimed all the best land.[84] The Office of Indian Affairs favored farming as the main economic activity through which to promote Native self-sufficiency, so perhaps low numbers of cattle reflect that persistent bias, even though the land and climate continually recommended otherwise, in the forms of punishing droughts.

In response, Indian Rights groups mobilized to lobby Congress on behalf of the welfare of all southern California Native peoples. Congress authorized Helen Hunt Jackson and Abbott Kinney to update the status of the Native groups. They published their report in 1883. Based roughly on the Jackson-Kinney report and decades of documented violations of their human rights, the U.S. Senate passed a law dedicated to the relief of southern California Indians. They passed the law three times in the 1880s. Three times the House of Representatives failed to even bring it to a vote. Finally, on January 12, 1891, the Fifty-First Congress passed *An Act for the Relief of the Mission Indians in the State of California*. Although much work lay ahead for the Indians of southern California, for the appointed Commissioners of Indian Affairs, and for numerous agents and superintendents, they had reached a pivot point from which they could begin to build better lives. In 1890, the Mission Tule River Agency reported that the people held 1,244 horses and 1,500 head of cattle. The numbers indicate that despite encroachments and other depredations by settlers, Serranos, Cahuillas, Cupeños, Luiseños, and Kumeyaay had not only survived, they had begun to revitalize their societies.[85]

NOTES

1. H. T. Liliencrantz, "Recollections of a California Cattleman: Three Chapters from the Memoirs of H. T. Lilienkrantz," *California Historical Society Quarterly* 38, no. 3 (September 1959): 259–268.
2. Pulling, "A History of California's Range-Cattle Industry," 338–339, 341.
3. Ibid., 74–77.
4. *Annual Report of the Commissioner of Indian Affairs for 1853*, hereafter *ARCIA*, 3; owing to ongoing violence and kidnappings, uncounted Native refugees on the move to escape the same, and the lack of personnel on the ground to conduct an accurate count, any estimate given must be considered a rough guess. See Russell Thornton, *American Indian Holocaust and Survival: A Population History Since 1492* (Norman, OK: University of Oklahoma Press, 1987), 109. Scholars on this subject estimate pre-contact Alta California Indians at 275,000–310,000, therefore the estimate of 100,000 represents a population loss of at least two-thirds. See also Clifford E. Trafzer and Joel R. Hyer, eds., *Exterminate Them!: Written Accounts of the Murder, Rape, and Enslavement of Native Americans during the California Gold Rush* (East Lansing, MI: Michigan State University Press, 1999); Trafzer and Hyer state that between 1848 and 1868, Indian communities lost a further 80 percent of their people to diseases, murders, and kidnappings.
5. James Gerber blames the combination of gold fever and Bonanza wheat farming for the updated uses of Spanish Indian labor practices, in James Gerber, "The Gold Rush Origins of California's Wheat Economy," *América Latina En La Historia Económica, Boletín de Fuentes* 34 (December 2010): 35–64. These early grain ventures came to be known as Bonanza Wheat Farms.
6. Cleland, *The Cattle on a Thousand Hills*, 102.
7. Hubert Howe Bancroft, *History of California, Vol. III, 1825–1840* (Santa Barbara, CA: Wallace Hebberd, 1966), 173–175; Dary, *Cowboy Culture*, 62–63; Jordan, *North American Cattle-Ranching Frontiers*, 243–245.
8. Cleland, *The Cattle on a Thousand Hills*, 104–106; Lawrence James Jelinek, "'Property of Every Kind': Ranching and Farming During the Gold Rush Era," *California History* 77, no. 4 (Winter 1998/1999): 233–234.
9. B .D. Wilson, *The Indians of Southern California in 1852*, ed. John Walton Caughey (Lincoln, NE: University of Nebraska Press, 1995), xvii.
10. Vernette Snyder Ripley, "The San Fernando Pass and the Pioneer Traffic that Went Over it," *Historical Society of Southern California* 29, no. 1 (March 1947): 12–17.
11. William L. Preston, "The Tulare Lake Basin: An Aboriginal Cornucopia," *California Geographical Society* 30 (1990): 1–24. Preston notes that Sherburne Cook determined that the population of 18,000 Yokuts represented perhaps half of the lush basin's carrying capacity. Preston also asserts that early European landings in California, by the likes of Cabrillo, Drake, and Viscaino, left behind the scourge of diseases that ravaged indigenous populations throughout California long before the 1770s.
12. James M. Jensen, "Cattle Drives from the Ranchos to the Gold Fields of California," *Arizona and the West* 2, no. 4 (Winter 1960): 341–345.

13. Jensen, "Cattle Drives from the Ranchos to the Gold Fields of California," 345–352.

14. M. Magliari, "Free Soil, Unfree Labor," *Pacific Historical Review* 73, no. 3 (August 2004): 373. The San Diego County grand jury issued no fewer than four separate indictments against Couts between 1855–1870, for homicide or violent assaults but he evaded accountability on all counts. Couts did stand trial for murder in 1866 for shooting Juan Mendoza in the back with a shotgun and killing him almost instantly. For the trial, in which the jury acquitted Couts, see Clare McKanna Jr., "An Old Town Gunfight: The Homicide Trial of Cave Johnson Couts, 1866," *The Journal of San Diego History* 44, no. 4 (Fall 1998): 259–273.

15. Carrico, *Strangers in a Stolen Land*, 97.

16. Ibid., 78, 96–100. See also Magliari, "Free Soil, Unfree Labor," 358–362.

17. Cleland, *The Cattle on a Thousand Hills*, 108–109.

18. Gilbert Cureton, "The Cattle Trail to California 1840–1860," *The Historical Society of Southern California Quarterly* 35, no. 2 (June 1953): 100.

19. Ibid., 102. Stolen or unbranded cattle come to mind as reasons to sell on the black market and therefore go uncounted.

20. Trafzer, *Yuma: Frontier Crossing of the Far Southwest*, 52–68. The Quechans fought numerous battles and skirmishes with U.S. Army units but hostilities with the Army mostly ended by 1852. The Quechans fought more bloody battles with their enemies, the Cocopa Indians, and in one campaign, fell into a deadly Cocopa trap, in which nearly all of a Quechan war party of 150 warriors met their deaths.

21. Cureton, "The Cattle Trail to California," 103–106.

22. *ARCIA 1848*, 407–408.

23. *ARCIA 1849–1850*, 17–20, 23, 26–27, 91–93.

24. George W. Barbour, [report] "No. 73," July 28, 1851, California Superintendency, *ARCIA, 1851*, 231–236. See also Rawls, *Indians of California*, 141–143. For approximate weights of the Spanish Longhorn breed in colonial California, see Webb, *Indian Life at the Old Missions*, 174.

25. Redick McKee, G. W. Barbour, and O. W. Wozencraft, "No. 70," May 15, 1851, California Superintendency, *ARCIA, 1851*, 224.

26. O. W. Wozencraft, "No. 71," May 18, 1851, California Superintendency, *ARCIA, 1851*, 225.

27. Phillips, *Chiefs and Challengers*, 103–105, 138–139.

28. Bibb, "Pablo Apis and Temecula," 264. See also "No. 19," Special Agent J.Q.A. Stanley, *ARCIA 1865*, 125. Stanley mentioned that Pablo Apis "died about ten years ago," but offered no documentation. Apis's hosting of the Treaty of Temecula and the attendance of so many important Native leaders testified to the respect accorded him among Indians. Pablo had also earned the trust and goodwill of the white population of the region. He refused to join the uprising supposedly instigated by Antonio Garra just two months prior, in November 1851; he had also captured a murderous Army deserter, among numerous other instances. On October 22, 1853, the *San Diego Herald* described him as "Pablo Apis: the celebrated Indian chief," in anticipation of a visit by him to the town.

29. Phillips, *Chiefs and Challengers*, 140–141; Rawls, *Indians of California*, 141–148; Carrico, *Strangers in a Stolen Land*, 59–60, 90–95; Farris, "Jose Panto, 'Capitan' of the Indian Pueblo of San Pascual, San Diego County," 118–120.

30. David Samuel Torres-Rouff, *Before L.A.: Race, Space, and Municipal Power in Los Angeles, 1781–1894* (New Haven, CT: Yale University Press, 2013), 55–56.

31. Wilson, *The Indians of Southern California in 1852*, xxxiv–xxxix, 24; "California Superintendency," ARCIA 1857, 387. The term "Extermination" appears sporadically in official reports describing the "miserable and degraded condition" of Indians who are dying from disease, starvation, and "the abuse of evil disposed white persons." Superintendent Thomas J. Henley's use of the term appears to stem more from despair rather than from genocidal intent on his part toward the Native Californians.

32. John Ryan Fischer, *Cattle Colonialism: An Environmental History of the Conquest of California and Hawai'i* (Chapel Hill, NC: University of North Carolina Press, 2015), 1–11; William Bauer, Jr., *We Were All Migrant Workers Here: Work, Community, and Memory on California's Round Valley Reservation, 1850–1941* (Chapel Hill, NC: University of North Carolina Press, 2009), 65; see also H. R. Harvey, "Population of the Cahuilla Indians: Decline and Its Causes," *Eugenics Quarterly* 14, no. 3 (1967): 185–198.

33. Cleland, *The Cattle on a Thousand Hills*, 108–111; Jelinek, "Property of Every Kind," 233–235.

34. Cleland, *The Cattle on a Thousand Hills*, 106–112. For a discussion of the stunting of California's economic growth due to its isolation, see Paul W. Rhode, "Learning, Capital Accumulation, and the Transformation of California Agriculture," *Journal of Economic History* 55, no. 4 (December 1995): 773–800.

35. Lugo, "Life of a Rancher," 236.

36. William Deverell, "The 1850s," in *A Companion to California History*, eds. William Deverell and David Igler, 161–174 (Malden, MA: Wiley-Blackwell).

37. William Duncan Strong, *Aboriginal Society in Southern California* (Banning, CA: Malki Museum Press, Morongo Indian Reservation, 1972), 145. See also Lowell John Bean, *Mukat's People: The Cahuilla People of Southern California* (Berkeley, CA: University of California Press, 1972), 70.

38. W. Turrentine Jackson, *Wagon Roads West: A Study of Federal Road Surveys and Construction in the Trans-Mississippi West, 1846–1869* (Berkeley, CA: University of California Press, 1952), 241–256. Beale included seventy-six camels in his first round-trip. The camels proved their supreme hardiness for desert travel. They carried water and grain for the other animals and needed little for themselves. Beale called the camel "an economical and noble brute." See also Odie B. Faulk, *The U.S. Camel Corps* (New York: Oxford University Press, 1976); and Gary Paul Nabhan, "Camel Whisperers: Desert Nomads Crossing Paths," *Arizona Journal of History* 49, no. 2 (Summer 2008): 95–118.

39. "Office of the Mendocino Indian Reservation," August 15, 1857, *ARCIA 1857*, 394–398.

40. Cureton, "The Cattle Trail to California," 99–101. Other immigrants brought small numbers of milk cows to provide milk, butter, and cheese to consume or to sell for income.

41. "California Superintendency, September 4, 1857," *ARCIA 1857*, 387–406; Cleland, *The Cattle on a Thousand Hills*, 110–111.
42. Carrico, *Strangers in a Stolen Land*, 118–119.
43. "Agent J.Q.A. Stanley Reports," ARCIA, 1865, 119–120.
44. Pulling, "A History of California's Range Cattle Industry," 107–108.
45. Ibid., 99–101.
46. Cleland, *The Cattle on a Thousand Hills*, 130–131. Burcham, *California Range Land*, 152. Sacramento received 36 inches of rain in the 1861–62 season.
47. Thornton, *American Indian Holocaust and Survival*, 125–126; Thornton sets the Cahuilla population in 1850 at 2,000–3,000. "No. 18," Special Agent W.E. Lovett, *ARCIA 1865*, 124. Accompanied by Stanley, Lovett met with and conducted a census of the former mission Indians of San Bernardino and San Diego Counties at Temecula on May 4, 1865, two years after the smallpox epidemic. The Cahuilla numbered just 703 men, women, and children, and possessed only 60 horses and cows combined. Lowell John Bean, Lisa J. Bourgeault, and Frank W. Porter III, *The Cahuilla* (New York: Chelsea House, 1989), 89. Bean et al. propose a pre-contact Cahuilla population of 6,000–10,000 and 2,500 after the epidemic.
48. Hanks, *This War is for a Whole Life*, 32.
49. Phillips, *Chiefs and Challengers*, 178–179, 372n147; Cleland, *The Cattle on a Thousand Hills*, 131–133.
50. Hanks, *This War is for a Whole Life*, 26–27.
51. Phillips, *Chiefs and Challengers*, 371, fn133.
52. *ARCIA 1867*, 393.
53. *ARCIA 1867*, 136–137; Pulling, "A History of California's Range Cattle Industry," 125.
54. Edward Everett Dale, *The Range Cattle Industry: Ranching on the Great Plains from 1865 to 1925* (Norman, OK: University of Oklahoma Press, 1930), 60, 83, 93, 104, 132–135. Cattle "die-ups" have occurred throughout the West, usually the result of some combination of overburdened range feed, too many animals, and a severe natural event, like drought or blizzard.
55. Jordan, *North American Cattle Ranching Frontiers*, 279–287; Rawls, *Indians of California*, 109–111.
56. Rawls, *Indians of California*, 171–176; Lowell John Bean and Harry W. Lawton, "Some Explanations For the Rise of Cultural Complexity in Native California With Comments on Proto-Agriculture and Agriculture," in *Before the Wilderness: Environmental Management by Native Californians*, eds. Thomas C. Blackburn and Kat Anderson (Menlo Park, CA: Ballena Press, 1993), 27–54, 53–54.
57. *ARCIA 1865*, 119–125; Phillips, *Chiefs and Challengers*, 59–62, 180–181.
58. Brigandi, *Temecula*, 33. When Wolf acquired Casilda Apis's share of Little Temecula in 1872, she kept a small 3-acre homestead that she also relinquished to Wolf in 1876.
59. Rawls, *Indians of California*, 109–112; "California Superintendency," *ARCIA 1871*, 329.
60. Pulling, "A History of California's Range Cattle Industry," 103.

61. Nordhoff, *California for Health, Pleasure, and Residence*, 185–187.
62. Bancroft, *History of California, Vol. III*, 744; James M. Jensen, "John Forster: A California Ranchero," *California Historical Society Quarterly* 48, no. 1 (March 1969): 40–41.
63. Nordhoff, *California for Health, Pleasure, and Residence*, 185–187.
64. Nordhoff, *California for Health, Pleasure, and Residence*, 239. *Sections 5, 6, and 7, of an Act concerning Judges of the Plains and defining their duties, passed April 25th, 1851, and the Amendment thereto.*
65. Ibid., 239.
66. Nordhoff, *California for Health, Pleasure, and Residence*, 188–190.
67. Ibid.,190–191.
68. Ibid., 191–194.
69. "Report of Special Agent John G. Ames in Regard to the Condition of the Mission Indians of California, With Recommendations," *ARCIA 1873*, 29–33.
70. *ARCIA 1873*, 33–34.
71. Luther E. Sleigh, Los Angeles, Cal., July 31, 1873, "Report of Special Agent John G. Ames in Regard to the Condition of the Mission Indians of California, With Recommendations," *ARCIA 1873*, 29–41.
72. Carrico, *Strangers in a Stolen Land*, 120–122.
73. "Report, Charles A. Wetmore, Special U.S. Commissioner of Mission Indians of Southern California" (Washington, DC: Government Printing Office, 1875), 8–9; Larry E. Burgess, "Commission to the Mission Indians, 1891," *San Bernardino County Museum Association Quarterly* 35, no. 1 (Spring 1988): 14.
74. *ARCIA 1875*, 9–12.
75. Hanks, *This War is for a Whole Life*, 40–44; Richard L. Carrico, "The Struggle for Native American Self-Determination in San Diego County," *Journal of California and Great Basin Anthropology* 2, no. 2 (Winter 1980): 199–201.
76. Phillips, *Chiefs and Challengers*, 210, 376n114.
77. Ibid., 210.
78. Ibid., 210–212; Hanks, *This War is for a Whole Life*, 46.
79. Tanis Thorne, "The Mixed Legacy of Mission Indian Agent S.S. Lawson, 1878–1883," *Journal of California and Great Basin Anthropology* 25, no. 2 (2005): 152.
80. *ARCIA 1879*, 246–247; *ARCIA 1880*, 258–259.
81. Ames, *Report,* 31–32; Wetmore, *Report*, 5.
82. "Mission Agency, San Bernardino, Cal., Aug.7, 1882." *ARCIA 1882*, 10–12.
83. *ARCIA 1881*, xi, reports 4,761 Natives in the sphere of the four agencies. Russell Thornton, Table 5–4: "California Indian Population History, Pre-European to 1980," in *American Indian Holocaust and Survival*,109. Thornton estimates the California Indian population at 20,500 in 1880.
84. *ARCIA 1881–1890*, "Mission Agency, California, Colton, August 14, 1886," *ARCIA 1886*, 43–46.
85. *ARCIA 1884*, xxxvii; *ARCIA 1886*, xlii; *ARCIA 1887*, li; *ARCIA 1889*, 59–60; *ARCIA 1890*, 466467; *Congressional Record*, "Fifty-First Congress, Session II, Chapters 64, 65," 712–714.

Chapter 6

"Subjects But Not Citizens," 1891–1920

At the end of the nineteenth century, the southern California cattle industry reflected profound changes that American rule had brought to the political, economic, social, and cultural life of the state. Ownership diffused from large land grant ranches to many smaller-scale but more intensively managed stock-raising farms, including small herds that California Indian cattlemen managed on the new reservations. However, these changes did not alter the fact that ranchers still needed skilled cowhands. Cowboys still branded and doctored calves, they turned colts into dependable cow ponies, and they herded steers and cows into cattle cars destined for the slaughterhouse.

By the passage of *An Act for the Relief of the Mission Indians in the State of California* in 1891, Native peoples of southern California had obtained federally recognized portions of their traditional lands. However, the Act did not put an end to threats to Indian lands in the 1890s and beyond. In the churn of immigration, business ambitions, population growth, and divisions among whites relating to reservations and land tenure, some southern California Indians lost homelands and faced removals and relocations, most notably the Cupeño. In those first decades of the new era, droughts and corrupt, biased, or ineffectual Office of Indian Affairs personnel continued to inflict suffering on Native peoples of the region. Poor quality and minimal quantity of those lands often limited their ability to support their families. Nonetheless, many Native people raised horses and cattle to provide food security and to renew their connection to the land. Indian cowboys also continued to find work on ranches owned by non-Native settlers. Thus, California Indians remained essential to the viability of the southern California cattle industry.

In addition to the difficulties related to making a living, reservation life itself posed a challenge, in the often paternalistic and oppressive expectations of American society for an assimilated Native population. The federal government expressed these expectations in laws and policies, carried out by the Office of Indian Affairs. Cahuillas, Luiseños, Kumeyaay, and Serranos adapted to these new realities and cooperated when they saw benefit but resisted what they perceived as being harmful to their survival and their sovereignty. Over the next three decades, southern California Indians worked hard to develop their reservation resources, to maintain a subsistence connection to the earth, and to control their borders. On each reservation, livestock herds increased as popular engagement increased and with at least average rainfall. Over time, that engagement declined and cattle ownership concentrated among a small cadre of cattlemen on most reservations. Although wage income far outpaced reservation income from stock sales, raising cattle had assumed an importance that cannot be measured by market currency. The currency of cattle ranching lies in staying connected to the land, cowboying with family members, and honoring a tradition that reaches back to that first Alta California Indigenous American who mounted up on a mission *estancia* some two and a half centuries ago, and started working the cattle.

Many of the cattle herds driven to California to satisfy the demands of the Gold Rush came from Midwestern states like Missouri, Illinois, and Iowa. They not only introduced American breeds like Durham and Angus, they also employed methods geared toward optimizing the welfare and quality of the animals. From settler families who drove a few head of seed cattle for their farm, to large herds assembled by speculators, the Midwestern breeds and practices generally displaced California ranching principles. Fences, upbreeding, winter feed grown in enclosed meadows, and disease controls all differed from the freewheeling Hispanic system. That system, born of necessity when Longhorns reproduced rapidly on California grasses, required the Franciscan padres to train and equip neophyte Indigenous men to work the herds as cowboys.[1]

Political power accompanied the rapid ascension of California's farm population during the early American period (1848–1891). New fence laws protected crops at the expense of cattlemen. "Limited range and expensive quartering and feeding cattle rendered unprofitable the raising of inferior stock, which in turn led to an emphasis on better grades of cattle."[2] In the last decade of the nineteenth century and the first of the twentieth, the California cattle industry transitioned from a range-cattle business to stock farming.[3]

The range cattleman gambled that he could raise large numbers of lower quality cattle (in beef per head) at low cost or on free pasturage. His business model compensated for lower market prices per animal with high-volume production. The hardy and half-wild Spanish Longhorns supported this method. Small stock farmers needed supplemental feed—hay, produced by extensive grain hay farming. Their higher cost of goods sold per unit (animal) forced them to turn to higher returning products (better breeds). New laws that required cattlemen to fence *in* their stock, upgrade their breeds, and control that process evened out the costs of producing high-quality beef cattle among larger and smaller stock farmers. The new conditions also encouraged the small stockmen to produce beyond their own family's needs. These upgrades also prompted a more localized processing infrastructure, in stock yards, local packinghouses, and refrigerated storage.[4]

In his 1891 annual report to the Secretary of the Interior, Commissioner of Indian Affairs Thomas J. Morgan declared that Indians were "subjects but not citizens." Morgan explained that Congress had made no provision for them in the Treaty of Guadalupe Hidalgo, even though the Republic of Mexico had proclaimed in 1821 that members of all races held citizenship in the new nation. Commissioner Morgan, who had commanded Black troops in the Civil War, and who had been a Baptist minister and an educator, also advocated for the moral uplift and civilizing potential of forced Indian attendance at day schools.[5] To Morgan, schooling accelerated the process for childlike Indians and that a good school "may thus bridge over for them the dreary chasm of a thousand years of tedious evolution."[6] Morgan's 1891 assessment of Indians indicated that field agents must supervise their charges as a parent does a child. Paternalism and self-interest pervaded the actions and words of Horatio Nelson Rust, agent for all southern California Indians from 1889 to 1893.

Rust administered the jurisdiction named the "Mission, Tule River (consolidated) Agency," based in Colton, California. It included all the reservations in southern California plus Tule River in the southern Sierra Nevada mountains and the Yuma reservation on the Colorado River. In 1891 Rust reported that he had charge of 3,999 women, men, and children, of which total the Yumas (Quechans) represented about one-fourth. Referring to the people on the Potrero (Morongo) reservation, he stated,

> These Indians are better situated than any of the twenty-one tribes under my charge ... [they are] three miles from Banning, a thriving fruit-growing colony, where many find employment. Charles O. Barker, manager of the [local] fruit-growing company finds them [to be] good help and pays men and women alike $1.50 per day. Some more reliable men get $2.

However, since much of the reservation lies five to six miles from the village and is without water, Rust seemed to believe that it was only good for dry farming barley.[7]

Rust paid no attention in his reports to the cattle that had remained a pillar in Morongo society—of food security, and of the autonomy promised by that security. Horses, cattle, and methods to control them had not really changed since the Spanish landed them on Hispaniola in 1493, but the men and women on southern California Indian reservations trained, rode, and herded in their own ways. Clearly, part of their identity as an autonomous people, within the political boundaries of the United States, had come from the horse and cattle culture.

Disputes emanated out of reservation boundaries that had not yet been surveyed and clearly marked. This lack of followthrough had the potential to incite angry disputes between southern California Indians and non-Natives who accidentally or purposely allowed their livestock to graze on reservation grass. In 1895, Francisco Estudillo (1893–1897) reported to the Commissioner that two men from the Cahuilla reservation went to prison for the offense of cattle theft, one for five years and the other sent up for eight years. Estudillo blamed the Office of Indian Affairs for the lack of surveyed and clearly marked boundary lines. Owing to this gap in legal protection for the Cahuilla, local law enforcement authorities gained jurisdiction in the case. "Before a jury it is almost a certain conviction for anyone accused of the offense of cattle stealing, especially so if he be an Indian." [8] Estudillo did not detail the facts of the case in his report, making it difficult to determine if the two Cahuilla men had in some way impounded trespassing cattle pending payment of a fine, or if they had other motives. In either case, the Cahuilla people linked the imprisonment of two of their family and tribal members to an undefined boundary. From their standpoint, the personal freedom of two men had been sacrificed by government negligence.[9]

Fenced boundaries kept out trespassing cattle to preserve the pasturage for Indian animals. Fences had also been used to deny Indian cattle access to water, critical to the survival of the people and their livestock on reservations. During the period 1891–1903, the Mission Tule River Agency included all reservations in the southern third of California. The agents reported few statistics and what they did report aggregated economic activities for the entirety of the agency, not yet differentiated by reservation. Nonetheless, the reports of Horatio N. Rust (1889–1892), Francisco Estudillo (1893–1896), and Lucius A. Wright (1897–1903) portrayed Native people who took advantage of the avenues of survival open to them. They made the best of poor conditions on the reservation. They also coped with the realities of administrative rules, paternalistic meddling, and outright racial prejudice at home and in the greater community. In every report submitted by the Mission-Tule River Mission agent, the issue of water hovers over every reservation: shortage of water, inadequate irrigation infrastructure, drought, and fights with settlers on the perimeters of reservations. In 1891, Rust declared most of the Morongo Reservation only good for dry farming.[10] In 1893, Estudillo described an industrious people who needed only trees and a better water supply to prosper.[11] In 1894, in describing a fractious Morongo community, Estudillo said that they are good farm hands and that they raised stock when and where practicable but that droughts compounded the suffering. "During the summer, they can get along from the fact that fruits furnish them with a living. The winter will be very severe upon these people. They cannot provide for themselves for the winter; it is impossible."[12]

Just two years later, Estudillo proclaimed the Morongo the best reservation in his care. The people had built their own stone irrigation ditch over the last two years, with but little help from the Office of Indian Affairs.[13] In 1899, though, drought returned and Lucius A. Wright observed that droughts are doubly hard on the poor Indians, who lose both their own crops and the chance to work for other farmers. They became destitute and needed subsistence aid.[14] These mostly dismal assessments revealed that the Indians had done their best to keep body and soul together while crops dried up and animals had to be slaughtered to reduce demand on forage. These assessments also revealed the inability of the Office of Indian Affairs to support Indian striving for self-sufficiency in the early years of the Mission Tule River Agency.

Agent Lucius A. Wright presented the stark reality of the Indian water situation in his 1902 "Report of Agent for Mission Tule River Agency." In addition to the number of acres, population, and distance from the agency, Wright characterized the land and water for each of thirty-two reservations. In almost all cases, he described "little water," "very little water," or "no water." Only Pala and Pauma in San Diego County had "good water." On four reservations in Riverside County (Agua Caliente, Cahuilla, Morongo, and Soboba), only Morongo received a rating of "fair land with water."[15] Thirty-three Agua Caliente (Palm Springs) Indians constantly fought with the surrounding whites over water that they had rightly and freely used before whites came.[16]

Raising any crops but dry-farmed grains required irrigation, placing arable land at a premium. Water shortages directly degraded the quality of reservation life. In 1905, Superintendent and Special Disbursing Agent Lucius A. Wright reported that Luiseños and Cahuilla on the Soboba reservation cultivated 150 acres in the attempt to support 144 people. The irrigation water for this small tract came from a small, spring-fed reservoir. To place this fact in perspective, a single family of homesteaders proved up title on 160 acres by working the land for five years. The Sobobas had to support 144 human beings on less than a homestead.[17] Overall, southern California Indians derived most of their income that year from wages, but the Palm Springs (Agua Caliente) Indians, all thirty-three of them, supported themselves almost entirely by outside wage work. In fact, Wright reported that "The Mission Indians obtain at least 75% of their own and their families' maintenance by working for white people in civilized pursuits." So many took up wage work off the reservation because much of the reservation lands are dry hills and mountains, and "only a small portion of the land is fit for cultivation."[18] But of that remaining 25 percent of annual income, the Natives of the region dry-farmed grains, nurtured fruit orchards, planted small gardens, and cowboys saddled up and rode out to tend the herds.

In the last third of the nineteenth century, while the few big cattle operations got bigger and industrialized in the Central Valley, southern California ranchers continued to find ranges for smaller herds and cowboys to work them. Many owners of the old land grant ranches, such as Rancho San Jacinto Viejo, sold or subdivided the land into smaller stock-raising farms and townships on which neighborhoods and towns appeared.[19] However, many cattlemen discovered pastures of last resort during the drought of the 1860s, in the mountain meadows in the San Bernardino and San Jacinto Mountain ranges.

James Houghton purchased 320 acres in the San Bernardino Mountains in 1870. On those acres, he established the Summit Valley Ranch, situated along the present-day state Highway 138, east of the Cajon Pass (and Interstate 15) and northeast of where the Cedar Springs Dam impounds the North Fork of the Mojave River. John Vole bought that ranch from Houghton in 1897. Over time, local people referred to the ranch as Los Flores, possibly alluding to the spring wildflower displays along the Mojave.[20] Cattle had grazed on the flowers and grasses of the mountain meadows as early as the late 1860s, and cattleman Augustus Knight, Sr. claimed that Indians ran off some of his herd. Knight pursued the claim with the Office of Indian Affairs and actually received an $8,000 reimbursement for his loss in 1896. Knight's complaint made no mention of which Indians ran off his cattle, or their motives or whether they stole to stave off hunger, to start a herd, or to trade. [21]

Cattle grazing in the San Bernardinos centered in the Bear Valley-Holcomb Valley area, north of Big Bear Lake. In 1906 Will Shay bought some land southeast of the lake in an area known as Moonridge, and in 1914, he partnered with Banning rancher and fruit grower Charles Omar Barker. Shay and Barker wintered their herd in the high desert of the Little San Bernardino Mountains in a northwest to southeast arc that took the cattle down along the Whitewater River.[22]

About five or six miles east of Baldwin Lake lay the Rose Mine holding pens. After a summer of feeding and fattening on the meadow vegetation, the cowboys got the cattle into those pens. Meat buyers from as far away as Los Angeles came in early September to bid on the best animals, weigh them, and settle accounts. Cowboys then drove those animals to the railroad at Victorville. By 1919, a real estate boom in the mountains foreclosed free-range grazing around Big Bear Lake.[23]

Cattle ranching in the San Jacintos also had its roots in the drought of the 1860s, and there too, the cattlemen found mountain valleys and settled in with their families. The proximity of the large Cahuilla Reservation south of the present-day towns of Anza and Mountain Center presented the possibility of a more cooperative engagement between Native people and, in truth, uninvited immigrants, all parties being willing.

Charles Thomas possessed a ranch and grist mill in Temecula in the 1860s and with the permission of the Cahuilla Indians, he built his ranch near the present-day Mountain Center, California, about twenty-four miles east of the city of San Jacinto and about three miles north of the Cahuilla Reservation. He reputedly paid the Cahuillas between twenty-two and two hundred head of cattle for the land. Some Cahuillas lived and worked on the ranch, so Thomas had ramadas constructed for them. He moved his wife and their nine children there in 1867. Thomas ran Durham "shorthorns" on the ranch, along with racehorses. Some forty years later (1907), Thomas sold his 1,700-acre spread to the very entrepreneurial cattle rancher Robert F. Garner. Then forty-five years old, Garner "at one time or another . . . owned the Los Flores Ranch in Summit Valley [San Bernardino Mountains], the Whitewater Ranch east of Banning and various other grazing lands in the San Bernardino and San Jacinto valleys." [24]

Garner built up the old Thomas Ranch from 1,700 acres to over 9,500 acres, carrying more than 1,500 head of cattle. He sold his mountain meadow-fed cattle in the fall, then restocked with new purchases in the spring. He preserved his range by rotating the herds on various pastures and by grazing fewer head than the carrying capacity of those pastures. Garner's cowboys included Cahuillas or men of Mexican-Indian blood. An old Cahuilla cowboy by the name of Santana led many of the drives from the San Jacinto Mountain ranch. Others included Dan Arnaiz, Gib Miller, and two cousins from Soboba, Adolfo Jauro and Joe John. Santa Rosa Reservation cowboys that worked for Garner included Ignacio Guanche, and John, Calistro, and Castro Tortes.[25]

Before R.F. Garner bought the Thomas Ranch on San Jacinto Mountain, he had his eye on the last of the big ranches in Riverside County: Rancho Temecula, Rancho Pauba, and Rancho Santa Rosa. However, he lost out in the bidding for those properties to Walter Vail.

Walter Vail was born to American parents in Nova Scotia, Canada in 1852, came out West at age twenty-one, and entered the cattle business on his homestead east of Tucson, Arizona. Starting with three hundred head of cattle, he built his land holdings and business into what he aptly named the Empire Ranch, fully eighteen thousand square miles in size.[26] In 1888, Vail and his finance partner C.W. Gates decided to sell into the California market. To that end, they leased the old Warner Ranch and shipped cattle by rail from Empire, east of Tucson to Warner's in order to fatten the cattle for sale. On one occasion Vail's cowboys actually drove a herd from Empire to Warner's, a distance of about four hundred miles over roughly the same route as Juan Bautista de Anza's parties had taken in the 1770s. From this base, they then purchased Santa Rosa Island in 1901. They bought thirty-eight thousand acres of Rancho Temecula and Rancho Pauba from a San Francisco bank in 1905, and the entire Rancho Santa Rosa and Little Temecula Ranch in 1906.[27] Ironically, Walter Vail died before he could savor the addition of the final piece of the empire that he had assembled in southern California.[28] Vail's sons assumed control and ran the ranches, operations, and pastures, including grazing in Imperial Valley until they sold off the Empire Ranch to consolidate in California. Mahlon Vail managed the big spreads on which present-day Temecula and Murrieta have been built, and Banning Vail took charge of the Imperial Valley properties. The Vails raised cattle on the Temecula and Pauba Ranches, and also planted crops to feed the cattle and even dairy cows. Early in the 1900s, they enjoyed plentiful water, pumped from the ground by windmills.[29]

Walter Vail held the lease on Warner Ranch (1888–1916) while the Cupeños were fighting their long and losing battle to stay on their traditional land, which included the hot springs. Vail submitted an affidavit to the judicial proceedings in the Superior Court of San Diego, in which he implied that the Cupeños, by their presence on the land, somehow prevented the full economic exploitation of the hot springs. His affidavit, one of several, likely did not solely influence the decisions of the courts but it added to the weight of popular (white) opinion seeking Cupeño removal, even though Indian cowboys worked for him on Warner Ranch.[30]

About twenty-five miles east-northeast of present-day Escondido and Interstate 15, four hundred Cupeños lived reasonably secure lives in their village of Cupa (Kupa). Owing to the hot mineral springs adjacent to the village, it also carried the Spanish name of Agua Caliente. The Cupeños shared relations by language and culture with both the Cahuillas to the north and the Kumeyaay to the south. They enjoyed good water that enabled them to live healthy lives on the land. Their village lay within the land granted by California Governor Pío Pico to John J. Warner in 1844. The Cupeños supplied the labor to plant crops, vineyards, and orchards for Warner. They worked Warner's cattle herds as *vaqueros* and continued to cowboy for Walter Vail, who had leased the ranch in 1888. And, they performed the same services for the succeeding owners of the ranch, including former Governor John G. Downey. The Cupeños also derived a significant income from visitors who paid to bathe in the hot springs and receive other services, such as food, among others. After Downey's death in 1894, his heirs sought the immediate removal of the Cupeños. Litigation ensued that went all the way to the U.S. Supreme Court. The Cupeños lost all appeals and suffered a forced removal in 1903 to Pala, some twenty-five miles to the northwest of their homeland. From a contented, thrifty, and peaceful life at Cupa, the devastated Cupeños entered into hunger and poverty at their new location at Pala, a place that held no ancient or sacred significance for them and which did not provide a ready income stream.[31]

Although histories of great ranches may not explicitly report on the ethnicities of their cowboys, by the 1890s, southern California Indians had built a record of excellent ranch work over several generations. From the missions to *ranchos* like San Jacinto Viejo, they had earned the reputation of top hands. In the American period, they readily found work on non-Native-owned ranches, such as the Garner Ranch on Mt. San Jacinto, and on the very largest ones, such as the Tejon Ranch in the southern San Joaquin Valley. Mission-Tule River agents like Lucius Wright reported on the high rate of wage work taken by the Indians of the agency in 1905. He provided no breakdown of that 75 percent of their income in wages but some of that likely came from work on non-Native ranches. A few Indian cowboys lived full time on big spreads like the Tejon Ranch. Cowboys there wanted the respect of their peers, as in any profession or occupation but for cowboys on the Tejon, the greatest compliment was to be described as "having been raised among the Indians."[32]

More commonly, families on the reservations needed transportation, which horses provided, and many families kept at least a few head of cattle. The aggregate statistics reported by the Mission-Tule River agents from 1891 to 1900 bear this out. Totals of horses and cattle, distributed among thirty-four reservations, average out to fifty-one horses and forty-nine head of cattle per reservation. Naturally, each location had its own unique combination of size, population, water, and forage resources, proximity to outside economic activity, and mindset about engaging in the work of livestock raising.[33] Nonetheless, horses and cattle were a common sight on many of the newly established reservations. The first California Indian cowboys had no prior experience with horses, except what they had observed of the Spanish soldiers and mission padres on horseback. But once their sons saw them mounted and working with cattle, they imitated what they saw in their child's play. Those "second-generation" Native boys grew up on horseback and, naturally then, assumed control of the horse and cattle herds. They learned to saddle and hobble a horse. From the platform of their horse, they learned to throw the *reata,* and from that, they threw, branded, and doctored calves and, in the old days at the missions or *ranchos*, even laid out the steers during *matanza* or slaughter.[34] Fathers passed these skills down to their sons, and over several generations, these cowboy ways took on the status of traditions and tribal identity.

The establishment of thirty-four reservations did not put an end to removals, and it certainly did not prevent water source diversions and boundary violations in the form of cattle trespass by neighboring non-Native ranchers. On the Morongo reservation east of Banning, Serrano and Cahuilla cattlemen and non-Natives shared the range and negotiated an uneasy peace through the Indian Office superintendents. In a series of communiqués from 1911 to 1913, R. F. Garner complained about Indian cattle on his side of the fence, agreed to pay a few dollars for more fence, built a gate for that fence, claimed he got the worst of the deal (and tried to renegotiate it), asked for more range, and identified Indian brands on his range. He generally lobbied Malki Superintendents William T. Sullivan (1910–1913) and Charles T. Coggeshall (1913–1916) to make sure that the Indians did their part to return his trespassing cattle and to keep theirs where they belonged. Garner's letters also indicate that he held realistic expectations for relations with his ranching neighbors, based on the nature of cattle and on his appreciation of the Indian cowboys who worked for him. For instance, he knew that some cattle from Agua Caliente (Palm Springs) had been driven up to Morongo and he therefore expected them to wander back toward their "home range," which lay eastward through his pastures. The records of these episodes did not include Morongo grievances against Garner but they likely had their own set of valid complaints that they may have made in person to Sullivan and Coggeshall.[35]

Harry E. Wadsworth (1916–1920) succeeded Harwood Hall (1912–1916) as Soboba Superintendent in September 1916. Baptista LaChappa complained to Wadsworth about a trespass on his pasture in the Santa Ysabel Reservation in north San Diego County. Wadsworth responded to the complaint by laying out the basic determinant of damages due to the owner of the violated pastures. If a cattleman had built a good fence and trespassing cattle broke through it to graze on his grass and drink his water, the owner of those trespassers must pay damages. "If the fence is not in good condition, however, no damages can be collected."[36] A good fence, described by the Office of Indian Affairs, consisted of three wires stapled onto wooden posts set eight feet apart, and, of course, upright. Wadsworth promised LaChappa that he would inspect the fence and assess any damages when next in his area, and if warranted, notify the owner to pay LaChappa. Failing that, he would refer the matter to the Commissioner's office.[37]

Up on the Santa Rosa reservation, the Cahuilla needed strong fencing and more to keep rancher Manuel Arnaiz's cattle off their pasturage. Arnaiz was born in San Francisco in 1856, and had grown up on the massive Miller and Lux Ranch in the upper San Joaquin Valley. In 1883, he moved to San Bernardino to marry and in search of land on which to build his own operation. He moved his family to a homestead in the Kenworthy area, north of the Cahuilla Reservation and less than a mile southwest of the Garner Ranch, along State Highway 74. That road is also known as the "Pines to Palms Highway." Arnaiz grazed cattle eastward of Kenworthy in the areas known as Upper Palm Canyon and Pinyon Flats.[38] Moving his herd in that direction put Arnaiz's cattle up against the Santa Rosa Indian Reservation. The Cahuillas there had their own herd and enough forage to feed their cattle but none to spare. In a letter to Superintendent Harry Wadsworth in October 1916, Arnaiz stated that there was no "lawful" fence and requested that the Indians be made to build one so that he would not have to pay damages.[39] As directed by the Commissioner's office, Wadsworth submitted an estimate for enough fencing materials and tools to build eight miles of fence around the Santa Rosa. He added forty man-days of labor to build the fence and twenty man-days of labor to haul the materials to the mountain. Cahuilla men needed the work. In explaining his motive, Wadsworth described the dilemma facing the Santa Rosa Cahuilla. "These Indians are anxious to help in the work, especially as it is for their own benefit, but they are poor, and are away from home practically all the time, seeking employment to support themselves and families. They have no means of supplying themselves with provisions while engaged in this [fencing] work."[40] Trespasses like Arnaiz's only added to Cahuilla anxiety, in that the violations occurred while the men were away and unable to protect their homes.

The Southern Pacific Railroad's claiming of alternating sections of land had created a checkerboard landscape in which Arnaiz had to run his cattle across Santa Rosa land to get them to the next section of range that he had leased from the Southern Pacific. Wadsworth flatly told the Commissioner that this configuration practically guaranteed friction between Arnaiz and the Cahuilla. He petitioned the Commissioner to explore the possibility of purchasing those problematic railroad sections, in order to make the reservation more compact and symmetrical (and less easily penetrated).[41] Three years later, Arnaiz's stock continued to trespass on Cahuilla land.[42]

California Indians quickly adopted new technologies that helped them better survive their new world, but fences proved to be a tool with mixed utility, one that hurt them as well as helped. Fences contained Indians in the reservation as much as they kept outsiders out.[43] Correspondence of the Soboba Superintendency reveals that individual tribal members occasionally used fences to enclose certain reservation lands for the exclusive use of their own grazing animals.[44] Although not the norm, such actions perhaps revealed an early and tacit acknowledgment that the traditional way of resource allocation would not work when fences and deeds and sheriffs denied Indian access to those resources. Over centuries, Indians had established territorial prerogatives, "recorded" in songs and physically marked by petroglyphs, stones, or significant landmarks.[45] Now, superintendents, inspectors, and attorneys became the arbiters of what was Indian range. The Southern Pacific's checker-boarded sections created friction between the Santa Rosa cattlemen and Manuel Arnaiz. No experienced cattleman realistically expected hungry cows and steers to make a right turn at a Santa Rosa fence instead of pushing through to the forage on the other side, especially in a time of drought. Superintendent Wadsworth persisted in lobbying the Indian Office to cancel the sections that the federal government granted to the Southern Pacific. In November 1919, Wadsworth reiterated this solution to the U.S. Indian Service supervising engineer in Los Angeles. This time, he advocated for the cancellation of the Southern Pacific sections based on affidavits that he believed established the prior use and occupancy of the land by the Cahuilla.[46]

Non-Native rancher Lester Reed obtained grazing permits on the Cahuilla Reservation in the early twentieth century and enjoyed good relations with the Cahuilla. "Some of the best beef I ever sold were fattened on meadows leased from the Indians, and after our cattle were taken out there was good feed for whatever cattle or horses they owned."[47] Lester's father, Quitman, migrated to southern California from Texas in 1867, eventually settling in the Sage-Aguanga area, just west of the Cahuilla Reservation. Lester was born in 1890, and grew up among Native and non-Native cattlemen, and some of both groups worked on his father's ranch as hired hands. Reed recalled that the Indians he knew owned good cattle, and many showed good Durham breeding from the Charlie Thomas Ranch in the San Jacinto Mountains.[48]

Reed remembered Gabriel Costo as a "good Indian cowboy on the Cahuilla," good with a big loop on his rawhide reata. A large man, Gabe always fashioned and placed special pads under his saddle to prevent soreness on his horse's back. In 1910, Gabe helped Lester and others drive a herd of 700 head of cattle from the Vail Ranch in Temecula to their range down in the Imperial Valley. Reed complained that instead of cowboys, the Vail people gave him "plowboys to do the work." Reed had Gabe Costo and one other cowboy. One took the lead and the other sat at the tail end of the herd. The plowboys just filled in on the flanks. By letting the cattle go at their own pace, they made the arduous drive that went through a portion of the Anza-Borrego Desert and only lost two bulls and one cow. The whole enterprise took thirteen days and nights to complete. Reed said that was just too many cattle for that sort of drive.[49]

In the second decade of the twentieth century (1911–1920), the federal government pushed hard for Native American self-sufficiency. The effort to assimilate American Indians, that is, to remake them into some version of Euro-American yeoman farmers, had not succeeded. Native traditions like fiesta did not fade away, and the social and cultural importance of those traditions persisted and possibly grew, as railroads, automotive vehicles, and settlements emerged around them. The new approach of the Office of Indian Affairs sought to make Indians self-sufficient as the precursor to the termination of government expenditures.

In 1913, President Woodrow Wilson appointed Californian Franklin K. Lane as Secretary of the Interior. In an early version of termination, Lane suggested that "The Indian Bureau should be a vanishing Bureau," once Indians competently managed their affairs just like white men.[50] New Commissioner

Cato Sells did not disagree; but for him, that mindset heightened the sense of urgency to increase funding for projects and programs intended to put Indians on the road to self-sufficiency. "In this connection, it should be remembered that the Indians, in a large number of cases, live far removed from railroad facilities, that they are handicapped by lack of adequate livestock and farming implements, and that they are living and working under conditions which would discourage even the most progressive white farmers."[51] To that end, Sells pledged the completion of the irrigation projects undertaken specifically for "the benefit of the Mission Indians and others in California," by the end of fiscal 1915.[52]

In the new world of the reservation situated within American society, and with uncertain means of subsistence, southern California Indian households, by necessity, became mixed economies. These economies consisted of at least five kinds of income: subsistence production in farming and ranching; wage work on- and off-reservation; made goods like basketry, wood cutting, and lacemaking; freighting; rent from grazing permits, and gifting and other means of redistributing wealth.[53]

Despite drought, the inadequacy of water and arable land, and off-reservation wage work, the Native people of the region continued to plant crops and raise stock, even if they could not entirely support themselves by doing so. They persisted because their connection to the land defined them, as it had done for their ancestors over many generations. They worked off-reservation out of need and some chose to remain in the outside world, but many returned. All Native peoples experience and cherish the same ancient connection to the land as southern California Indians. For instance, Diné (Navajo) people who worked for wages off-reservation in northern Arizona returned to fulfill kinship obligations. A son has an obligation to his mother, ensuring there is enough firewood for the winter.[54] In the reservation household, families pooled and redistributed resources, especially those derived from the land. For the Diné, the importance of that connection with the land outweighed its portion of household production.[55]

Similarly, Cahuilla or Serrano or Kumeyaay households in California mixed off-reservation work with subsistence crops like apricots and almonds, horses and cattle, crafts, and income from grazing permits. But the produce of their land enabled them to redistribute those resources in a reciprocal way, according to social customs. Lineages that host a celebration of the dead make gifts and feed their guests from local plants and minerals, their crops, and their animals. In the next year, they become recipients of gifts and food from the next hosting group. In the social custom of gift-giving, receiving a gift graciously carries the same importance as the giving. Subsistence resources played an important cultural role, regardless of the size of their contribution to the household economy.[56]

Beginning in 1911, the fortunes of all the Native groups in the administrative districts of the Malki and Soboba Superintendencies began to improve and saw dramatic increases in the mixed economic revenue streams of wage work, crop income, and stock sales. Table 6.1 (page 123) shows the combined Total Incomes for Malki and Soboba at just under $22,000 in 1911. That income then doubled for three straight years, reaching nearly $200,000 in 1915. Incomes declined in 1916–1917, at least partly attributable to what Commissioner Sells called "the greatest flood known in recent years," that destroyed irrigation projects on the Morongo, Soboba, Palm Springs, and Pala reservations, among others.[57] Incomes then rebounded with the American entry into the Great War. War mobilization generated demand for mass quantities of American farm and ranch products, bumping Malki-Soboba incomes again to nearly $200,000.

Wages and crops increased commensurately over the decade of 1911–1920: crop income averaged 34.5 percent of income while wages averaged 52.8 percent. Just as droughts doubly punished the Indian populations, abundant rains produced bumper crops on- and off-reservations that Indians picked, packed, dried, canned, and sold. Sales of livestock averaged only 7 percent of total income for 1914–1920 and significantly less in absolute dollars, than crops and wage work.[58] However, the importance of this particular part of southern California Indian life carried a value disproportionate to its income contributions.

Over the many generations of Spanish colonization, Mexican *ranchos*, and American settler colonialism, cattle ranching's significance to Natives of southern California evolved from a survival strategy to new-traditional.[59] Because stock raising is a complex business, the rancher does not measure this year's success or failure by a single measure, for instance, gross income from sales. Higher stock sales might be attributed to higher prices on the beef market or reflect a severe shortage of forage due to drought, hence a need to reduce the herd. Conversely, building a herd of animals takes time and patience, so lower stock sales in one year holds the promise of much higher sales in coming years—diseases, rainfall, and downed fences notwithstanding. Building a herd takes time because only cows and heifers can reproduce, and only if a bull has successfully bred them. In aggregate, Indian cattle in the Malki and Soboba Superintendencies increased to as many as 1,716 head in 1919 and averaged 1,303 head during the decade. However, the dispersal of those 1,300 head among thirty-two locations, each with unique feed, water, and breeding conditions, denied all locations the benefits of a large gene pool.[60] The average of forty-one head per reservation also attests to the meager carrying capacity of Indian rangelands.

Like farming, water inputs directly affect livestock yields. Unlike farm crops, heifers, cows, steers, and bulls serve different functions during their

Table 6.1 Combined Total Incomes in Dollars, of Malki and Soboba Superintendencies, 1911–1920

Year	Combined Total Incomes in dollars, of Malki and Soboba Superintendencies[a]	Crop Income in Dollars	Crop Income as % of Total Income	Wage Work in Dollars	Wage Work as % of Total Income	Stock Sold in Dollars	Stock Sold as % of Total Income
1911	21,858	7,000	32%	12,263	56%	NR*	
1912	45,861	18,608	41%	21,794	48%	NR	
1913	88,143	29,937	34%	44,993	51%	NR	
1914	174,618	62,078	36%	82,661	48%	16,650	10%
1915	199,609	67,251	34%	98,939	49%	16,289	8%
1916	133,120	27,175	20%	90,341	68%	11,973	9%
1917	137,440	36,915	27%	77,816	57%	10,890	8%
1918	197,792	67,349	34%	108,928	55%	14,530	7%
1919	190,605	75,488	40%	94,087	49%	12,150	6%
1920	110,684	52,250	47%	52,270	47%	4,630	4%

Source: Annual Report of the Commissioner of Indian Affairs, 1911–1920.
* Not Reported.
[a] ARCIA, 1911–1920.

lives and at varying rates of productivity in their purpose. They do this for a number of years, and then go on the market as merchandise. Heifers must mature until they can produce a calf, at which point they are a productive unit called a cow. Steers do not reproduce; but their singular "job" is to grow to about a thousand pounds and go to the stockyards. Some cows produce milk and when they stop making milk, they too go to market as beef. Bulls turn heifers into cows and have a productive life from age two until the ripe old age of five or six years. Then they too head for the stockyards.[61] The stockman's business does suffer during drought but they can provide water and bank extra feed for these crises, if they have surplus funds to do it.[62] They must make good choices in purchasing breeding stock that return well on the investments, and they have to be on the constant lookout for predators, whether two-legged, four-legged, or microbial. Then, having navigated successfully through those hazards, they find themselves at the mercy of large market forces, over which they have even less control.[63]

For Native men and boys, running cattle helped replace the traditional hunting role that requires acute attention to the land and the animals, respecting the animals, and sharing, so that many could feed their families. To succeed in his cattle operation and feed his family, the Native cattleman needed to master the complex nature of raising and breeding animals in an unpredictable ecosystem and under the influence of changeable markets. The ranching business demands intelligence, patient determination, an extraordinary work ethic, and some help from nature. Thus, over time, the factors listed above took a toll and forced some families out of the business. Those that survived usually ran larger herds.

Despite these challenges, cattle ranching occupied a special place in California Native American economies and cultures of the early twentieth century; it also held a similar place in the heart of Commissioner Cato Sells (1913–1921), a rancher himself. Sells authored an article entitled "Indians as Producers of Live Stock." In it, he formalizes the seven-point plan by which any American rancher could maximize their yield from cattle and other types. Sells directed superintendents to increase the carrying capacity of Indian grazing with efforts to improve the water supply and to build and maintain strong fences. When possible, Sells wanted them to provide winter protection and feed, eliminate predators, and eliminate wild and worthless horses, and "scrub" stock that consumed forage meant for high beef-producing cattle. Sells noted in his article that individual herds accounted for a much higher percentage of Indian stock than did tribal herds.[64]

Office of Indian Affairs programs, the Great War in Europe, and reservation communities themselves stimulated the burst of economic growth of 1911–1920 (See Table 6.2, page 126). Southern California Indians combined subsistence from the land, wage work, and their other economic resources, at first to survive and stay on the land, and then to improve their condition and live as they decided, free from outside interference.

The Indian Office established the position of Farming Agent in 1910 (some held the title of Expert Farmer) to help the Indians learn and apply the best and latest practices in farming and animal husbandry. In March and July 1910, the Civil Service Commission held examinations to find and hire qualified candidates, whose "theses" proved their "practical knowledge of the art."[65] The Office also hired thirty-seven stockmen in 1913 who specialized in that important industry but for smaller reservations or herds, the farming agent handled both farming and stock responsibilities. These agents helped Indian farmers set out orchards of peaches, apricots, and almonds, and to plant both subsistence and cash crops, and then assisted them in selling their produce. They advised on seed selection and supervised the upbreeding of herds.[66]

The U.S. Indian Service periodically sent bulletins to the farmers, sharing suggestions from fellow farmers around the country. Since Indians did not automatically welcome the farmers' input, Expert Farmer Marion E. Waite reported that he had to "lead off" or demonstrate new techniques first if he expected the Native farmers to give it a try. "They watch critically all your movements and if you can 'do' it then they may follow if it is to their advantage."[67] At times, farmers provided leadership for the economic well-being of their Indian clients. In June 1916, Farmer Adrian F. Maxwell advised Malki Superintendent James Jenkins that he intended to supervise a roundup on the Agua Caliente reservation. They planned to count all head of cattle and to "sort out the runts and matured ones for the market." Maxwell asked Jenkins to notify the butcher in case he wanted any of the animals. They also planned to round up horses and sell off all but what they needed for transport. Maxwell reiterated the urgent need to take action quickly in order to head off the starvation that loomed due to the scarcity of grass that summer.[68] Unlike the administratively burdened superintendent, Maxwell had inspected the range and knew what was coming if they did not act. His preemptive slaughter and sell-off kept the best animals alive, and saved the many by sacrificing the few.

In 1911, the Indian Service introduced government "financing" in the form of the Reimbursement program, under the administration of Commissioner Robert Valentine. The program enabled Indians to use reimbursable funds to purchase livestock, agricultural implements, hay balers, seeds, wagons, sewing machines, housing improvements, fence wire, and to dig wells. Occasionally, agencies purchased rations to sustain families until their investments began to show results and provide income.[69]

The program required that the "borrower" pay or reimburse in currency for most purposes, but for animals, Indian stockmen reimbursed in kind. When a tribal member decided to start a new herd or increase their existing one, they

Table 6.2 Rapid Expansion of Reservation Farm and Ranch Productivity during the Great War[a]

Year	Acreage Cultivated	Value of all Crops	Value of all Stock	Value of Native Wares	Native Wage Earners
1911	388,025	$1.95 MM	$900K	$847,556	3,200
1917	678,529	$5.29 MM	$4.58 MM	$1.72 MM	6,900

Source: Annual Report of the Commissioner of Indian Affairs, 1911–1917. [a] ARCIA 1911–1920.

applied for and received, in essence, the loan of a calf. The superintendent drew up a promissory note, consistent with getting a bank loan, which all parties then signed and notarized. The new owner raised that calf into a mature heifer and bred her with a bull. Soon after the birth of her calf, the owner handed the newborn to the agency and, by doing so, had paid his note in full. The agency then loaned that calf to another applicant to start or increase his or her own herd. This policy fit well with Indian identity in that by repaying the loan, that tribal member reciprocated to the government and provided a new animal to another tribal member. The borrower had truly paid forward that first calf by giving the opportunity of new or additional ownership to another member, thus continuing the reimbursable cycle.[70]

Commissioner Sells saw the potential of this policy and embraced it with increased funding year after year. From an initial appropriation in 1911 of $30,000, Sells asked for $100,000 in 1913 and then announced that the expenditure for 1914 would be $750,000, the "largest appropriation ever for the advancement of [Indian] industry and self-support." But then in 1915, he doubled the appropriation again to $1.5 million for reimbursable economic activity. The Office of Indian Affairs took a flexible stance in making terms with tribal members who made an earnest effort to repay the loans, often extending the term when climatic conditions ruined crops or killed stock. The reimbursable funds program also enjoyed wide support among southern California Indians and, in the future, helped cattlemen stay afloat in the midst of a drought during the Great Depression.[71]

In 1918 the war effort continued to trump most other considerations and Sells continued to tout the patriotic support of the Indian population as an affirmation of the policy strategies of the Office of Indian Affairs. Indians stepped into the breach of the labor shortage, not only in their continued work to grow their own crops and raise their own stock, but also in working off-reservation on farms and ranches.

Despite the predominance of wage work in Native household economies, subsistence derived from cattle and crops continued to satisfy the Indians' need to stay connected to the land and to receive nourishment of body and spirit from its gifts. They continued the tradition of resource redistribution when one tribal member donated a steer to be slaughtered for a fiesta or other significant social events. The mounted cowboy played a role in the continuity of the new-traditional horse and cattle culture. He mastered his horse, and together they branded, raised, and herded cattle, just as their ancestors had done at the missions and *ranchos*. According to a story in the *San Pedro Daily News*, the 1919 Hollywood movie *The Lone Star Ranger* used actual footage of Morongo Reservation cowboys moving their cattle on the range.[72]

Under the weight of the American government and its restrictive policies, southern California's Native peoples adopted new technologies like fences and seized new opportunities to improve their standard of living, usually off-reservation. Young Indian men brought home cash from their ranch or farm work, but some also carried freight, sold hay, and learned useful and marketable skills as watermen, masons, and carpenters. These new arrangements also adversely affected Indian societies. When young Native women sought domestic work in the homes of white families, they learned new ways, but at the same time absented themselves from the reproductive pool by delaying or even denying marriage within the traditional structure.

In the last few years of the period 1891–1920, Native Americans all around the United States benefited from the huge demand generated by the Great War in Europe. Locally, Kumeyaay, Luiseños, Cahuillas, and Serranos sold more produce and beef, grew more crops, and earned higher wages than ever before. In the process, they proved their own great capacities to pursue any economic opportunity, on- or off-reservation, for their own satisfaction and to bring those benefits home to their families and communities.

NOTES

1. Jordan, *North American Cattle-Ranching Frontiers*, 267–287.
2. Pulling, "A History of California's Range-Cattle Industry," 192.
3. Dary, *Cowboy Culture*, 310–311. When California state lawmakers shifted the burden of protecting crops to the cattlemen, especially in the semi-arid southern counties, they placed a burden on ranchers who lacked the resources to build a "lawful" fence, that is "five feet high and sufficiently close to turn stock." Without plentiful stone or wood, and before the invention and spread of barbed wire in 1874, cowboys had to ride the imaginary line of demarcation between their employer's range and the neighbor's, especially farmland. By patrolling this way, they turned back wandering or trespassing cattle. These lonesome "line riders" rarely saw another human being and bunked in a small line shack that at least offered shelter from a storm. Barbed wire not only kept the ranch's cattle in and trespassers out, it facilitated the segregation needed to improve the breed of the herd.
4. Pulling, "A History of California's Range Cattle Industry," 334–336

5. Frederick E. Hoxie, *A Final Promise: The Campaign to Assimilate the Indians, 1880–1920* (Lincoln, NE: University of Nebraska Press, 2001), 64–66.
6. *Annual Report of the Commissioner of Indian Affairs* (hereafter *ARCIA*) *1891*, five, 26–37.
7. "Report of Agent Horatio N. Rust," *ARCIA 1891*, 221–223.
8. "Report of Mission-Tule River Agency," August 31, 1895, *ARCIA 1895*, 132.
9. Tanis C. Thorne, "The Death of Superintendent Stanley and the Cahuilla Uprising of 1907–1912," *Journal of California and Great Basin Anthropology* 24, no. 2 (2004): 237–240.
10. *ARCIA, 1891*.
11. *ARCIA, 1893*.
12. "Report of Mission-Tule River Consolidated Agency," *ARCIA, 1894*, 118–124.
13. Ibid., 126–130.
14. Ibid., 171–172.
15. Ibid., 171–172.
16. "Report of Superintendent in Charge of Mission Indians," *ARCIA, 1905*, 191–192.
17. Ibid., 191–192.
18. Ibid., 193.
19. David Igler, *Industrial Cowboys: Miller & Lux and the Transformation of the Far West. 1850–1920* (Berkeley, CA: University of California Press, 2001).
20. Robinson, *The San Bernardinos*, 83–84.
21. Ibid., 85.
22. "C.O. Barker, Pioneer Citizen of Banning A Half Century, Answers The Last Summons," *Palm Springs* (CA) *Desert Sun* 8, no. 26 (February 1, 1935); Robinson, *The San Bernardinos*, 86–87.
23. Robinson, *The San Bernardinos*, 87–88.
24. John W. Robinson and Bruce D. Risher, *The San Jacintos: The Mountain Country from Banning to Borrego Valley* (Arcadia, CA: Big Santa Anita Historical Society, 1993), 41, 49–52.
25. Robinson and Risher, *The San Jacintos*, 60–62.
26. Brigandi, *Temecula*, 78.
27. Ibid., 79. The Warner Ranch, originally granted by Governor Pío Pico to John J. Warner in 1844, has for many years served as a resort built around the mineral hot springs that the Cupeño Indians still claim as a sacred site. Santa Rosa Island lies about twenty-six miles offshore of Santa Barbara. At about 53,000 acres in area, it is the second largest of the Channel Islands.
28. Ibid., 79.
29. Ibid., 80.
30. Phillips, *Chiefs and Challengers*, 281, 386n31.
31. "Their Birthplace. Aged Indians Testify Of Their Lives on Warner's Ranch," *San Diego* (CA) *Union and Bee* 38, no. 8981 (July 19, 1893); "Not Cattle Thieves: Warner's Ranch Indians Still Persecuted, Former Chief Sent To Jail On Flimsy Pretext," *Los Angeles Herald* 30, no. 167 (March 23, 1903); Carrico, *Strangers in a Stolen Land*, 149–162; Steven M. Karr, "The Warner's Ranch Removal: Cultural

Adaptation, Accommodation, and Continuity," *California History* 86, no. 4 (2009): 32–36; Phillips, *Chiefs and* Challengers, 78–82, 272–292.

32. Rojas, *The Vaquero*, 24–25.
33. *ARCIA, 1891–1900*.
34. Mora, *Californios*, 47–52.
35. R. F. Garner to William T. Sullivan and R. F. Garner to Charles T. Coggeshall, 1911–1913, Box 346, Malki Superintendency Miscellaneous Records, 1908–1920, Record Group (RG) 75, National Archives and Records Administration, hereafter NARA, Riverside, California; "Thinks Water Already Taken: Banning Paper [*Banning* (CA) *Herald*, quoted in article] Does Not Take Stock in Proposed Water Storage Scheme Which Is Being Exploited," *Riverside* (CA) *Daily Press* 32, no. 30 (December 18, 1917); Lester Reed, *Old Time Cattlemen and Other Pioneers of the Anza-Borrego Area*, 3rd ed. (Borrego Springs, CA: Anza-Borrego Natural History Association, 2004. First Published 1963), 8. Cattle get used to the diet provided them by the grasses in their specific home pasture; a new diet affects their digestive systems. As a result, they eat less and drop weight, which certainly reduces their sale value.
36. Harry E. Wadsworth to Baptista LaChappa, August 29, 1918, Box 6, Soboba Superintendency, General Correspondence 1892–1920, RG 75, NARA Riverside, California. See also "Indian Family War Has Been Averted," *Riverside* (CA) *Enterprise* 55, no. 6 (October 25, 1919); "Big California Indian Feud Averted By U.S. Men," *Los Angeles Herald* 44, no. 303 (October 21, 1919). Even between Native American cattlemen, friction sometimes developed over unpaid pasturage consumption.
37. Wadsworth to the Commissioner of India Affairs, October 24, 1916, Box 3, Soboba Superintendency, General Correspondence 1892–1920, RG 75, NARA Riverside, California.
38. Robinson and Risher, *The San Jacintos*, 56–59. The Miller and Lux Ranch is the focal point of David Igler's *Industrial Cowboys*, cited earlier in this chapter.
39. Manuel Arnaiz to Department of the Interior, U.S. Indian Service, San Jacinto, California, October 18, 1916, Box 3, Soboba Superintendency, General Correspondence 1892–1920, RG 75, NARA Riverside, California.
40. Wadsworth to Commissioner of Indian Affairs, October 24, 1916, Box 3, Soboba Superintendency, General Correspondence 1892–1920, RG 75, NARA Riverside, California.
41. Ibid.
42. Wadsworth to Arnaiz, October 18, 1919, Box 3, Soboba Superintendency, General Correspondence 1892–1920, RG 75, NARA Riverside, California.
43. Lyn Ellen Bennett and Scott Abbott, *The Perfect Fence: Untangling the Meanings of Barbed Wire* (College Station, TX: Texas A&M University Press, 2017), 187–189.
44. Thomas M. Games to Superintendent Harwood Hall, April 8, 1916, Box 2, Soboba Superintendency, General Correspondence 1892–1920, RG 75, NARA Riverside, California.
45. Bean, *Mukat's People*, 125–126.

46. Wadsworth to Herbert V. Clotts, November 7, 1919, Box 9, Soboba Superintendency, General Correspondence 1892–1920, RG 75, NARA Riverside, California.

47. Lester Reed, *Oldtimers of Southeastern California* (San Francisco, CA: American Indian Historical Society, 1967), 1.

48. Ibid., 1.

49. Ibid., 3–4. Brigandi, *Temecula*, 82.

50. Hoxie, *Final Promise*, 178–179.

51. *ARCIA, 1914*, 3.

52. Ibid., 3, 38.

53. Colleen O'Neill, *Working the Navajo Way: Labor and Culture in the Twentieth Century* (Lawrence, KS: University Press of Kansas, 2005), 3; see also William J. Bauer Jr., *We Were All Like Migrant Workers Here: Work, Community, and Memory on California's Round Valley Reservation, 1850–1941* (Chapel Hill, NC: University of North Carolina Press, 2009), and Immanuel Wallerstein, *World Systems Analysis: An Introduction* (Durham, NC: Duke University Press, 2004). The game of *peon* provides an example of other means of redistributing wealth and is played during the celebrations of the dead, misnamed by the Spanish as Fiesta.

54. O'Neill, *Working the Navajo Way*, 19–20.

55. Ibid., 28.

56. Ibid., 29. See also Lowell John Bean, *Mukat's People: The Cahuilla Indians of Southern California* (Los Angeles: University of California Press, 1972), 122–125.

57. *ARCIA 1916*, 44.

58. *ARCIA, 1914–1920*; stock sales amounted to over $16,000 in 1914 and 1915, and just under $15,000 in 1918 but lower in all other years.

59. Jordan, *North American Cattle Ranching Frontiers*, 241–243.

60. Russell H. Bennett, *The Compleat Rancher* (New York: Rinehart and Company, 1946), 217–225.

61. Ibid., 34–50.

62. Ibid., 123–124.

63. Ibid., 218–224.

64. *ARCIA, 1918*, 47–52, *ARCIA 1920*, 27–28.

65. "Education—Industries," November 7, 1910, Box 1583, General Service—Agricultural Training, Central Classified Files (CCF) 1907–1939, RG-75, National Archives Building (NAB), Washington, DC.

66. Ibid.

67. Bulletin No. 3, "Progress in Indian Farming," United States Indian Service, January 16, 1911, Box 1583, General Service—Agricultural Training, CCF 1907–1939, RG-75, NAB, Washington, DC.

68. Adrian F. Maxwell to James E. Jenkins, June 5, 1916, Box 346 Malki Superintendency, RG 75, NARA Riverside, California.

69. *ARCIA 1915*, 21.

70. *ARCIA 1914*, 18–20; *ARCIA 1915*, 7, 21–22.

71. Ibid.

72. "At The Empire Today," *San Pedro* (CA) *Daily News* 19, no. 172 (July 26, 1920).

Chapter 7

A New Economy Based on Cattle, 1921–1941

At the dawn of the twentieth century, southern California Indians had worked as *vaqueros* on mission *estancias*, then on the *ranchos* formed out of mission lands, and finally, they ran their own herds on those small portions of their ancient lands that the U.S. government recognized. The Serrano and Cahuilla Indians of the San Gorgonio Pass had worked on ranches of the San Gabriel mission at Yucaipa, and at Rancho San Gorgonio. They had also worked on ranches owned by Americans, including founding families of the region, like the Gilmans and Charles O. Barker. The vast rolling grasslands of the pass lay between two massive peaks that bound it, Mount San Gorgonio to the north and Mount San Jacinto to the south. On the reservations, persistent enforcement of boundaries kept out trespass cattle that might have fed on grass meant for Morongo reservation cattle. Survival and sovereignty go hand in hand. Each enables the other. Raising cattle provided some food security but also a measure of independence. Family members who cowboyed together enjoyed that process and found a sense of community with other families. Over generations, fathers, sons, mothers, and daughters added to longstanding family traditions centered on managing herds of cattle. Native mothers owned cattle too, and in the roundup, women sometimes tended the fires that kept the branding irons at just the right intensity. Daughters, too, rode horses and learned to throw a reata.

The Armistice of November 11, 1918, had mercifully put an end to the slaughter of the Great War in Europe. Accordingly, the prosperity of 1911–1920 receded in the following decade. Demand for American agricultural products declined, including beef. Severe drought further reduced reservation economic output and income, which prompted decisions to explore the options of off-reservation work and relocation. In the late 1920s and the 1930s, support for range management and rejuvenation also crystallized,

Figure 7.1 Roundup on the Morongo Reservation, Banning, CA. *Source*: Image Provided by Banning Library District.

affecting all California ranchers. Under the auspices of the U.S. Forest Service, the Indian Office gave support to relieve the depletion of southern California Indian ranges that had been feeding domesticated animals for a century and a half.

In the 1930s, New Deal policies reversed a century of blatant hostility, economic marginalization, and assimilation goals by lessening the pressures on Native peoples of the region to give up their social and cultural traditions. The highly activist administration of Franklin D. Roosevelt (1933–1945) offered emergency lifelines to help American Indians cope with the Great Depression and reversed policies that continued to take Indigenous American lands. Some of the policies aligned with Native modes of governance and social organizing, such as the advent of cattlemen's associations. These groups advanced agendas for herd management, cooperative marketing of cattle, work distributions, and the maintenance of good relations with reservation families who raised crops instead of livestock. The Associations also shaped a particular sense of community among cowboys within the larger reservation society. By the end of the decade, as another world war loomed, horse and cattle culture persisted among Cahuillas, Serranos, and others, but not solely as a form of subsistence in diverse reservation household economies. Indian cowboys continued the traditions of riding, roping, and branding that formed part of tribal identity: adapting to survive and a means through which to assert sovereignty.

In the early 1920s, Annual Reports of the Commissioner of Indian Affairs showed marked changes to Indian economies. The reports did not break out numbers of cattle and horses on each reservation. Rather, they aggregated all Mission Indian Agency livestock as a measure of wealth. In 1922, Commissioner Charles H. Burke's report set the total wealth of all Mission Indian Agency livestock at $182,000. This number dropped to $152,000 in 1923 and to $117,000 in 1924. Livestock value continued to decrease year by year until the value of all horses, cattle, sheep, hogs, and poultry bottomed out at $95,000 in 1927, an average of $3,000 when divided among thirty-two reservations. Larger reservations like the Morongo likely surpassed the average value of livestock, and small ones likely had much less. Post-war decline in demand caused some of the decrease but a 50 percent decline suggests that some southern California Indians simply decided to get out of the cattle business. The all-too-familiar scourge of drought struck the American Southwest again in 1921, one that Burke called "the most trying and disastrous in history." As usual, the drought forced all California cattlemen, including Indians, to reduce their herds. Drought robbed Native workers of even a meager income from their crops, and reduced off-reservation work on non-Native farms and ranches.[1]

By the 1920s, zeal for the dogma of assimilation had also waned. For Commissioner Burke, assimilation still held the key to the dissolution of the Office of Indian Affairs. But while Indians readily adapted to new economies like cattle operations, they held to their cultural traditions and religious practices. Scientists and politicians mistook a lack of interest in being part of a homogeneous American society for ineptitude. They blamed Indians themselves for the poverty, diseases, and suffering that came from being relegated to vestiges of their traditional homelands. Raising horses and cattle continued to hold a significant place in the mixed household economies of Luiseños, Kumeyaay, and other Indians, despite droughts, fluctuating cattle prices, and the lure of life and work off the reservation.[2]

An unsigned 1922 report, likely compiled by Farmer Arthur F. Johnson, listed cattle sales made by seven members of the Morongo reservation that year. Four men and three women sold thirteen cows, eight steers, and eight calves, altogether twenty-nine head, for a grand total of $952.00. The average of $24.41 per head harkens back to prices from the late Gold Rush years after massive imports of cattle had glutted the market. This example illustrates the steep post-war decline in demand, assuming that the Morongo stock-raisers had gotten true market value for their animals.[3]

Non-Native cattleman Lester Reed's family had immigrated from Texas in 1867. They settled in what became known as Reed Valley, on land to the southeast of Hemet, eastward of Sage, and northwest of the Cahuilla Reservation and Highway 371. Born into a ranching family in 1890, Lester and his brothers learned to ride and rope from early childhood. Cahuilla Indians worked for Lester's father Quitman and Lester knew many of them. Augustine Apapas often visited the Reeds and told of an old Cahuilla village at a place called Rock Spring. *Metates,* or grinding holes, in the boulders above the spring substantiated prior Cahuilla habitation. Lester and his brother Gib bought their first cattle from Augustine Apapas's grandson Ambrosio. They raised the twelve yearling steers and sold them as beef animals at three years old.[4]

Bonds formed among and between Native and non-Native cattlemen that came from shared dangers and long days in the saddle. One day, when working with his cattle, Quitman's horse fell, severely injuring the old Texan. Cahuilla cowboy Servante Lubo raced home to inform Mrs. Reed that "Boss" was down. She followed Servante with her buckboard to bring Quitman back home. Quitman lay unconscious for four days but recovered and went back to work. Lester said, "Servante never spoke to my father or about him in any name other than 'Boss.'" They developed the short-hand communication of old friends. If Servante wanted some of the nice vegetables from the Reed garden, he need only preface the request by saying that his baby was sick. Servante also broke horses for ranchers of the region and used a technique reminiscent of the days of Spanish rule. The sons of the old *ranchero Dons* had chased and roped wild horses at breakneck speed in the upper San Joaquin Valley, and their lives depended on staying mounted.

> The first time that he [Servante] rode a horse he had taken to break [,] he liked to take it into a sand-wash, tie a rope around the horse's body pretty tight, yet so that he could get his knees underneath the rope with knees bent, and then hold the rope with one hand. The horse that threw him had to be better than average.

Quitman Reed often paid Servante for this service with a horse or a cow.[5]

Reed also told of how the Cahuilla cowboy, Pat Cassero, worked for his father before Lester was born in 1890 and that Lester also worked cattle with Cassero as a young man. Reed said that "Pat Cassero was one of the very best I have ever known with the long rawhide riata [sic] as a working cowboy." He also knew that Cassero worked for a rancher in Coyote Canyon on the Cahuilla reservation, when past the age of eighty.[6]

Despite post-war depression, drought, and the lure of off-reservation wage work, Indians on Riverside and San Diego County reservations continued to raise and herd as many cattle as their ranges could carry. The 1925 Census of Agriculture affirms this maximum effort. On the Morongo Reservation—nearly 27,000 acres in size at that time—they planted but

640 acres in crops. However, they pastured 288 head of cattle, from bulls to calves, and 183 horses and mules. The Indian Service agent counted 162 men, women, and children on the reservation. At Agua Caliente (Palm Springs), the 46 tribal members planted crops on only 29 acres out of their total of over 31,000. Like the people of Morongo, they herded 153 head of cattle and 48 horses. By comparison, 74 Soboba members lived on 4,179 acres, harvested crops from 50 acres, and had 60 acres worth of crops fail. But like at Morongo and Palm Springs, they ran a high number of horses and cattle in proportion to their populations, at 89 and 84, respectively. The 525 total cattle on all three reservations represented 1.86 head of cattle per capita, for each of the 282 men, women, and children, a rate four times the national average. This statistic indicates that Native cattlemen continued to maximize the cattle on their marginal ranges. In a cycle of drought, their cattle represented food security and perhaps higher income on stock sales if demand exceeded supply once other ranchers drastically reduced their herds.[7]

During the 1920s, Lester Reed and his brothers continued to raise cattle. They also supplied bucking horses and steers for roping and "bulldogging" at the Hemet rodeo and for the Cahuilla Fiestas.[8] Unfortunately, the Reeds went broke in 1929 at the outset of the Great Depression, forcing Lester to go to work on the Vail Ranch at Pauba, adjacent to Temecula.[9] When Reed reported to foreman Jack Roripaugh and ranch owner Mahlon Vail at Pauba, he rode the last surviving horse of the stock that his parents had brought from Comanche County, Texas in 1867. "She was all I had saved out of the wreck when going broke in the cattle business."[10]

In the 1930s, Native cattlemen faced problems that also threatened the viability of their businesses. The depletion of their rangelands reduced or even threatened their ability to produce quality beef cattle. Second, selling their cattle individually and locally to traveling buyers guaranteed below-market prices. Each problem required changes to their ways of doing business.

By 1930, the California cattle economy had reached a turning point. Economic depression heightened awareness that California ranges did not possess the fuel to maximize the productivity of livestock, at a time when southern California Indians truly needed food security. In April, the Secretary of the Interior directed the forestry branch of the Indian Service to address the depletion of Indian rangelands. Recognizing that the range resource fueled food and income, the forestry branch first determined to examine the range on each reservation, then develop a plan that allowed some portion of the ranges to recover without crippling production. By making extensive surveys of all ranges, "it will be possible to relieve range depletion, gradually restore the native grasses, and check the erosion that has become, in recent years, increasingly destructive on Indian reservations in the Southwest."[11]

In order to reinvigorate grazing lands, forestry scientists began research to identify the contents of virgin rangeland and the process of degradation under human and animal consumption, that is, farming and ranching. By the time of these studies, more than five hundred non-Native plants had been introduced into California and had thrived uncultivated. The California Experiment Station joined with the U.S. Forest Service to understand the forage resource completely. In the spring of 1931, forestry personnel submitted reports on forty widely separated reservations throughout the United States. They provided enough information to generate regulations to prevent over-grazing, the first step in conserving the resource.[12] With funding drying up due to the deepening economic depression, southern California Indian cattlemen faced the hard choice of either finding ways to let pastures recover or making significant herd reductions.[13]

The Annual Report of the Commissioner of Indian Affairs for 1932 showed that 296 Indian people had enrolled on the Morongo reservation, an 83 percent increase from the 162 people counted in the Census of 1925. A 1928 law that required all Indians to officially enroll in their tribal register may explain some of the surge. However, the worst economic disaster in American history also reduced off-reservation work for Indians, especially when destitute white Californians or migrants from the drought-ravaged "Dust Bowl" states crowded into California's farms and orchards.[14]

The Civilian Conservation Corps-Indian Division provided wages for Native men during the 1930s and coupled the goals of improving infrastructure with money to buy groceries. Originally set up in 1933 as Indian Emergency Conservation Work, funding actually continued until 1942. Within the Mission Indian Agency, Native men improved roads, built culverts, created fire breaks, set about reducing rodent populations, and even set up telephone lines. In 1933, they also cleared ninety-nine springs, built one small dam, cut over six thousand fence posts, and installed over thirty-six miles of fencing. In these last tasks, their work directly improved the viability of their cattle economies, as a subsistence connection with the land, and to secure sovereignty over their pastures and water sources. In his December 1933 message to the people, Superintendent John W. Dady lauded the efforts of four Indian foremen, thirty Indian sub-foremen, and the approximately six hundred Indian workingmen.[15]

Although people on the Morongo reservation preferred to stay among family, finding wage work of any sort off the reservation had to take precedence. If one had the means of getting to a distant job site, it increased the odds that the family had enough to eat. It also reduced the number of jobless on the reservation. Whether Superintendent Dady had any of this in mind or not, in the August 1934 issue of the locally printed newsletter the *Mission Indian*, he announced that "Mr. and Mrs. Henry Pablo have purchased a Ford Sedan" and that "Mr. and Mrs. John Morongo have a new Chevrolet Coupe." Working for wages meant regular working hours and days off, distinct advantages compared to the full-time occupation of raising livestock on the reservation. Raising cattle entails strenuous and at times dangerous work, in addition to the risks posed to the rancher's capital by droughts and external market forces.[16]

Drought beleaguered southern California Indians once again in 1934–1935, this time forcing the government to take drastic action. In April 1935, Superintendent Dady reported to Commissioner of Indian Affairs John Collier that the State of California Emergency Relief Administration had purchased ninety-one head of cattle from Indians in Riverside County, and then turned them back to the Indians for slaughter and distribution of the meat among those same people. Farmer Joseph K. Hall of the Morongo Sub-Agency reported to Dady that forty-seven hides had also been sold to the government at $0.50 per hide. Farmer Arthur F. Johnson of the Pala Sub-Agency reported the slaughter of thirty-four head of at-risk cattle in San Diego County. Dady notified the State Emergency Relief Administration in December 1934 of the shipment of replacement cattle from Denver, Colorado, decided upon after early season rainfall had begun to relieve the drought.[17]

Native Americans adopted any New Deal program that helped them to make a living, on or off the reservation, but raising cattle and horses allowed individual family members to work together in the family business. They worked roundups and moved herds to the higher pastures as spring turned to summer and the lower ranges dried up. Ranching families cooperated and normally ran their cattle together. The spring roundup was a community event. Men brought in the cattle, and women not only brought up food and coffee but also tended the coals to keep the branding irons at just the right temperature. Morongo elder Tyron Linton recalled roundup events. "Oh yeah, at noon some people would bring lunch up and were there most of the rest of the day. My aunt, that's Frances Bosley, was the one that used to handle the brands, coming out of the fire because it had to be somebody who could tell when the brand was hot and not too hot."[18]

Some Morongo women also owned cattle. In 1938, Frances Bosley applied for her own cattle brand to the California Department of Food and Agriculture, among eight other members on the Morongo reservation. Mrs. Doris Sanchez's elderly aunts owned cattle and Morongo cowboys took care of them. They branded calves and did any doctoring that the animals needed. The aunts brought up lunch and dinner for the cowboys as a way to reciprocate.[19]

A successful family cattle business rewarded the hard work with some measure of financial independence. It also reaffirmed family traditions and tribal identity. During the Great Depression, southern California Indians battled the elements, such as drought, high winds, and floods that washed out crops and damaged homes. They faced the tough choices of raising as many head of cattle as their ranges could carry without depleting the range. Therefore, they could not afford to sell their cattle at below-market prices. Cattle buyers who traveled out to the country went in search of bargains, not to pay top dollar. Native American hesitance to leave the reservation played into that plan when buyers also transported the purchased cattle from reservation to market. Just as in better range management, Morongo Indian cattlemen and others had to change their ways of doing business to maximize their return on investment. The answer lay in cooperative marketing but they had to overcome internal obstacles. Decades of meddling and exploitation by strangers, and even their own agents from the Office of Indian Affairs, had engendered Native suspicion of outside entities.[20]

However, in 1934–1935, Farming Agent J. K. Hall began the process of placing sixty head of reimbursable cattle in the hands of "Indians of the district." [Morongo Sub-Agency] He reiterated to Superintendent Dady his intention to introduce Morongo cattlemen to the wider marketplace. To that end, he organized a visit by a group of those cattlemen to the Union Stockyards in Los Angeles in April 1936. While there, they learned that buyers had to make the highest bid against other buyers to acquire Morongo cattle, that it is "a cash market every day in the year," and that the central market is "an outlet for all classes of livestock."[21]

With Hall's help, the Morongo cattlemen "made the first cooperative shipment of [their] Indian cattle to a central market." In 1937 they sold their cattle for double the prices that they had gotten from traveling buyers on the reservation. The import of this move cannot be underestimated. Not only did such a profitable sale get their attention, it inspired a more communal spirit in addressing better range management practices. Hall believed that the sale opened the door to the formation of a cattlemen's association in 1938. Range management, in the broader terms of the Indian Office, meant conserving the forage by keeping the number of head of cattle below the range's ability to support or "carry" all of them. In a cooperative organization, it means apportioning range feed so that the cattlemen needed to work out an equitable sharing of available range forage among a diverse group of cattle owners with diverse objectives for their cattle. They each owned a mix of numbers of animals across different ages and types (heifers, cows, steers, etc.). For instance, if an owner had just two or three head that were approaching maturity, their objective would be to "finish" those animals, that is, to fatten them for market. Another owner with dozens of animals has decisions to make about prioritizing or culling his herd, especially in a time of drought. Pursuant to their establishing the association, the Morongo tribal council voted to build a modern corral "with cattle squeeze and loading facilities," and to buy registered bulls. To maximize their new assets, they developed a twenty-acre field in which they grew alfalfa to feed the bulls, and obtained a team of draft horses to work the ground.[22]

In the spring of 1939, "The Morongo Livestock Association . . . assessed the membership to defray the cost of a full-time herder, in order to provide better distribution of livestock on the range and to protect the stock from cattle thieves." By definition, the tribal herder's job required him to move and distribute cattle to optimize range management—that is, to decide where the cattle should go. The job also required him to decide where the cattle must not go—near crops, gardens, and orchards. The first imperative helped to keep the peace among cattlemen and the second one helped keep the peace between members who raised livestock and those who raised crops. The monthly newsletter *Mission Indian* added that Indian Emergency Conservation Workers had constructed fencing to keep cattle away from the cultivated areas.

In general practice, the Livestock Association operated more on an ad hoc basis than as a formal institution. Former Morongo Chairman Robert Martin explained that when issues arose that needed group action, the cowboys often gathered on horseback, talked out the options, decided on what had to be done, and then went back about their business.[23]

The measures taken by the Morongo Tribal Council and the Livestock Association improved the cattle business and, by extension, life on that reservation. Although it is doubtful that by the hiring of the tribal herder, no cow or steer ever got into a private garden again, the proactive nature of the new policy communicated clearly that cattlemen respected the rights of the farmers, gardeners, and orchardists.

The experiences of the Yokut people living on the Tule River reservation offer a cautionary tale about the potential risks that cattlemen's (or Stockmen's) associations posed to the cohesion of Native American societies. Tule River members had run horses and cattle since the early years of the reservation in the 1850s, and in 1922, they held in aggregate, one thousand horses, cattle, sheep, and hogs. By the 1930s, a small minority of Tule River Indians held the majority of the livestock, and those few resisted the potential loss of their individual property in any sort of tribal herd or sharing of the range. Those members who did not own cattle may have worked off-reservation or subsisted on crops in a semi-arid climate with little level land. Some may also have worked for the cattle owners setting up potential conflicts over private benefit derived from tribal assets.[24]

A forest ranger assessed the carrying capacity of the reservation at 1,200 cattle and 1,500 sheep but in 1936, the Tule River stockmen had only 800 cattle and 150 sheep on the range. Since the Office of Indian Affairs personnel favored the establishment of a cattlemen's association, they unilaterally imposed conservation measures and recommended the distribution of some 500 cattle under the Reimbursement Program. In that program, recipients of new heifer calves bred them to a bull and reimbursed the Indian Service "loan" by turning the first calf over to another member who wished to start or increase their herd. Members of the community voted 24–17 to negotiate a tribal Constitution according to the Indian Reorganization Act but the tribal chairman and council held powerful sway over many members. The few large cattle owners held firm in opposition to any communal arrangement. With such deep divisions, the cattlemen's association did not last, and the many members who might have enjoyed some benefit as a small stakeholder in a larger enterprise lost that opportunity to the political and financial power of the few. The meddling of an over-zealous Indian Service also played a role in the ultimate end of a cattlemen's association at Tule River.[25]

The controversy experienced by the Tule River reservation people and their attempt to establish a more equitable cattle business did not predict the same results for the people of the Morongo reservation. A wider participation in cattle raising at Morongo averted conflict brought on by a small and powerful minority against the many.

In 1936, 297 men, women, and children lived on the Morongo reservation in forty-seven families. The 1937 Industry and Extension Report (for the year 1936) counted twenty-nine Morongo owners of beef cattle and five owners of dairy cattle. Assuming that each family had one owner for the records, thirty-four of forty-seven families, or seventy-two percent of families, owned, raised, or earned income from cattle. The Morongo's 32,000 acres supported many more cattle than the smaller reservations and enabled such widespread involvement in the industry. On the Morongo, the cattle business represented a major portion of subsistence and had begun to form a community among all who worked in it and all who depended on it, especially in a year like 1936.

The apricot crop basically failed that year caused by a mild winter. Stone fruits like cherries, peaches, plums, and apricots must experience extended cold and go dormant. In a warm winter, wet or not, the blossoms can appear too early and be blown off by high and hot winds, or ruined by a late spring snowfall. At Morongo in 1936, the trees did not even defoliate, most of the blossoms fell off, and those that bees did pollinate produced weak fruits that dropped before ripening. Dried apricots on Morongo brought in significant income in most years but not in 1936. The almond crop performed much better and, because of higher prices than in 1935, filled some of the void left by apricots.[26] Cattle prices had also surpassed those of the prior year and, as had been the case for more than a century and a half, provided food security for southern California Indians.

The idea of a cattlemen's association had been proposed and ten inches of rain had fallen in December 1936, contributing to a bright outlook for 1937.

With good pasturage to be had, cows and heifers would come through winter into spring well-fed and strong, and birth strong and healthy calves. Better than average rains foretold abundant crops on the Morongo and jobs off the reservations as well.[27]

Native adaptability began to emerge on a different economic path for the Cahuillas at Palm Springs (Agua Caliente). The Agua Caliente Cahuillas had lived for thousands of years in equilibrium with their Colorado desert ecosystem, until newcomers by the thousands poured into their domain. In 1936, they had no irrigated farm or grazing lands but they did have "environmental proximity to a highly publicized and fast-growing fashionable playground and resort." Seizing their best economic opportunity, they agreed that year to lease out forty acres of tribal land for the construction of an airport to fly in the tourists.[28]

The construction of an airport and hotels on Agua Caliente lands foretold a new and very different sort of prosperity for the Cahuilla people there, but Indian horse and cattle culture persisted. Alvino Siva was born in Palm Springs in 1923 and was only thirteen years old in 1936. By that age, Siva had already been roping for five years. He ran cattle throughout his life, and his extended family ran cattle on the Los Coyotes Reservation during the 1920s and 1930s. Los Coyotes is situated in northern San Diego County, just eastward of Warner's Ranch. The Cahuilla there moved their herds with the seasons—to the mountains for summer grazing and then in winter, down to the desert pastures of Coyote Canyon on the eastern side of their reservation. Siva recalled that many small subsistence herds were the rule on San Diego reservations in those inter-war years. He also noted that "when men left for World War II in the 1940s, several of the herds were dispersed . . . and after the war many of the families never restarted their cattle herds." He also "lived his life learning and performing the Cahuilla Indian ceremonial bird songs." Like his sister Katherine Siva Saubel and his cousin Ernest Siva on the Morongo Reservation, Alvino Siva honored his Native culture, and shared a lifetime of knowledge and wisdom with younger tribal members. He loved the old cowboy ways, and knew old-time cowboys who braided reatas the same way that the mission Indian *vaqueros* had done. He also served his larger country for twenty years in the U.S. Army during World War II and in Korea.[29]

Not all California Indian people raised and herded cattle on the reservations. The Kumeyaay Ponchetti family started out in the cattle business on the Mesa Grande reservation. A man on the reservation named Louis Cassou received three head of reimbursable cattle in 1915, on behalf of the family matriarch Barbara Ponchetta [sic].[30] When Mrs. Ponchetti's boys were still young, Mexican *vaqueros* visited their ranch, perhaps to work for Mrs. Ponchetti. While there, they taught the boys how to make the braided leather ropes known as *reatas*. Barbara also taught her boys how to doctor their horses, using medicines derived from plants and minerals in their environment. She learned this vital knowledge and ability from a Kumeyaay doctor. Veterinarians did not live close by. On a remote and mostly mountainous reservation, Indian cattlemen and cattlewomen had to care for and heal their animals. When her three sons came of age, Mrs. Ponchetti divided the herd and gave each of her sons sixty head of cattle, proving that she had indeed been running a successful operation. With that seed cattle, each son established their own ranch.[31]

Son Charlie and his wife Bernyce first started a ranch on Mesa Grande and named it *Hopyall*, which in English translates to "The Place of the Big Rocks." The couple later decided to venture outside the reservation and leased the J-9 Ranch from a non-Native rancher named Ralph Jasper, which they renamed "Ranchita." The ranch lies south of the Los Coyotes Reservation and northeast of Mesa Grande near Highway S22. If success can be measured by following a road less traveled to pursue a lifelong dream, then the Ponchettis did indeed achieve success, and all the hard work involved in running their own ranch had been a labor of love and had paid off big.[32]

With the fall of France to Hitler in June 1940, the threat to the United States and other democracies in the Western Hemisphere finally became clear. President Franklin D. Roosevelt and the U.S. Congress passed multiple bills to rapidly mobilize the military, the American people, and the national economy. When the government drafted more than a million men into active service, they reduced the civilian workforce significantly and stimulated the economy with the new spending. Defense contracts to buy 50,000 airplanes per year and build a two-ocean navy demanded skilled labor in high-paying jobs to produce all manner of vehicles, weapons, ammunition, uniforms, and supplies, among others.[33]

These pre-war preparations looked modest in hindsight compared to the total mobilization that came after the United States entered the war. However, they reverberated throughout the national economy and increased demand that brought better beef prices for southern California Indian cattle. Stories in the 1941 issues of the *Mission Indian* newsletter offer a window into this fundamental shift.

In the January issue of *Mission Indian*, "Cattle prices advanced during the first week of the new year and are averaging substantially higher than a year ago." It certainly did not hurt that December 1940 had been a wet month. Range Investigator Hugh Harvey and two botanists spent two days on the Morongo Reservation, with the intent of increasing range feed, fencing out trespass cattle, and developing added watering spots. One botanist sought to identify poisonous plants, for the general knowledge of all concerned.[34]

Walter Linton, president of the Cattle Association, reported in February that a dearth of jackrabbits on the range put calves at risk for coyote attacks. One did occur, although the bite did not prove to be fatal, in large part because the tribal herder witnessed the attack and rescued the calf. The Cattle Association also announced their intent to trade their eight four-year-old bulls to any other ranch, Native or non-Native. After three years, the gene pool needed refreshing. *Mission Indian's* editor also noted that Californians consumed 151 pounds of beef per capita in 1940, a rate 20 percent above the national average.[35]

"Fed" steers drew the highest price since 1937, at $11.85 per hundredweight. Steers easily exceeded one thousand pounds, so even a smaller steer conservatively yielded $120 per animal. Three or four animals sold on this basis pushed yearly income for the Indian cattle ranching family into the $360–$480 range for beef cattle alone. The strong market also encouraged families to sell their undesirable cows and steers. Cattle-raising families and the Farming Agents still waited for the Range Management Survey report. They hoped for an upgrade in range feed quantity and quality per pasture that would translate into sustaining cows through the winter at healthy weights, and consequently, raise the percentage of healthy calf births to 80 percent or above.[36]

The May 1941 newsletter told how "permanent pasture mix" test plots on a ranch near the Soboba Reservation had produced impressive weight gains. One group of yearling heifers weighed in at 375 pounds on average on June 1, and weighed out on September 25 at 750 pounds. However, the article mentioned no plans to test these findings on the reservations. The Morongo cattlemen's association met in the Sub-Agency office there and decided to hold their spring roundup on May 3–4. Each person received an assigned job for the event and the Farmer ordered Blackleg vaccine.[37]

Results of the Morongo roundup appeared in the June issue of *Mission Indian* and revealed an exciting statistic: 191 cows gave birth to 187 calves, an astounding 97.9 percent calf crop. The people attributed this achievement to two factors: the herder "being with the herd constantly and culling unproductive cows."[38]

The December issue of the newsletter topped off a very good year for the Morongo cattle business. Thirty-one members sold sixty head of steers, thirty-one head of cows, five bulls, thirty-one calves, and seventy hogs. All told, those tribal members netted over $6,000. If the Morongo cattlemen had interest, the newsletter announced the Great Western Livestock Show, scheduled for December 2–7, at the Union Stockyards in Los Angeles.[39]

Five years prior, Serrano and Cahuilla stock-raisers on the Morongo Reservation sold their cattle at bargain prices to traveling buyers. They did not care to travel to Los Angeles but despite their misgivings about new ways to do business, they traveled to the stockyards in Los Angeles and almost immediately started selling their cattle for the best market prices. They had moved

Figure 7.2 Roundup on the Morongo Reservation, Banning, CA. *Source*: Image provided by Banning Library District.

out of a bare subsistence mode to a highly efficient tribal operation, with better bulls, more productive cows, and an increased calving efficiency that hit its peak, as seen in the 1941 roundup. They formed a cattlemen's association that hired a professional herder to improve range management, guard the calves from predators, and keep trespassers out. Once again, the ability to adopt ideas and processes that provided real benefit resulted in progress for the Native peoples in southern California, strengthened their sovereignty, and re-affirmed their identities as Indian cowboys and cattlemen.

NOTES

1. *Annual Report of the Commissioner of Indian Affairs 1921–1927*, hereafter *ARCIA*. Peter Iverson, *When Indians Became Cowboys*, 2, 116–150.

2. Cathleen D. Cahill, *Federal Fathers and Mothers: A Social History of the United States Indian Service, 1869–1933* (Chapel Hill, NC: University of North Carolina Press, 2011), 236–266.

3. "Cattle sold on the Morongo Reservation during week ending August 5th., 1922," Box 65 Mission Indian Agency, Central Classified Files, 1920–1953, Record Group (RG)-75, National Archives Building (NAB), Washington, DC; Arthur Ferdinand Johnson, Personnel Information Sheet, National Personnel Records Center, St.

Louis, Missouri. Johnson served at the Morongo Sub-Agency of the Mission Indian Agency from 1921–1930, facilitating and supervising the planting, cultivation, and harvesting of fruit, grain, and feed crops, as well as the stock raising on the Morongo and six other reservations.

4. Reed, *Oldtimers of Southeastern California*, 2.
5. Ibid., 7–8; Davis, *Seventy-Five Years in California*, 27–29.
6. Reed, *Oldtimers of Southeastern California*, 4.
7. "United States Census of Agriculture, 1925" Morongo, Palm Springs, and Soboba Reservations, Box 65 Central Classified Files, 1920–1953, RG 75, National Records and Archives Administration (hereafter NARA) Riverside, California; Pulling, "A History of California's Range-Cattle Industry," 107–108.
8. Reed, *Oldtimers of Southeastern California*, 16–17. Bulldogging is a rodeo event in which the competing cowboy jumps off a running horse to tackle a running steer, and by twisting the steer's horns and neck, he throws the animal to the ground. He wins the event by throwing the steer in the shortest time compared to all the competitors.
9. Brigandi, *Temecula*, 81.
10. Lester Reed, "Cowboy on the Pauba," *High Country* 57 (Winter 1981): 32.
11. *ARCIA, 1930*, 17–18; Burcham, *California Range Land*, 185–191.
12. *ARCIA, 1931*, 24.
13. Burcham, *California Range Land*, 214–223.
14. *ARCIA, 1932*, 26, 36; "United States Census of Agriculture, 1925" Morongo, Palm Springs, and Soboba Reservations, Box 65 Central Classified Files, 1920–1953, Record Group (hereafter RG) 75, National Records and Archives Administration (hereafter NARA) Riverside, CA; see also Walter Stein, *California and the Dust Bowl Migration* (Westport, CT: Greenwood Press, 1973).
15. *The Mission Indian* 2, no. 6 (December 1933), E98 S7 M58 1933, Autry Museum, Los Angeles, California; see also Thomas Biolsi, *Organizing the Lakota: The Political Economy of the New Deal on the Pine Ridge and Rosebud Reservations* (Tucson, AZ: University of Arizona Press, 1992), 113–115.
16. *The Mission Indian* 3, no. 1 (August 1934), E98 S7 M58 1933, Autry Museum, Los Angeles, California; Harlan Lanas Hoffman, "In the Shadow of the Mountain: The Cahuilla, Serrano, and Cupeño People of the Morongo Indian Reservation, 1885–1934," PhD Dissertation (Riverside, CA: University of California Riverside, 2006), 133–135.
17. Joseph K. Hall to Dady, April 11, 1935; Arthur F. Johnson to Dady, April 16, 1935; Dady to Collier, April 18, 1935; Dady to State Emergency Relief Administration, December 3, 1935; Box 68 "Cattle," Mission Indian Agency, Central Classified Files 1920–1953, RG-75, NARA Riverside, California.
18. Interview of Roderick Tyron Linton with David Shanta, November 6, 2015, Morongo Indian Reservation, Banning, California; hereafter cited as "Linton Interview."
19. "Stock Shipment," *San Bernardino (CA) Sun* 44 (August 7, 1938); Interview of Mrs. Doris Sanchez with David Shanta, September 9, 2015, Morongo Indian Reservation, Banning, California; hereafter cited as "Sanchez Interview."

20. *The Mission Indian* 4, no. 4 (March 1936), University of California Riverside, Special Collections and University Archives, E98 S7 M58 1936, Riverside, California.

21. Ibid.; Joseph Karl Hall, Qualification Record, National Personnel Records Center, St. Louis, Missouri. Hall succeeded A.F. Johnson as Farming Agent for the Morongo Sub-Agency, in 1930; Hoffman, "In the Shadow of the Mountain," 157–161.

22. Hall, Qualification Record; Bennett, *The Compleat Rancher*, 34–77.

23. Hall, Qualification Record; Interview of Robert Martin with David Shanta, May 8, 2015, Morongo Indian Reservation, Banning, California; hereafter cited as "Martin Interview."

24. Kumiko Noguchi, "From Yokuts to Tule River Indians: Recreation of the Tribal Identity on the Tule River Indian Reservation in California from EuroAmerican Contact to the Indian Reorganization Act of 1934," PhD Dissertation (Davis, CA: University of California, Davis, 2009), 208–210.

25. Noguchi, "From Yokuts to Tule River Indians," 211–220. Four stock raisers owned 90 percent of the cattle on the reservation ranges.

26. 1937 Annual Extension Report, Morongo Reservation, Box 10, Mission Indian Agency, Central Classified Files, 1920–1953, RG-75, NARA Riverside, California.

27. Ibid.

28. Ibid.

29. "1923–2009: Tribal Elder Alvino Siva Taught Cahuilla Songs, Traditions," *Banning* (CA) *Record Gazette,* July 10, 2009; Interview of Ernest Siva with David Shanta, May 1, 2018, Dorothy Ramon Learning Center, Banning, California, hereafter cited as "Siva Interview;" Sue A. Wade, Stephen R. Van Wormer, and Heather Thomson, "240 Years of Ranching: Historical Research, Field Surveys, Oral Interviews, and Management Recommendations for Ranching Districts and Sites in the San Diego Region" (Save Our Heritage Organisation, September 2009), 26. https://sohosandiego.org/images/240yearsofranching.pdf.

30. "Reimbursable Transactions," Box 11, Soboba Superintendency, General Correspondence 1892–1920, RG-75 NARA Riverside, California.

31. Trafzer, *American Indians as Cowboys,* 33–38.

32. Trafzer, *American Indians as Cowboys*, 33–38.

33. William E. Leuchtenburg, *Franklin D. Roosevelt and the New Deal 1932–1940* (New York: Harper, 1963), 299–310.

34. *Mission Indian* 8, no. 1 (January 1941), Box 69 "Cattle," Mission Indian Agency, Central Classified Files 1920–1953, RG-75, NARA Riverside, California; see also Burcham, *California Range Land,* 214–219.

35. *Mission Indian* 8, no. 2 (February 1941), Box 69 "Cattle," Mission Indian Agency, Central Classified Files 1920–1953, RG-75, NARA Riverside, California.

36. *Mission Indian* 8, no. 3 (March 1941), Box 69 "Cattle," Mission Indian Agency, Central Classified Files 1920–1953, RG-75, NARA Riverside, California.

37. *Mission Indian* 8, no. 5 (May 1941), Box 69 "Cattle," Mission Indian Agency, Central Classified Files 1920–1953, RG-75, NARA Riverside, California. Pulling, "A History of California's Range-Cattle Industry," 244–249. Blackleg or Hemorrhagic

Septicemia attacks fat, young cattle at a rate of over 20 percent if not vaccinated. Vaccinated herd rates drop below 4 percent.

38. *Mission Indian* 8, no. 6 (June 1941), Box 69 "Cattle," Mission Indian Agency, Central Classified Files 1920–1953, RG-75, NARA Riverside, California.

39. *Mission Indian* 8, no. 12 (December 1941), Box 69 "Cattle," Mission Indian Agency, Central Classified Files 1920–1953, RG-75, NARA Riverside, California.

Conclusion

Two and one-half centuries after the Spanish landed on the mainland of New Spain in 1519, Colonel Gaspar de Portolá and Father Junípero Serra led the Sacred Expedition to extend Spanish rule and the Catholic faith into Alta California in 1769. They arrived at San Diego Bay and claimed land for God and king that the Native peoples had inhabited for thousands of years. The relatively low numbers of people in the expedition's two parties included Cochimí Indians from central Baja California, who blazed the trail for the Spanish and helped to care for the horses and mules. In 1770, they returned to Baja with Captain Juan Rivera and drove about 160 head of Spanish Longhorn cattle onto the plains surrounding San Diego Bay.

The animals fed on annual California grasses and other perennial types of vegetation. They multiplied rapidly and moved ever outward from the coastal plains to the interior hills and valleys, and in the process, they consumed Indigenous food sources. As Indigenous food availability declined, Native dependence on meat from cattle, hogs, goats, and chickens increased.

The rapid growth of the domesticated animals displaced native vegetation with new species, incidentally and purposefully, but the impact forced California Indians to adapt to the European diet. The cattle increased rapidly in numbers beyond the control of the padres and soldiers. This forced them to select trusted Indian neophytes or converts and train them to mount horses and control the cattle herds spreading across southern California.

Padres established *estancias* or cattle ranches that kept the cattle far from crops and with enough space to move the cattle from one grazing area to another, and to preserve the range resources. Within the mission social structure, the first neophyte Indian cowboys had been elevated from field work and seated on a tall horse. As mounted herders, they wore *pantalones*, shoes, and a leather jacket. They carried the responsibility of managing and preserving the valuable mission assets that fed and clothed mission populations and provided tallow, rawhide, and leather that filled a multiplicity of needs in mission life.

When the father-general of the Franciscan padres decided that existing mission resources had reached a level that could support donations for the next new mission, Indian cowboys from nearby missions separated out and drove seed cattle to the new site. Some of those Indian cowboys stayed to teach the local Natives how to ride, rope, brand, and slaughter cattle. This process of building a new mission from the donated assets of existing ones, replayed from San Diego all the way north to San Francisco de Solano, situated north of the San Francisco Bay, established in 1823. This process filled the coastal ranges with Spanish Longhorn cattle and established some of the local Natives as trained and experienced cowboys.

By the time that secularization of the mission lands became law in 1833, California Indian cowboys formed a ready-made workforce for the new proprietors of the mission lands, land grant *rancheros* who called themselves Californios. Many Native families had established *rancherías* or villages near the missions and therefore within the bounds of the *ranchos*. Indian cowboys and ranch workers played an essential role in producing hundreds of thousands of hides and thousands of large *botas* (bags) of tallow that fueled the international market from the 1820s to the California Gold Rush beginning in 1848. Few Indian families obtained land grants and so shared little in the prosperity of that brief era but Indian families in *rancherías*, or back in their home villages, had learned to keep some cattle as food security for survival. Tribal herds afforded not just food security but some level of economic autonomy or sovereignty as well.

Ranchers reaped even greater profits in this new period because hungry gold rush immigrants wanted beef and cared little for a cowhide. While southern California *rancheros* made tens of thousands of dollars on herds driven north, their Indian cowboys often struggled with the debt peonage that kept them on the ranch, making fortunes for their masters.

The Gold Rush and the influx of so many immigrants began to change the face of the California population and to transform the cattle industry. Speculators had driven herds of American breed cattle into California from the Midwest and Texas all during the 1850s, and in fact, glutted the market. The wide imbalance between an overabundant supply and crashing demand threatened California ranges before flood and drought in the 1860s wiped out half of all cattle in the state. Like a pruned tree, the California cattle industry grew back but resembled little the old ranges crowded with Spanish Longhorns. Open-range cattle ranching declined and the more intensive processes of stock raising replaced it. Bigger and higher beef-producing animals became the norm, often raised on many small family spreads that emerged from the subdivision of the big ranches.

Southern California Native peoples had at least found some stability in living on the *ranchos*, and kept their families together. However, amid the flood of American immigrants and the diffusion of ranch ownership during the 1870s and 1880s, even finding wage work on an off-reservation ranch required individual effort that did not guarantee a safe haven for the worker's family. At home, Indians had even less security as settlers relentlessly tried to preempt their land, squat on it, or just let their livestock feed on Indian pastures and drink Indian water. These degenerative conditions threatened to irreparably tear the family fabric of Native societies and alarmed many concerned special agents of the Indian Service, and civilian visitors, activists, and residents. As never before, southern California Indians had to fight to survive and kept small herds of livestock where possible. In their fight for sovereignty, they argued their grievances in the American legal system and confronted trespassers. The struggle for survival and freedom in any group of human beings at some point becomes a part of their history and embedded in their group identity. California Indian cowboying and cattle raising had remained a constant all through the night and when a glimmer of light arrived in an Act of Congress to provide relief for the Indians of southern California in 1891, hope came with it.

During the years after the land grant ranches broke up and non-Natives moved into the state, the denial of sovereignty threatened the cohesion of Indigenous societies and the survival of the people. Yet Native cowboys had not forgotten how to ride and rope and drive herds. The culture of cattle, even on the lands over which the Native peoples had only a tenuous hold, persisted as a means of feeding families and of working for other ranchers. Among Native and non-Native cowboys who worked together, respect and fellowship existed alongside the wider societal disrespect for their basic human rights and general racial animus.

In the early years of the twentieth century, the old challenges continued to try the spirits of the southern California Indians but real boundaries had been drawn. When surveyed and patented, the newly drawn reservations acquired the status of private property, and as such, were protected under American property and contract law. Moral sovereignty had been joined to legal sovereignty.

The Office of Indian Affairs had stubbornly pursued goals of assimilation well into the twentieth century with predictable results. Indian Office policies and personnel often caused more suffering and lost the trust of the people they had hoped to integrate into American society. However, some policies produced benefits and some of the personnel did serve their clients well. The Reimbursable program and the addition of Expert Farming Agents, both in the 1910s, extended economic opportunities with loans to start or expand new ventures, and provided expertise that built, expanded, or optimized the returns on investment of cattle ranching and many other economic ventures. The Great War of 1914–1918 brought a surge in demand for southern California Indian beef cattle that lasted through 1920.

In the 1920s, a post-war drop in demand coupled with droughts depressed Native American economies through most of the decade but nothing like the crash of the economy that developed into the Great Depression in the early 1930s. New Deal programs provided emergency relief for at-risk Indian communities and offered structures to improve reservation resources and produce a more profitable cattle business. Judging by the examples of the Morongo cattlemen in the latter 1930s, Native groups who worked cooperatively in their cattle operations produced more and higher-quality cattle, that sold for high market prices. Southern California Indian cattle herds not only provided subsistence to feed families, but they sustained and strengthened their spiritual connection to the land, one that has existed for thousands of years.

Survival through the cattle industry among California Indians enabled Indigenous peoples to assert their personal and tribal sovereignty and to continue the family traditions of cowboying together (See figure 8.1, page 152), which had become part of tribal traditions and identity. Indian cowboys and their families reflect the innovative nature of southern California Indians. As their ancient economies declined due to immigrant settlement on Native

Figure 8.1 Cahuilla Indian Cowboys, Cahuilla Reservation. *Source*: Permission provided by Anthony Madrigal Sr., Tribal Historic Preservation Officer for the Cahuilla Band of Indians at Anza.

lands and preemption of resources, the people drew on their experiences in the missions and on the *ranchos* to carve out a new economy based on cattle. The original *vaqueros* of California throughout the Spanish and *rancho* periods were Native Americans from many tribes. They adapted the ways of the Mexican *vaqueros* and developed a robust and successful life in the cattle business that continues today.

Bibliography

PRIMARY SOURCES

Government Documents

An Act for the Relief of the Mission Indians in the State of California, United States Congressional Record, January 12, 1891.
National Archives and Records Administration (NARA), Riverside, California.
National Archives and Records Administration, Mission Indian Agency. *Mission Indian* 8, nos. 1–3, 5–8 (January-March, May, June, October, December 1941), Box 69 "Cattle," Mission Indian Agency, Central Classified Files 1920–1953, Record Group-75, NARA Riverside, California.
National Archives and Records Administration, *The Mission Indian* 2, no. 6 (December 1933): E98 S7 M58 1933, Autry Museum, Los Angeles, California.
National Archives and Records Administration, *The Mission Indian* 3, no. 1 (August 1934): E98 S7 M58 1933, Autry Museum, Los Angeles, California.
National Archives and Records Administration, *The Mission Indian* 4, no. 4 (March 1936): E98 S7 M58 1936, University of California Riverside, Special Collections and University Archives, Riverside, California.
National Archives and Records Administration, Mission Indian Agency, Central Classified Files, 1920–1953, Record Group-75.
National Archives and Records Administration, National Archives Building, Washington, DC.
National Archives and Records Administration, Soboba Superintendency, General Correspondence 1892–1920, Record Group-75.
National Personnel Records Center, St. Louis, Missouri.
National Personnel Records Center, Arthur Ferdinand Johnson, Personnel Information Sheet.
National Personnel Records Center, Joseph Karl Hall, Qualification Record.

United States Bureau of the Census, *Population of States and Counties of the United States, 1790–1990.*
United States Interior Department, Office of Indians Affairs. *Annual Report of the Commissioner of Indian Affairs, 1848–1932.*

Non-Government Primary Sources

Rupert and Jeannette Costo Collection, Rupert Costo Library, Special Collections, University of California Riverside.
William Weinland Collection, The Huntington Library, San Marino, California.

PUBLISHED PRIMARY SOURCES

Dana, Richard Henry. *Two Years Before the Mast and Twenty-Four Years After.* New York: P. F. Collier and Son, 1937.
Davis, William Heath. *Seventy-Five Years in California: Recollections and Remarks by One Who Visited These Shores in 1831, and Again in 1833, and Except When Absent on Business Was a Resident From 1838 Until the End of a Long Life in 1909.* Edited by Harold A. Small. San Francisco, CA: John Howell-Books, 1967.
Kino, Eusebio Francisco, S. J. *Kino's Historical Memoir of Pimería Alta: A Contemporary Account of the Beginnings of California, Sonora, and Arizona, By Father Eusebio Francisco Kino, S.J., Pioneer Missionary, Explorer, Cartographer, and Ranchman, 1683-1711.* Translated and Edited by Herbert Eugene Bolton. Berkeley, CA: University of California Press, (1919) 1948.
Liliencrantz, H. T. "Recollections of a California Cattleman: Three Chapters from the Memoirs of H.T. Lilienkrantz." *California Historical Society Quarterly* 38, no. 3 (September 1959): 259–268.
Loveland, Cyrus C. *California Trail Herd: The 1850 Missouri-to-California Journal of Cyrus C. Loveland.* Edited and Annotated by Richard H. Dillon. Los Gatos, CA: Talisman Press, 1961.
Lugo, Don Jose del Carmen Lugo. "Life of a Rancher." *The Historical Society of Southern California Quarterly,* 32 no. 3 (September 1950): 185–236.
Nordhoff, Charles. *California for Health, Pleasure, and Residence: A Book for Travellers and Settlers.* New York: Harper and Brothers, 1882.
Painter, C. C. *The Condition of Affairs in Indian Territory and California.* Philadelphia, PA: Indian Rights Association, 1888.
Quinn, Harry M. "A Cowboy Memory," *Heritage Keepers,* 6 no. 3 (Spring 2009).
Reed, Lester. "Cowboy on the Pauba." *High Country,* 57 (Winter 1981): 31–37.
Reed, Lester. *Old Time Cattlemen and Other Pioneers of the Anza-Borrego Area.* 3rd ed. Borrego Springs, CA: Anza-Borrego Desert Natural History Association, (1963) 2004.

Reed, Lester. *Oldtimers of Southeastern California.* San Francisco, CA: American Indian Historical Society, 1967.

Robinson, Alfred. *Life in California, During a Residence in that Territory, Comprising a Description of the Country and the Missionary Establishments.* New York: Da Capo Press, 1969.

Rojas, Arnold R. *Lore of the California Vaquero.* Fresno, CA: Academy Library Guild, 1958.

Rojas, Arnold R. *The Vaquero.* Charlotte, NC: McNally and Lofton, 1964.

Salvatierra, Juan Maria de. *Report on How the First Cattle Came to California. A Missionary Letter.* Riverside, CA: Rivera Library, University of California Riverside, 1709.

Wetmore, Charles A. "Report of Charles A. Wetmore, Special Commissioner of Mission Indians of Southern California." Washington, DC: Government Printing Office, 1875.

Wilson, B. D. *The Indians of Southern California in 1852.* Edited by John Walton Caughey. Lincoln, NE: University of Nebraska Press, 1995.

Southern California Newspapers

Courtesy of the California Digital Newspaper Collection, Center for Bibliographic Studies and Research, University of California, Riversidehttp://cdnc.ucr.e.

Banning (CA) Herald
Banning (CA) Record Gazette
Los Angeles Herald
Palm Springs (CA) Desert Sun
Riverside (CA) Daily Press
Riverside (CA) Enterprise
San Bernardino (CA) Sun
San Diego (CA) Union and Bee
San Pedro (CA) Daily News

INTERVIEWS

Roderick Tyron Linton with David Shanta, November 6, 2015, Morongo Indian Reservation, Banning, California.

Tribal Chairman Robert Martin with David Shanta, May 8, 2015, Morongo Indian Reservation, Banning, California.

Mrs. Doris Sanchez with David Shanta, September 9, 2015, Morongo Indian Reservation, Banning, California.

Ernest Siva with David Shanta, May 1, 2018, Dorothy Ramon Learning Center, Banning, California.

SECONDARY SOURCES

Adams, Andy. *Log of a Cowboy*. New York: Houghton Mifflin, 1931.

Álvarez-Nogal, Carlos and Leandro Prados Álvarez De La Escosura. "The Rise and Fall of Spain (1270-1850)." *The Economic History Review* 66, no. 1 (February 2013): 1–37.

Anderson, Virginia DeJohn. *Creatures of Empire: How Domesticated Animals Transformed Early America*. New York: Oxford University Press, 2004.

Aviles, Brian A. and Robert L. Hoover. "Two Californias, Three Religious Orders, and Fifty Missions: A Comparison of the Missionary Systems of Baja and Alta California." *Pacific Coast Archaeological Society Quarterly* 33, no. 3 (Summer 1997): 1–28.

Baillargeon, Morgan and Leslie Tepper. *Legends of Our Times: Native Cowboy Life*. Seattle, WA: University of Washington Press, 1998.

Baker, Charles C. "Mexican Land Grants in California." *Annual Publication of the Historical Society of Southern California* 9, no. 3 (1914): 236–243.

Bakken, Gordon Morris. "Mexican and American Land Policy: A Conflict of Cultures." *Southern California Quarterly* 75, no. 4 (Fall/Winter 1993): 237–262.

Bancroft, Hubert Howe. *California Pastoral, 1769-1848*. San Francisco, CA: History Company, 1888.

Bancroft, Hubert Howe. *History of California Vols. 1-7., 1542-1890*. Santa Barbara, CA: Wallace Hebberd, 1966–1970.

Bannon, John Francis. "Black-Robe Frontiersman: Pedro Mendez, S.J." *The Hispanic American Historical Review* 27, no. 1 (February 1947): 61–86.

Barger, William J. "Merchants of Los Angeles: Economics and Commerce in Mexican California." *Southern California Quarterly* 82, no. 2 (Summer 2000).

Barrows, David Prescott. *The Ethno-Botany of the Coahuilla Indians of Southern California*. Chicago, IL: University of Chicago Press, 1900.

Bauer, William Jr. "Native Californians in the Nineteenth Century." In *A Companion to California History*, edited by William Deverell and David Igler, 192–214. Malden, MA: Wiley-Blackwell, 2008,

Bauer, William Jr. *We Were All Migrant Workers Here: Work, Community, and Memory on California's Round Valley Reservation, 1850-1941*. Chapel Hill, NC: University of North Carolina Press, 2009.

Bean, Lowell John. "Morongo Indian Reservation: A Century of Adaptive Strategies." In *American Indian Economic Development*, edited by Sam Stanley 159–236. Chicago, IL: Mouton Publishers, 1978.

Bean, Lowell John. *Mukat's People: The Cahuilla People of Southern California*. Berkeley, CA: University of California Press, 1972.

Bean, Lowell John, Lisa J. Bourgeault and Frank W. Porter III. *The Cahuilla*. New York: Chelsea House, 1989.

Bean, Lowell John and Harry W. Lawton, "Some Explanations for the Rise of Cultural Complexity in Native California With Comments on Proto-Agriculture and Agriculture." In *Before the Wilderness: Environmental Management by Native*

Californians, edited by Thomas C. Blackburn and Kat Anderson, 27–54. Menlo Park, CA: Ballena Press, 1993.

Bean, Lowell John and Katherine Siva Saubel. *Temalpakh: Cahuilla Indian Knowledge and Usage of Plants*. Banning, CA: Malki Museum Press, Morongo Indian Reservation, 1972.

Bell, James G. and J. Evetts Haley. "A Log of the Texas-California Cattle Trail, 1854." *The Southwestern Historical Quarterly* 35, no. 3 (January 1932): 208–237.

Bennett, Lyn Ellen and Scott Abbott. *The Perfect Fence: Untangling the Meanings of Barbed Wire*. College Station, TX: Texas A&M University Press, 2017.

Bennett, Russell H. *The Compleat Rancher*. New York: Rinehart and Company, 1946.

Bibb, Leland. "Pablo Apis and Temecula," *Journal of San Diego History* 37, no. 4 (1991): 256–271.

Billington, Ray Allen and Martin Ridge. *Westward Expansion: A History of the American Frontier*. 5th ed. New York: Macmillan, 1982.

Biolsi, Thomas. *Organizing the Lakota: The Political Economy of the New Deal on the Pine Ridge and Rosebud Reservations*. Tucson, AZ: University of Arizona Press, 1992.

Bishko, Charles Julian. "The Peninsular Background of Latin American Cattle Ranching." *The Hispanic American Historical Review* 32, no. 4 (November 1952): 491–515.

Blackburn, Thomas C. and Kat Anderson. *Before the Wilderness: Environmental Management by Native Californians*. Menlo Park, CA: Ballena Press, 1993.

Bolton, Herbert Eugene. *Anza's California Expeditions, Vol.1: An Outpost of Empire*. Berkeley, CA: University of California Press, 1930.

Bolton, Herbert Eugene. "The Mission as a Frontier Institution in the Spanish-American Colonies." *American Historical Review* 23, no.1 (October 1917), 42–61.

Bolton, Herbert Eugene. *The Padre on Horseback: A Sketch of Eusebio Francisco Kino, S.J., Apostle to the Pima*. San Francisco, CA: The Sonora Press. Reprint, Chicago, IL: Loyola University Press, (1932) 1963, 1986.

Bolton, Herbert Eugene. *Rim of Christendom: A Biography of Eusebio Francisco Kino Pacific Coast Pioneer*. New York: The MacMillan Company. Reprint, Tucson, AZ: University of Arizona Press, (1936) 1984.

Bolton, Herbert Eugene. *The Spanish Borderlands: A Chronicle of Old Florida and the Southwest*. New Haven, CT: Yale University Press, 1921.

Boulé, Mary Null. *California Native American Tribes: Chumash Tribe*. Vashon, WA: Merryant, 1992.

Brand, Donald D. "The Early History of the Range Cattle Industry in Northern Mexico." *Agricultural History* 35, no. 3 (July 1961): 132–139.

Brigandi, Phil. *Temecula: At the Crossroads of History*. Encinitas, CA: Heritage Media, 1998.

Brigandi, Phil. "The Outposts of Mission San Luis Rey." *San Diego Historical Society Quarterly* 45, no. 2 (Spring 1999): 106–112.

Brinckerhoff, Sidney B. and Odie B. Faulk. *Lancers for the King: A Study of the Frontier Military System of Northern New Spain, With a Translation of the Royal Regulation of 1772*. Phoenix, AZ: Arizona Historical Foundation, 1965.

Brown-Coronel, Margie. "Intimacy and Family in the California Borderlands: The Letters of Josefa Del Valle Forster, 1876-1896." *Pacific Historical Review* 89, no. 1 (2020): 74–96.

Brumgardt, John R. "Pioneer by Circumstance: James Marshall Gilman and the Beginnings of Banning." *Southern California Quarterly* 62, no. 2 (Summer 1980): 143–159.

Burcham, L. T. [Lee T.] *California Range Land: An Historico-Ecological Study of the Range Resource of California.* Sacramento, CA: Division of Forestry, Department of Natural Resources, State of California, 1957.

Burcham, L. T. "Cattle and Range Forage in California: 1770-1880" *Agricultural History* 35, no. 3 (July 1961): 140–149.

Burgess, Larry E." Commission to the Mission Indians, 1891." *San Bernardino County Museum Association Quarterly* 35, no.1 (Spring 1988): 3–46.

Butzer, Karl W. "Cattle and Sheep from Old to New Spain: Historical Antecedents." *Annals of the Association of American Geographers* 7, no. 2 (March 1988): 29–56.

Carrasco, David. "Cortes and the Sacred Ceiba." In *The History of the Conquest of New Spain* by Bernal Diaz del Castillo, edited by David Carrasco, 399–404. Albuquerque, NM: New Mexico University Press, 2008.

Carrico, Richard L. *Strangers in a Stolen Land: Indians of San Diego County from Prehistory to the New Deal.* 2nd ed. San Diego, CA: Sunbelt Publications, 2008.

Carrico, Richard L. "The Struggle for Native American Self-Determination in San Diego County." *Journal of California and Great Basin Anthropology* 2, no. 2 (Winter 1980): 199–213.

Chaput, Donald. "Horatio N. Rust and the Agent-As-Collector Dilemma." *Southern California Quarterly* 64, no. 4 (Winter 1982): 281–295.

Chardon, Roland. "The Elusive Spanish League: A Problem of Measurement in Sixteenth-Century New Spain." *The Hispanic American Historical Review* 60, no. 2 (May 1980): 294–302.

Cleland, Robert Glass. *The Cattle on a Thousand Hills: Southern California, 1850-1880.* Reprint, San Marino, CA: The Huntington Library, (1941) 1990.

Condé, Bruce. "Santa Ana of the Yorbas: Which Might Have Become California's Greatest Semi-Feudal Hacienda." *Historical Society of Southern California Quarterly* 22, no. 2 (June 1940): 70–79.

Coolidge, Dane. *Old California Cowboys.* New York: Dutton. Reprint, *California Cowboys.* Tucson, AZ: University of Arizona Press, (1939) 1985.

Crosby, Harry W. *Antigua California: Mission and Colony on the Peninsular Frontier, 1697-1768.* Albuquerque, NM: University of New Mexico Press, 1994.

Crosby, Harry W. *Gateway to Alta California: The Expedition to San Diego, 1769.* San Diego, CA: Sunbelt Publications, 2003.

Curiel, José Refugio De La Torre. "Franciscan Missionaries in Late Colonial Sonora: Five Decades of Change and Conflict." In *Alta California: Peoples in Motion, Identities in Formation, 1769-1850*, edited by Steven W. Hackel, 47–78. Berkeley, CA: University of California Press and San Marino: Huntington Library, 2010.

Dale, Edward Everett. *The Indians of the Southwest: A Century of Development Under the United States.* Norman, OK: University of Oklahoma Press, 1949.

Dale, Edward Everett. *The Range Cattle Industry: Ranching on the Great Plains from 1865 to 1925.* Norman, OK: University of Oklahoma Press, 1930.

Dary, David. *Cowboy Culture: A Saga of Five Centuries.* New York: Alfred A. Knopf, 1981.

Davis, Dave D. "The Strategy of Early Spanish Ecosystem Management on Cuba." *Journal of Anthropological Research* 30, no. 4 (Winter 1974): 294–314.

Denevan, William M. "The Pristine Myth: The Landscape of the Americas in 1492." *Annals of the Association of American Geographers* 82, no. 3 (September 1992): 369–385.

Denhardt, Robert Moorman. "Driving Livestock East from California Prior to 1850." *California Historical Society Quarterly* 20, no. 4 (December 1941): 341–347.

Deverell, William, Editor. *A Companion to the American West.* Malden, MA: Blackwell, 2004.

Deverell, William. "The 1850s." In *A Companion to California History*, edited by William Deverell and David Igler, 161–174. Malden, MA: Wiley-Blackwell, 2008.

Diamond, Jared. *Guns, Germs, and Steel: The Fates of Human Societies.* New York: W. W. Norton, 1999.

Díaz del Castillo, Bernal. *The History of the Conquest of New Spain*, Translated and Edited by Davíd Carrasco. Albuquerque, NM: University of New Mexico Press, 2008.

Dobie, J. Frank. *A Vaquero of the Brush Country: Partly from the Reminiscences of John Young.* Boston, MA: Little, Brown, 1929.

Dunne, Peter Masten. *Black Robes in Lower California.* Berkeley and Los Angeles, CA: University of California Press, 1968.

Farris, Glenn J. "Jose Panto, 'Capitan' of the Indian Pueblo of San Pascual, San Diego County," *Journal of California and Great Basin Anthropology* 16, no. 2 (1994): 149–161.

Faulk, Odie B. *Crimson Desert.* New York: Oxford University Press, 1974.

Faulk, Odie B. *Land of Many Frontiers: A History of the American Southwest.* New York: Oxford University Press, 1968.

Faulk, Odie B. "Ranching in Spanish Texas." *The Hispanic American Historical Review* 45, no. 2 (May 1965): 257–266.

Faulk, Odie B. and Sidney B. Brinckerhoff. *Lancers for the King: A Study of the Frontier Military System of Northern New Spain, With a Translation of the Royal Regulations of 1772.* Phoenix, AZ: Arizona Historical Foundation, 1965.

Faulk, Odie B. and Sidney B. Brinckerhoff. *The U.S. Camel Corps.* New York: Oxford University Press, 1976.

Fischer, John Ryan. *Cattle Colonialism: An Environmental History of the Conquest of California and Hawai'i.* Chapel Hill, NC: University of North Carolina Press, 2015.

Freedman, Russell. *In the Days of the Vaqueros: America's First True Cowboys.* New York: Clarion Books, 2001.

Geiger, Maynard J. *As the Padres Saw Them.* Santa Barbara, CA: Santa Barbara Bicentennial Series, 1976.

Gerber, James. "The Gold Rush Origins of California's Wheat Economy." *América Latina En La Historia Económica, Boletín de Fuentes* 34 (December 2010): 35–64.

Getty, Harry T. "Development of the San Carlos Apache Cattle Industry." *Kiva* 23, no. 3 (February 1958): 1–4.

Gilman, Carolyn and Mary Jane Schneider. *The Way to Independence: Memories of a Hidatsa Indian Family 1840-1920.* St. Paul, MN: University of Minnesota Press, 1987.

Gonzales, Manuel G. *Mexicanos: A History of Mexicans in the United States.* Bloomington, IN: Indiana University Press, 2009.

Grunberg, Bernard. "The Origins of the Conquistadores of Mexico City," *The Hispanic American Historical Review* 74, no. 2 (May 1994): 259–283.

Guedea, Virginia. "The Process of Mexican Independence," *American Historical Review* 105, no. 1 (February 2000): 116–130.

Guinn, J. M. "The Passing of the Cattle Barons of California." *Annual Publication of the Historical Society of Southern California* 8, no. 1 and 2 (1909–1910): 51–60.

Haas, Lisbeth. *Conquests and Historical Identities in California, 1769-1936.* Berkeley, CA: University of California Press, 1995.

Haas, Lisbeth. "'Raise Your Sword and I Will Eat You': Luiseño Scholar Pablo Tac, ca. 1841." In *Alta California: Peoples in Motion, Identities in Formation, 1769-1850*, edited by Steven W. Hackel, 79–110. Berkeley, CA: University of California Press and San Marino: Huntington Library, 2010.

Hackel, Steven W. *Children of Coyote, Missionaries of Saint Francis: Indian-Spanish Relations in Colonial California, 1769-1850.* Chapel Hill, NC: University of North Carolina Press, 2005.

Hackel, Steven W., Editor. *Alta California: Peoples in Motion, Identities in Formation, 1769-1850.* Berkeley, CA: University of California Press and San Marino: Huntington Library, 2010.

Hackel, Steven W. "Land, Labor, and Production: The Colonial Economy of Spanish and Mexican California." *California History* 76, nos. 2–3, "Contested Eden: California Before the Gold Rush" (Summer-Fall 1997): 111–146.

Hague, Harlan. "The Search for a Southern Overland Route to California." *California Historical Quarterly* 55, no. 2 (Summer 1976): 150–161.

Hanks, Richard A. *This War is for a Whole Life: The Culture of Resistance Among Southern California Indians, 1850-1966.* Banning, CA: Ushkana Press, 2012.

Hanks, Richard A. "Vicissitudes of Justice: Massacre at San Timoteo Canyon." *Southern California Quarterly* 82, no. 3 (Fall 2000): 233–256.

Harvey, H. R. "Population of the Cahuilla Indians: Decline and Its Causes." *Eugenics Quarterly* 14, no. 3 (1967): 185–198.

Harley, R. Bruce. "Did Mission San Gabriel Have Two Asistencias?: The Case of Rancho San Bernardino." *San Bernardino County Museum Association Quarterly* 36, no. 4 (Winter 1989): 1–69.

Harley, R. Bruce "The San Jacinto Rancho." San Bernardino, CA: Diocesan Heritage Series, Catholic Diocese of San Bernardino, 1985, pp. 1–6.

Holmes, Elmer Wallace, Editor. *History of Riverside County, California*. Los Angeles, CA: Historic Record Company, 1912.

Hornbeck, David. "Land Tenure and Rancho Expansion in Alta California, 1784-1846." *Journal of Historical Geography* 4, no. 4 (1978): 371–390.

Hundley, Norris, Jr. "The Dark and Bloody Ground of Indian Water Rights: Confusion Elevated to Principle." *Western Historical Quarterly* 9, no. 4 (October 1978): 454–482.

Hundley, Norris, Jr. *The Great Thirst: Californians and Water, 1770s-1990s*. Berkeley, CA: University of California Press, 1992.

Igler, David, "Alta California, the Pacific, and International Commerce Before the Gold Rush." In *A Companion to California History*, edited by Deverell, William and David Igler, 116–126. Malden, MA: Wiley-Blackwell, 2008.

Igler, David. *Industrial Cowboys: Miller & Lux and the Transformation of the Far West. 1850-1920*. Berkeley, CA: University of California Press, 2001.

Iverson, Peter. *When Indians became Cowboys: Native Peoples and Cattle Ranching in the American West*. Norman, OK: University of Oklahoma Press, 1994.

Ives, Ronald L. "Kino's Route Across Baja California." *Kiva* 26, no. 4 (April 1961): 17–29.

Jackson, Robert H. "Epidemic Disease and Population Decline in the Baja California Missions, 1697-1834." *Southern California Quarterly* 63, no. 4 (Winter 1981): 308–346.

Jackson, Robert H. and Edward Castillo. *Indians, Franciscans, and Spanish Colonization: The Impact of the Mission System on California Indians*. Albuquerque, NM: University of New Mexico Press, 1995.

Jackson, W. Turrentine. *Wagon Roads West: A Study of Federal Road Surveys and Construction in the Trans-Mississippi West 1846-1869*. Berkeley, CA: University of California Press, 1952.

Jelinek, Lawrence James. "'Property of Every Kind': Ranching and Farming During the Gold Rush Era." *California History* 77, no. 4 (Winter 1998/1999): 233–249.

Jensen, James M. "Cattle Drives from the Ranchos to the Gold Fields of California." *Arizona and the West* 2, no. 4 (Winter 1960): 341–352.

Jensen, James M. "John Forster: A California Ranchero." *California Historical Society Quarterly* 48, no.1 (March 1969): 37–44.

Johnson, John J. "The Introduction of the Horse into the Western Hemisphere." *The Hispanic American Historical Review* 23, no. 4 (November 1943): 587–610.

Jordan, Terry G. *North American Cattle-Ranching Frontiers: Origins, Diffusion, and Differentiation*. Albuquerque, NM: University of New Mexico Press, 1993.

Jordan, Terry G. "The Origin of Anglo-American Cattle Ranching in Texas: A Documentation of Diffusion from the Lower South." *Economic Geography* 45, no. 1 (January 1969): 63–87.

Karr, Steven M. "The Warner's Ranch Removal: Cultural Adaptation, Accommodation, and Continuity." *California History* 86, no. 4 (2009): 24–43, 82–84.

Kessell, John L. *Friars, Soldiers, and Reformers: Hispanic Arizona and the Sonoran Mission Frontier, 1767-1856*. Tucson, AZ: University of Arizona Press, 1976.

Kessell, John L. "Friars Versus Bureaucrats: The Mission as a Threatened Institution on the Arizona-Sonora Frontier, 1767-1842." *Western Historical Quarterly* 5, no. 2 (April 1974): 151–162.

Kessell, John L. *Spain in the Southwest: A Narrative History of Colonial New Mexico, Arizona, Texas, and California*. Norman, OK: University of Oklahoma Press, 2002.

Kessell, John L. and Fray Bartholeme Ximeno. "San José De Tumacácori-1773: A Franciscan Reports from Arizona." *Arizona and the West* 6, no. 4 (Winter 1964): 303–312.

Lawton, Harry, Philip J. Wilke, Mary DeDecker and William M. Mason, "Agriculture Among the Paiutes of Owens Valley." In *Before the Wilderness: Environmental Management by Native Californians*, edited by Thomas C. Blackburn and Kat Anderson, 329–377. Menlo Park, CA: Ballena Press, 1993.

Lewis, David Rich. *Neither Wolf Nor Dog: American Indians, Environment, and Agrarian Change*. New York: Oxford University Press, 1994.

Lewis, Henry T. *Patterns of Burning in California: Ecology and Ethnohistory*. Ramona, CA: Ballena Press, 1973.

Liss, Peggy K. *Isabel the Queen: Life and Times*. Rev. ed. Philadelphia, PA: University of Pennsylvania Press, 2004.

Madrigal, Anthony. *Sovereignty, Land and Water: Building Tribal Environmental and Cultural Programs on the Cahuilla and Twenty-Nine Palms Reservations*. Riverside, CA: California Center for Native Nations, 2008.

Magliari, M. "Free Soil, Unfree Labor." *Pacific Historical Review* 73, no. 3 (August 2004): 349–390.

Mathes, Valerie Sherer and Phil Brigandi. *Reservations, Removal, and Reform: The Mission Indian Agents of Southern California, 1878-1903*. Norman, OK: University of Oklahoma Press, 2015.

Mathwich, Nicole and Barnet Pavao-Zuckerman. "Bureaucratic Reforms on the Frontier: Zooarchaeological and Historical Perspectives on the 1767 Jesuit Expulsion in the Pimería Alta." *Journal of Anthropological Archaeology* 52 (2018): 156–166.

McCarthy, Helen. "Managing Oaks and the Acorn Crop." In *Before the Wilderness: Environmental Management by Native Californians*, edited by Thomas C. Blackburn and Kat Anderson, 213–228. Menlo Park, CA: Ballena Press, 1993.

McCoy, Joseph G. *Historic Sketches of the Cattle Trade of the West and Southwest*. Kansas City, MO: Ramsey, Millett & Hudson, 1874.

McKanna, Clare V. Jr. "An Old Town Gunfight: The Homicide Trial of Cave Johnson Couts." *The Journal of San Diego History* 44, no. 4 (Fall 1998): 259–273.

Merriam, C. Hart. "The Indian Population of California." *American Anthropologist* 7, no. 4 (October–December 1905): 594–606.

Meyer, Michael C. *Water in the Hispanic Southwest: A Social and Legal History 1550-1850*. Tucson, AZ: University of Arizona Press, 1984.

Militello, Teresa. "Horatio Nelson Rust and His Contributions to the Development of American Archaeology." *Pacific Coast Archaeological Society Quarterly* 41, no. 1 (April 2009): 1–57.

Miner, H. Craig. "The Dream of a Native Cattle Industry in Indian Territory." In *Ranch and Range in Oklahoma*, edited by Jimmy M. Skaggs, 18–29. Oklahoma City, OK: Oklahoma Historical Society, 1978.

Monroy, Douglas. *Thrown Among Strangers: The Making of Mexican Culture in Frontier California*. Berkeley, CA: University of California Press, 1990.

Mora, Jo. *Californios: The Saga of the Hard-Riding Vaqueros, America's First Cowboys*. Garden City, NJ: Doubleday, 1949.

Mora, Jo. *Trail Dust and Saddle Leather*. New York: C. Scribner's Sons, 1950.

Morison, Samuel Eliot. *Admiral of the Ocean Sea: A Life of Christopher Columbus*. Boston, MA: Little, Brown, 1942.

Morrisey, Richard J. "Colonial Agriculture in New Spain." *Agricultural History* 3, no. 3 (July 1957): 24–29.

Morrisey, Richard J. "The Northward Expansion of Cattle Ranching in New Spain, 1550-1600." *Agricultural History* 25, no. 3 (July 1951): 115–121.

Myres, Sandra L. "The Ranching Frontier: Spanish Institutional Backgrounds of the Plains Cattle Industry." In *The Walter Prescott Webb Memorial Lectures: Essays on the American West*, edited by Harold M. Hollingsworth and Sandra L. Myres, 19–39. Austin, TX: University of Texas Press, 1969.

Nabhan, Gary Paul. "Camel Whisperers: Desert Nomads Crossing Paths." *Arizona Journal of History* 49, no. 2 (Summer 2008): 95–119.

Nuttall, Donald A. "Gaspar de Portolá: Disenchanted Conquistador of Spanish Upper California." *Southern California Quarterly* 53, no. 3 (September 1971): 185–198.

Officer, James E. "Kino and Agriculture in the Pimeria Alta." *The Journal of Arizona History* 34, no. 3 (Autumn 1993): 287–306.

Ogden, Adele. "Boston Hide Droghers Along California Shores." *California Historical Society Quarterly* 8, no. 4 (December 1929): 289–305.

Ogden, Adele. "Hides and Tallow: McCulloch, Hartnell and Company 1822-1828." *California Historical Society Quarterly* 6, no. 3 (September 1927): 254–264.

O'Neill, Colleen. *Working the Navajo Way: Labor and Culture in the Twentieth Century*. Lawrence, KS: University Press of Kansas, 2005.

Patencio, Chief Francsico, as told to Margaret Boynton. *Stories and Legends of the Palm Springs Indians*. Los Angeles, CA: Times-Mirror, 1943.

Pavao-Zuckerman, Barnet. "Missions, Livestock, and Economic Transformations in the Pimería Alta." In *New Mexico and the Pimería Alta: The Colonial Period in the American Southwest*, edited by John G. Douglas and William M. Graves, 289–309. Louisville, CO: University Press of Colorado, 2017.

Phillips, George Harwood. *Chiefs and Challengers: Indian Resistance and Cooperation in Southern California, 1769-1906*. 2nd ed. Norman, OK: University of Oklahoma Press, 2014.

Phillips, George Harwood. *Vineyards and Vaqueros: Indian Labor and the Economic Expansion of Southern California, 1771-1877*. Norman, OK: University of Oklahoma Press, 2010.

Powell, Philip Wayne. "Presidios and Towns on the Silver Frontier of New Spain, 1550-1580." *Hispanic American Historical Review* 24, no. 2 (May 1944): 179–200.

Powell, Philip Wayne. "Spanish Warfare Against the Chichimecas in the 1570s." *Hispanic American Historical Review* 24, no. 4 (November 1944): 580–604.

Preston, William L. "Serpent in Eden: Dispersal of Foreign Diseases into Pre-Mission California." *Journal of California and Great Basin Anthropology* 18, no. 1 (1996): 2–37.

Preston, William L. "The Tulare Lake Basin: An Aboriginal Cornucopia." *California Geographical Society* 30 (1990): 1–24.

Pubols, Louise. "Becoming Californio: Jokes, Broadsides, and a Slap in the Face." In *Alta California: Peoples in Motion, Identities in Formation, 1769-1850*, edited by Steven W. Hackel, 131–156. Berkeley, CA: University of California Press and San Marino: Huntington Library, 2010.

Quinn, Harry M. "A Cowboy Memory." *Heritage Keepers* 6, no. 1 (Autumn 2009): 1.

Ratekin, Mervyn. "The Early Sugar Industry in Española." *The Hispanic American Historical Review* 34, no. 1 (February 1954): 1–19.

Rawls, James. *Indians of California: The Changing Image*. Norman, OK: University of Oklahoma Press, 1984.

Reuther, Walter, Herbert John Webber and Leon Dexter Batchelor, Editors. *The Citrus Industry, Vol. 1: History, World Distribution, Botany and Varieties*. Rev. ed. Berkeley, CA: University of California Press, 1967.

Rhode, Paul W. "Learning, Capital Accumulation, and the Transformation of California Agriculture." *Journal of Economic History* 55, no. 4 (December 1995): 773–800.

Ripley, Vernette Snyder. "The San Fernando Pass and the Pioneer Traffic that Went Over it." *Historical Society of Southern California* 29, no. 1 (March 1947): 7–48

Robinson, John W. *The San Bernardinos: The Mountain Country from Cajon Pass to Oak Glen, Two Centuries of Changing Use*. Arcadia, CA: Big Santa Anita Historical Society, 1989.

Robinson, John W. and Bruce D. Risher. *The San Jacintos: The Mountain Country from Banning to Borrego Valley*. Arcadia, CA: Big Santa Anita Historical Society, 1993.

Robinson, W. W. "The Story of Rancho San Pasqual." *Historical Society of Southern California Quarterly* 37, no. 4 (December 1955): 347–353.

Roberts, Elizabeth Judson. *Indian Stories of the Southwest*. San Francisco, CA: Harr Wagner Publishing, 1917.

Rodero, A., J. V. Delgado and E. Rodero. "Primitive Andalusian Livestock and Their Implications in the Discovery of America." *Archivos de Zootecnia* 41, no. 154 (1992): 383–400.

Romero, John Bruno. *The Botanical Lore of the California Indians: With Side Lights on Historical Incidents in California*. New York: Vantage Press, 1954.

Saavedra, Yvette J. "Making the Region: The Mission Economy, Independence, and Liberalism." In *Pasadena Before the Roses: Race, Identity and Land Use in Southern California, 1771-1890*, 42–56. Tucson, AZ: University of Arizona Press, 2018.

Sample, L. L. "Trade and Trails in Aboriginal California." University of California Archaeological Survey, Report No. 8 (September 15, 1950). https://digitalassets.lib.berkeley.edu/anthpubs/ucb/text/ucas054-001.pdf.

Sandos, James A. "'Because He is a Liar and a Thief': Conquering the Residents of 'Old' California, 1850-1880." *California History* 79, no. 2 (Summer 2000): 86–112.

Sandos, James A. and Larry E. Burgess. *The Hunt for Willie Boy: Indian-Hating and Popular Culture*. Norman, OK: University of Oklahoma Press, 1994.

Santiago, Mark. *Massacre at the Yuma Crossing: Spanish Relations with the Quechans, 1779-1782*. Tucson, AZ: University of Arizona Press, 1998.

Saunt, Claudio. "My Medicine is Punishment: A Case of Torture in Early California, 1775-1776." *Ethnohistory* 57, no. 4 (Fall 2010): 679–708.

Savage, William W. Jr. "Indian Ranchers." In *Ranch and Range in Oklahoma*, edited by Jimmy M. Skaggs, 30–44. Oklahoma City, OK: Oklahoma Historical Society, 1978.

Shipek, Florence C. "A Native American Adaptation to Drought: The Kumeyaay as Seen in the San Diego Mission Records 1770-1798." *Ethnohistory* 28, no. 4 (Autumn 1981): 295–312.

Shipek, Florence C. "Kumeyaay Plant Husbandry: Fire, Water, and Erosion Management Systems." In *Before the Wilderness: Environmental management of Native Californians*, edited by Thomas C. Blackburn and Kat Anderson, 379–388. Menlo Park, CA: Ballena Press, 1993.

Shipek, Florence C. *Pushed Into the Rocks: Southern California Land Tenure, 1769-1986*. Lincoln, NE: University of Nebraska Press, 1988.

Shipek, Florence C. "Saints or Oppressors: The Franciscan Missionaries of California." In *The Missions of California: A Legacy of Genocide*, edited by Rupert Costo and Jeannette Henry Costo, 29–47. San Francisco, CA: Indian Historian Press, 1987.

Slatta, Richard W. *Comparing Cowboys and Frontiers*. Norman, OK: University of Oklahoma Press, 1997.

Slatta, Richard W. *The Cowboy Encyclopedia*. New York: W. W. Norton, 1994.

Smith, Dean Howard. *Modern Tribal Development: Paths to Self-Sufficiency and Cultural Integrity in Indian Country*. Walnut Creek, CA: Alta Mira Press, 2000.

Sneve, Virginia Driving Hawk. *Grandpa Was a Cowboy & and Indian and Other Stories*. Lincoln, NE: University of Nebraska Press, 2000.

Stampa, Miguel Carrera. "The Evolution of Weights and Measures in New Spain." *The Hispanic American Historical Review* 29, no. 1 (February 1949): 2–24.

Stephenson, Terry E. "Tomás Yorba, His Wife Vicenta, and His Account Book." *Historical Society of Southern California Quarterly* 23, nos. 3 and 4 (September–December 1941): 127–156.

Street, Richard Steven. *Beasts of the Field: A Narrative History of California Farmworkers, 1769-1913*. Stanford, CA: Stanford University Press, 2004.

Strong, William Duncan. *Aboriginal Society in Southern California*. Banning, CA: Malki Museum Press, Morongo Indian Reservation, 1972.

Svingen, Orlan J. "Reservation Self-Sufficiency: Stock Raising vs. Farming on the Northern Cheyenne Indian Reservation, 1900-1914." *Montana, The Magazine of Western History* 31, no. 4 (Autumn 1981): 14–23.

Thorne, Tanis C. "The Death of Superintendent Stanley and the Cahuilla Uprising of 1907-1912." *Journal of California and Great Basin Anthropology* 24, no.2 (2004): 233–258.

Thorne, Tanis C. "The Mixed Legacy of Mission Indian Agent S.S. Lawson, 1878-1883." *Journal of California and Great Basin Anthropology* 25, no. 2 (2005): 147–168.

Thornton, Russell. *American Indian Holocaust and Survival: A Population History Since 1492.* Norman, OK: University of Oklahoma Press, 1987.

Torres-Rouff, David Samuel. *Before L.A.: Race, Space, and Municipal Power in Los Angeles, 1781-1894.* New Haven, CT: Yale University Press, 2013.

Trafzer, Clifford E. *American Indians as Cowboys.* Newcastle, CA: Sierra Oaks Publishing, 1992.

Trafzer, Clifford E. *As Long as the Grass Shall Grow and the Rivers Flow: A History of Native Americans.* Belmont, CA: Wadsworth, 2000.

Trafzer, Clifford E. *The People of San Manuel.* Patton, CA: San Manuel Band of Mission Indians, 2002.

Trafzer, Clifford E. *Yuma: Frontier Crossing of the Far Southwest.* Wichita, KS: Western Heritage Books, 1980.

Trafzer, Clifford E. and Joel R. Hyer, Editors. *Exterminate Them!: Written Accounts of the Murder, Rape, and Enslavement of Native Americans during the California Gold Rush.* East Lansing, MI: Michigan State University Press, 1999.

Trafzer, Clifford E. and Jeffrey Smith. *Native Americans of Riverside County.* San Francisco, CA: Arcadia Publishing, 2006.

Van Evera, Stephen. "Offense, Defense, and the Causes of War." *International Security* 22, no. 4 (Spring 1998): 5–43.

Vélez, Karin. *The Miraculous Flying House of Loreto: Spreading Catholicism in the Early Modern World.* Princeton, NJ: Princeton University Press, 2019.

Wade, Sue A., Stephen R. Van Wormer, and Heather Thomson. "240 Years of Ranching: Historical Research, Field Suveys, Oral Interviews, and Management Recommendations for Ranching Districts and Sites in the San Diego Region." Save Our Heritage Organisation, September 2009, pp. 1–175. https://sohosandiego.org/images/240yearsofranching.pdf.

Watahomigie, Lucille J., Malinda Powskey, Jorigine Bender, Josie Uqualla and Philbert Watahomigie, Sr. Recounted in Hualapai by Elnora Malpatis, Everette Manakaja, Sr., Weldon Mahone and Grant Tapija, Sr., *Waksi: Wich: Hualapai Cattle Ranching.* Peach Springs, AZ: Peach Springs School District, 1983.

Wallerstein, Immanuel. *World-Systems Analysis: An Introduction.* Durham, NC: Duke University Press, 2004.

Webb, Edith Buckland. *Indian Life at the Old Missions.* Los Angeles, CA: Warren F. Lewis, 1952.

Webb, Walter Prescott. *The Great Plains.* Waltham, MA: Blaisdell Publishing, 1931.

Wencke, Elisabet V. and Xavier López-Medellín. "Historical Water Pulses in the Central Desert Region: Following the Paths of the Missionaries' First Explorations of Northern Baja California." *Journal of the Southwest* 57, no. 1 (Spring 2015): 145–162.

White, Richard. *"It's Your Misfortune and None of My Own": A New History of the American West.* Norman, OK: University of Oklahoma Press, 1991.

White, Richard. *The Roots of Dependency: Subsistence, Environment, and Social Change Among the Choctaws, Pawnees, and Navajos.* Lincoln, NE: University of Nebraska Press, 1983.

Woolsey, Ronald C. "Pioneer Views and Frontier Themes: Benjamin Hayes, Horace Bell, and the Southern California Experience." *Southern California Quarterly* 72, no. 3 (Fall 1990): 255–274.

Worster, Donald. *Rivers of Empire: Water, Aridity, and the Growth of the American West.* New York: Pantheon Books, 1986.

Theses and Dissertations

Hoffman, Harlan Lanas III. "In the Shadow of the Mountain: The Cahuilla, Serrano, and Cupeño People of the Morongo Indian Reservation, 1885-1934." PhD diss., University of California Riverside, Riverside, CA, 2006.

Noguchi, Kumiko. "From Yokuts to Tule River Indians: Re-creation of the Tribal Identity on the Tule River Indian Reservation in California from Euroamerican Contact to the Indian Reorganization Act of 1934." PhD diss., University of California Davis, Davis, CA, 2009.

Perez, Robert Cristian. "Indian Rebellions in Northwestern New Spain: A Comparative Analysis, 1695-1750s." PhD diss., University of California Riverside, Riverside, CA, 2003.

Pulling, Hazel Adele. "A History of California's Range-Cattle Industry 1770-1912." PhD diss., University of Southern California, Riverside, CA, 1944.

Index

Acâgchemem Indians (Juaneños), 2, 7, 8
Acapulco, 17, 19
Act for the Government and Protection of Indians (*1850*), 84
Act for the Relief of the Mission Indians in the State of California, An (1891), 5, 84, 102, 109
administradores, 73
Agua Caliente Indians (Palm Springs), 97, 100, 113, 116, 118, 125, 135, 141. See also Warner Hot Springs
aguardiente, 77, 82n48
alcalde, 73, 75
Altar, 38, 39, 44, 47n30
Ames, John G. (Agent (Reverend)), 98, 100
Andalucía, 1, 10, 12, 25n2, 26n9
Andalusian (persons, horses), 26n11, 10
Annual Report of the Commissioner of Indian Affairs, 88, 98, 103n4, 123, 126, 136
Antilles, Greater, 1, 2, 13, 14, 21, 58, 61
Antillón, Admiral Isidro de Atondo, 16
Antonio, Juan (Cahuilla Indian Paramount Chief) (*Cusuhatna*), 75, 76, 81n44, 91, 93, 94
Anza, Juan Bautista de (Lieutenant Colonel), 19, 37–44, 47n30, 68, 69, 86, 115

Apache Indians, 17, 35, 41, 46n16
Apapas, Ambrosio, 134
Apapas, Augustine, 134
Apis, Casilda Coyote de (wife of Pablo), 96
Apis, Pablo, 73, 75, 83, 89, 95, 96, 99, 100, 104n28. See also Little Temecula *ranchería*
Arguello, Luís Antonio (Governor Don), 52
Armas, Armitas, 53–54
Arnaiz, Dan, 115
Arnaiz, Manuel, 118, 119
arriero, 33, 38
arroba, 56, 66
Arroyo Seco, 60
Asistencia, 59
Aztec Indians (Empire), 2, 13–15, 50

Baegert, Jacobo (Father), 21
Bahia de Los Angeles, 22
Barbour, George W. ((Treaty) Commissioner), 89
Barker, Charles O., 111, 114, 131
Beale, Edward Fitzgerald, 74, 90, 92, 105n38
The Black Death, 25n2
Blackleg Vaccine, 143, 146n37
Bosley, Frances, 137

botas, 54, 56, 57, 71, 150
Bryant and Sturgis, 52, 66, 67, 69, 70
Bucareli, Antonio (Viceroy), 38, 40, 41, 44
bulldogging, 135, 145n8

caballada, 53, 58
caballo, 12
Cabezon, 98
Cahuenga, 70
Cahuilla Indians, 75, 76, 83, 89, 91, 93–95, 98, 100, 106, 112–15, 117–21, 131, 134, 135, 141, 143. See also language; Reservation
Calabasas, 42
Calac, Luiseño Headman Olegario, 5, 98–101
Caldera, Miguel, 15
California, State of Emergency Relief Administration, 137
camels, 105n38
Canary Islands, 1, 12
Capitana, 19, 29n54
caravel, 11, 26n9
Carlos III, King, 31, 33, 35, 37
carne seca, 56
Cassero, Pat, 134
Cassou, Louis, 141
Cattlemen's Associations, 6, 132, 138–40, 143, 144
chapareras/chaparajos (chaps), 53, 54
chaqueta de cuera, 20, 50
charro, 54
Cherokee Indians, 88
Chichimeca Indians, 15, 27n31, 36, 50. See also Huachichil Indians
Chubasco, 24, 28n53
Chumash Indians, 42, 48n45
Civilian Conservation Corps–Indian Division, 6, 136
Cochimí Indians, 18, 20, 23, 32–34, 36, 37, 39, 50, 51, 149
Collier, John (Commissioner of Indian Affairs), 137
Colonization Act of 1824, 65, 70. See also Supplemental Regulations of 1828

Columbus, Christopher, 1, 9, 11–13, 26n9
Comisionados, 25
Compostela, 22
Conchó, 18
Conquistadores, 10
Consag, Francisco (Father), 22, 23
Constantinople, 11
Cortés, Hernán (Capitan-General), 13–16, 18, 19, 31
Costansó, Miguel, 38
Costo, Gabriel, 120
Couts, Cave Johnson, 87, 97, 104n14
Coyote Canyon, 40, 134, 141
Crespí, Juan (Father), 33
Croix, Teodoro de (Comandant-General), 43, 44
Cuba, 1, 2, 11, 13
Cuesta Grade, 42, 68, 87
Culiacan, 41
Cupeño Indians, 100, 102, 109, 116, 128n27. See also Warner Hot Springs and Warner's Ranch
Cupeño Indians (Kupa), 116

Dady, John W. (Superintendent), 136–38
Dana, Richard Henry, 67
Davis, William Heath, 55, 58
Delaware Indians, 88
Diné Indians (Navajo), 39, 121
diseño, 70
Dolores, Mission Nuestra Señora de Los, 15–18
Domínguez, Juan José, 59
Dominican (clerical order), 36, 46n21
Dominican Republic, 9

Eixarch, Tomás (Father), 41
El Camino Real, 68, 86, 87
El Sur de California (El Sur), 21, 22, 29n60, 29n62, 32
encomienda, 12, 13, 26n13
Esplandián, 14
estancia, 3, 13, 15, 16, 110, 131, 149
Esténaga, Tomás (Father), 72, 73, 80n27

Index

Estudillo, Francisco (Agent), 112
Estudillo, Jose A. (Juez de Campo), 97
Executive Order reservations, 3, 84, 100, 102
Extremadura (Extremadurans), 10, 13

Fages, Pedro (Captain and Governor), 44, 50, 51, 59, 60, 80n14
Farming Agents, Farmers, Expert Farmers (employed by the Office of Indian Affairs), 6, 125, 133, 137, 138, 143, 151
Fernando, King of Aragon, 1, 11, 13, 22
fierro, 55
Figueroa, José (Governor), 72, 80n14
Font, Francisco (Father), 41, 43, 48n45
Forster, Don Juan, 97
Forster, F. P., 97
Forster, Isadora Pico, 97
Francisco Xavier, 44, 45
Fremont, John C., 88

Galleons, Manila, 19, 37
Galvéz, José de (Visitador General), 24, 31
Garcés, Francisco (Father), 19, 37, 38, 41, 44, 47n30
Garcia, Gabriel, 77, 78
Garner, Robert F., 115, 118
garrocha, 53
gente de razón, 71, 72
gente sin razón, 72
Gila River, 16, 18, 36, 39, 41, 47n30
Gold Rush, 62–63n11, 71, 83–87, 90, 95, 103n5, 110, 133, 150
Granada, 10–12
Grant, Ulysses S. (President of the United States), 99, 100
Great War (World War I), 6, 122, 124, 126, 127, 131, 152
Guadalupe Hidalgo, Treaty of, 4, 83, 85, 111
Guanche, Ignacio, 115
Gulf of California, 18, 20. *See also* Sea of Cortes

hacendados, 76
Haiti, 9
Hall, Harwood (Superintendent), 118
Hall, Joseph K. (Farmer), 137, 138
Harvey, Hugh, 142
Hayes, Benjamin (Judge), 94
hidalgos, 12
hides and tallow (trade in), 4, 14, 43, 49, 55, 56, 61, 62, 65–67, 69, 73, 78, 79n1, 83, 85, 88, 91, 95
Hispaniola, 9, 11–13, 34, 36, 111
Holy Brotherhood of Granada, 12
Hopyall, 142
Horcasitas, San Miguel de, 41
Huachichil Indians, 15, 27n31

Iberia, Iberian (Peninsula), 1, 9–11, 13, 20, 53
Indian Reorganization Act, 140
indigenes, 61
Irving, John "Red," 76, 91
Isabel, Queen of Castile, 1, 11, 12
Isla Angel De La Guarda, 22

Jackson, Helen Hunt, 5, 102
Jamaica, 1, 2, 13
Jasper, Ralph (J-9 Ranch), 142
Jauro, Adolfo, 115
Jenkins, James (Malki Superintendent), 125
Jesuits (Society of Jesus clerical order), 15–19, 21–25, 29n62, 35
John, Joe, 115
Johnson, Arthur F. (Farmer), 133, 137, 146n21, 144n3
Johnston, Adam (California Sub-agent), 88
Judges of the Plains (*Jueces de Campo*), 54, 55, 97, 98
Jurupit, 70
justicia mayor, 22

Kearny, Stephen Watts (General), 74
Kinney, Abbott, 102
Kino, Eusebio (Father), 15–19, 23, 37, 45, 50

Index

Kumeyaay Indians (Diegueño), 2, 5, 7, 8, 36, 42, 57, 61, 74, 93, 99, 100, 102, 110, 116, 121, 133, 141, 142

LaChappa, Baptista, 118, 129n36
Lane, Franklin K. (Secretary of Interior), 120
Las Marismas, 53
Lasuén, Fermín Francisco de (Father), 50, 51
Lawson, Samuel (Agent), 101
Linck, Wenceslao (Father), 22, 23, 33
Linton, Tyron Roderick, xii
Linton, Walter, 142
Little Temecula *rancheria*, 75, 95, 96, 99, 101, 102, 106n58, 116
Longhorn Cattle, Spanish, 2, 9, 32, 55, 66, 69, 85
Los Coyotes (Reservation), 141, 142
Los Flores (Summit Valley) Ranch, 114, 115
Lovett, W. E. (Agent), 95, 106n47
Lubo, Servante, 134
Lugo, Don Jose Del Carmen, 75, 92
Luiseño Indians (language), 75, 89, 95, 96, 98–102, 110, 113, 127, 133

majordomo, 3, 21, 51, 54, 73, 85
Malki Superintendency, 118, 125, 129n35
Manifiesto a la República Mejicana, 72
manteca, 56
Manuel Nieto, 59
Mariné, Juan, 73
Martin, Robert (Morongo Tribal Chairman), xiii, 139
matanza, 2, 3, 49, 55, 66, 68, 71, 117
Maxwell, Adrian F. (Farmer), 125
McCulloch, Hartnell and Company, 66, 67, 79n1
McKee, Redick ((Treaty) Commissioner), 89
Mesa Grande, 141, 142
Meseta Region, 10, 25n2
Metates, 134

MHA Nation (Mandan, Hidatsa, Arikara), 7
Miller, Gib, 115
Mission Indian (newsletter), 142, 143
Mission Nuestra Señora de Loreto Conchó (Loreto), 18–22, 24, 25, 32–34
Mission San Antonio de Padua, 44
Mission San Bruno, 16
Mission San Buenaventura, 52, 68
Mission San Carlos Borromeo (Monterey), 43
Mission San Diego de Alcalá, 34, 42, 74
Mission San Fernando, 34, 60, 70
Mission San Francisco de Borja (Borja), 34
Mission San Gabriel, 36, 40, 52, 59, 62n11, 70, 72, 80n27
Mission San Jose del Cabo, 24, 29n60
Mission San Juan Capistrano, 69
Mission San Luis Obispo, 42, 87
Mission San Luis Rey, 59, 69, 75
Mission Santa Clara de Asís, 37
Mission Santa María, 23, 32, 34
Mission San Xavier del Bac, 17, 18, 38
Mission Tule River (consolidated) Agency, 102, 111–13
Monquí Indians (Guaycurá), 20
Morgan, Thomas J. (Comissioner of Indian Affairs), 111
Mormons, 111, 127
Morongo (Reservation), xiii, 6, 100, 102, 111–13, 117, 118, 122, 127, 131–43, 144n3, 152
Morongo, Mr. and Mrs. John, 137
Morongo Tribal Council, 138, 139
Muslim, 1, 10, 11, 25n2

National Congress of American Indians, 7
National Museum of the American Indian, 7
neophytes, 2, 3, 9, 14, 17, 20, 23, 31, 35, 37, 40, 44, 51, 55, 58, 60, 61, 71–74, 78, 99, 149

Index

New Deal, 6, 132, 137, 152
Nordhoff, Charles, 96, 98

Office of Indian Affairs (Indian Office/ Indian Service), 6, 73, 84, 88, 93, 95, 102, 109, 110, 112–14, 118–20, 124–26, 132, 133, 135, 138–40, 151
Olleyquotequiebe, Quechan Chief, 39. See also Palma, Salvador
Ottomans, 11
Ovando, Gobernador Nicolás de (of Hispaniola), 12

Pablo, Mr. and Mrs. Henry, 136
Palma, Salvador (Quechan Chief), 39, 44, 45
Panto, José, 5, 74, 83, 89, 90, 93, 95, 98, 99
peonage, debt, 4, 72, 76, 79, 81n32, 84, 150
Perez, Eulalia, 73
Pericú Indians, 20
peso, 66, 77, 79n1
Peyri, Antonio (Father), 69
Philippine Islands, 19
Piccolo, Padre Francisco María, 18
Pico, Andres, 74, 77
Pico, Pío (Governor), 73, 75, 116, 128n22
Pima Indians (Piman language), 16, 28n43, 35, 45, 47n30
Pimería Alta, 16–18, 21, 34, 35, 37, 39, 46n16
Politana, 75
Ponchetti, Barbara, 141, 142
Ponchetti, Charlie and Bernyce, 142
Portolá, Gaspar de (Governor), 9, 24, 25, 32–34, 36–38, 42, 69, 149
presidio(s), 2, 10, 14, 15, 18, 21, 22, 24, 29n62, 31, 35–41, 43, 44, 49, 50, 59, 60, 97
pueblo(s), 10, 14, 15, 31, 34, 42–44, 49, 54, 59, 60, 69, 71, 74, 99
Puerto Rico, 1, 2, 13
Puerto Yaqui, 19

Quechan Indians (Yumas), 38–41, 44, 45, 47n30, 48n52, 104n20
Quitman Reed Ranch Indian cowboys, 120, 134. See also Apapas, Augustine; Cassero, Pat; Costo, Gabriel; Lubo, Servante

R.F. Garner Ranch Indian Cowboys, 115. See also Arnaiz, Dan; Guanche, Ignacio; Jauro, Adolfo; John, Joe; Miller, Gib; Santana; Tortes, Calistro; Tortes, Castro; Tortes, John
ranchería(s), 3, 4, 15, 19, 22, 23, 35n15, 46n15, 60, 70, 73, 78, 89, 95, 98, 99, 150
rancho del rey, 12, 13, 50, 54
Rancho Domínguez, 60, 69, 70, 80n14
Rancho Pauba, 115, 116
Rancho San Gorgonio, 76, 131
Rancho San Jacinto Viejo, 97, 114
Rancho San Pasqual (allotted from Mission San Gabriel), 73, 80n27
Rancho San Pedro, 60, 80n14
Rancho Santa Gertrudas, 60
Rancho Santa Rosa, 115, 116
Rancho Santiago de Santa Ana, 72
Rancho Temecula, 74, 115, 116
Range Management Survey Report, 143
reale, 77
reata (la reata), 3, 6, 10, 53, 54, 57, 58, 68, 117, 120, 131, 141, 142
Reconquista, 1, 10, 12, 61
Reed, Lester, 120, 129n35, 133, 135
Reed, Quitman (Reed's), 120, 133–35, 145n8
Reimbursement Program, 6, 125, 126, 138, 140, 141, 151
repartimiento, 73, 81n32
Riva, *Teniente* (Lieutenant) Pedro de la, 22
Rivera y Moncada, Captain Fernando, 22, 32–34, 39, 43, 44, 47n30, 149
Robinson, Alfred, 52, 67
Rodríguez, Bernardo (Captain), 22
Rodríguez, Esteban (Captain), 21, 22

Roripaugh, Jack, 135
Ruiz, Catarina Lisalde de, 77
Ruiz, Jose Antonio, 77
Rust, Horatio Nelson (Agent), 111, 112

Sacred Expedition, 33, 34, 149
Sahatpa, 76, 94. See also San Timoteo Canyon
Salinas River, 42, 69, 87
Salvatierra, Juan Maria de (Father), 17–19, 21, 23
San Bernardino Mountains, 6, 114, 115
San Blas, 24, 37
San Bruno, 16, 18, 19
San Carlos Pass, 40
Sanchez, José Bernardo (Father), 73
Sanchez, Mrs. Doris, xii, 137
San Gorgonio (Mount, Pass), 6, 59, 83, 94, 98, 131
San Jacinto (Mount, village), 69, 70, 94, 97, 114, 115, 117, 120
San Jacinto Mountains, 6, 114, 115
San Joaquin Valley, 43, 58, 86, 87, 89, 94, 117, 118
San Pascual (village, allotted from Mission San Diego), 74, 77, 89, 92, 93, 95, 98, 99
Santa Lucia Mountains, 42
Santana, 115
Santa Olaya, 41
Santa Rosa Island, 116
Santa Rosa Reservation, 115, 118, 119
Santa Ysabel, Treaty of, 89
San Timoteo Canyon, 70, 76, 81n44, 94. See also Sahatpa
Santo Domingo, 13
Saubel, Katherine Siva, 141
Sea of Cortes, 16, 18, 19. See also Gulf of California
sebo, 56
Secularization Act of 1833, 65, 70
Sells, Cato (Commissioner of Indian Affairs), 121, 122, 124, 126
señores de hato, 10

Serra, Junípero (Father), 9, 32, 34, 37, 38, 51, 149
Serrano Indians, 2, 5, 7, 8, 61, 89, 100, 117, 121, 131, 143
serviente, 77
Shay, Will, 114
Siva, Alvino, 141
Siva, Ernest, xii
Smiley Commission, 100
Smith, Edward P. (Commissioner of Indian Affairs), 100
Soboba (Reservation, Superintendency), 113, 115, 118, 119, 122, 123, 135, 143
soldados de cuera, 20, 33, 38, 60
Sonora (Sonoran), 2, 15–20, 24, 31, 34, 37–41, 43, 45, 49, 54, 58, 69, 84, 88, 91
Southern Pacific Railroad, 119, 120
Stanley, J. Q. A. (Agent), 95, 104n28, 106n47
steatite (soapstone), 42, 48n45
stock raising farms (*vs.* open-range ranching), 109–11, 114, 122, 130n58, 130n60–64, 144–45n3, 146–47n37, 150
Supplemental Regulations of 1828, 65, 70

Taino Indians, 11–13, 36
tapaderas, 54
Tarabal, Sebastian, 34, 39, 41, 47n30
Tejon Pass, 89, 93, 117
Tejon Ranch, 117
Temecula, Treaty of, 89, 104n28
Templo Mayor, 14
Tenochtítlan, 14
Thomas, Charles, 115
Tlaxcalan Indians, 13–15, 36
Todos Santos, 21, 22
Tongva Indians (Gabrieleños), 2, 7, 8, 40, 59, 61
Tortes, Calistro, 115
Tortes, Castro, 115
Tortes, John, 115

Index 177

Tribal Alliance of Sovereign Indian Nations, 7
Tubac, 35, 38, 39, 41, 43, 47n30
Tucson, 18, 115
Tulare Lake, 86, 103n11
Tule River Reservation, 139, 140

Uchití Indians, 20–22
Ulloa, Francisco de, 14
Union Stockyards (Los Angeles), 138, 143

Vail, Banning, 116
Vail, Mahlon, 116
Vail, Walter, 115, 116
Vancouver, George (Captain), 52
Velásquez, Diego (Governor), 13
Velicatá, 23, 33, 34, 36, 39
Ventura, 42
Vera Cruz, 13, 16
Verdugo, José María, 59

Wadsworth, Harry E. (Superintendent), 118–20, 129n36
Waite, Marion E. (Expert Farmer), 125
Ward, John S. (Agent), 102
Warner Hot Springs, 101, 115
Warner, John J., 116, 128n27
Warner's Ranch, 97, 115, 116, 128n27, 141

Wetmore, Charles A., 100
Whitewater Ranch, 114, 115
Wilson, Benjamin Davis (Sub-agent), 73, 86, 90
Wilson, Ramona Yorba, 90
Wolfskill, William, 62–63n11
Wozencraft, Oliver M. ((Treaty) Commissioner), 89
Wright, Lucius A. (Agent), 112, 113, 117

Ximeno, Fray Bartholome (Father), 35, 46n15

Yankee (traders), 4, 52, 56, 65–67, 84
Yaqui Indians, 88
yegua, 12
Yellow Bird, Michael Dr., 7
Yokut Indians, 87, 103n11, 139
Yorba, Bernardo, 70, 72, 73
Yorba, José Antonio (Sergeant), 69, 72
Yorba, Tomás, 69, 70, 77, 79n12
Young, Ewing, 86
Yucaipat, 70, 76
Yuman Indians (language), 16, 20, 36, 39, 47n33, 111. *See also* Quechan

Zalvidea, José (Father), 74
zanja, 60

About the Author

David G. Shanta is a lecturer in the Department of History at California State University, San Bernardino.

www.ingramcontent.com/pod-product-compliance
Lightning Source LLC
LaVergne TN
LVHW051818060925
820435LV00002B/20